**Effective Master Data Management
with SAP® NetWeaver MDM**

 PRESS

SAP PRESS is a joint initiative of SAP and Galileo Press. The know-how offered by SAP specialists combined with the expertise of the Galileo Press publishing house offers the reader expert books in the field. SAP PRESS features first-hand information and expert advice, and provides useful skills for professional decision-making.

SAP PRESS offers a variety of books on technical and business related topics for the SAP user. For further information, please visit our website: www.sap-press.com.

Andrew LaBlanc
Enterprise Data Management with SAP NetWeaver MDM
2007, 584 pp.
978-1-59229-115-1

Bernd Schloemer
Mastering SAP NetWeaver Master Data Management
2008, 76 pp.
978-1-59229-176-7

Heilig, Karch, Böttcher, Hofmann, Pfennig
SAP NetWeaver Master Data Management
2007, 331 pp.
978-1-59229-131-7

Andy Walker, Jagadeesh Ganapathy

Effective Master Data Management with SAP® NetWeaver MDM

Bonn • Boston

ISBN 978-1-59229-223-3

© 2009 by Galileo Press Inc., Boston (MA)

1st Edition 2009

Galileo Press is named after the Italian physicist, mathematician and philosopher Galileo Galilei (1564–1642). He is known as one of the founders of modern science and an advocate of our contemporary, heliocentric worldview. His words *Eppur si muove* (And yet it moves) have become legendary. The Galileo Press logo depicts Jupiter orbited by the four Galilean moons, which were discovered by Galileo in 1610.

Editor   Meg Dunkerley
Copy Editor   Julie McNamee
Cover Design   Tyler Creative
Cover Image   Photos.com
Layout Design   Vera Brauner
Production   Kelly O'Callaghan
Typesetting   Publishers' Design and Production Services, Inc.
Printed and bound in Canada

Contents at a Glance

Contents

5 Mobilizing for MDM: People and Planning 173

PART II SAP NetWeaver MDM Technical Framework and Solution Architecture

6 Developing an SAP NetWeaver MDM Architecture for an Enterprise 205

7 Converting and Maintaining Master Data 233

8 The SAP NetWeaver MDM Landscape, Data Modeling, and Data Maintenance 261

9 SAP NetWeaver MDM Data Integration and Enrichment 299

Acknowledgments

We were motivated to write this book because we are both passionately enthusiastic about the subject of MDM and believe that it is an exciting subject area that offers considerable business opportunities in the future. The solution we describe and the technology we are using is very much "leading edge," which will make this book invaluable to you as you embark on your various MDM journeys.

We have both learned a great deal about the skills required in writing a book during the past few months. We thank Meg Dunkerley, the Assoc. Acquisitions Editor for Galileo Press, Inc., for her wise advice concerning how to develop our ideas into structured chapters that are interesting and informative.

Special thanks also to Kevin Brimberry and to Dun & Bradstreet for allowing us access and permission to use their materials. The D&B services are described in Chapter 4 and forms an integral part of our story.

Andy: I'd especially like to thank my family for their patient support over the past few months, to allow me the necessary time to write this. Thanks to my wife, Kate, for recognizing why I wanted to write and for unquestioningly giving me the space to do so. Thanks to my sons, Luke and Edward, and to my daughters, Georgia and Bobbie — now, we can once again play our football in the backyard and go for long bike rides around the Windsor Great Park. And finally to my Dad, Brian, in Denstone, North Staffordshire, England, who follows everything that I do with great interest, I hope you will be proud to see my latest efforts!

Jagadeesh: I often complain to my wife Kavitha that she does not give me enough gifts. I have to stop that now, because the invaluable support and motivation that she gave me while I embarked on this journey to become an author is the best gift yet in my life. Nandini, my two-year-old daughter, is my prime inspiration for writing this book, but she was less than inspired by the sight of her Daddy brooding over a laptop for endless hours in the past few months. Having finished the MDM story now, I will get back to telling her simpler and more action-packed stories! The good wishes from my parents and my sister Hema also made the book-writing journey more pleasant. Finally, I don't know if I am breaching any protocol here, but I can't shy away from thanking my co-author, Andy Walker. Without his coaching, guidance, and motivation, I would not have completed this task, and working with him was a great learning experience that I will always cherish.

PART I
MDM Business Background and Skills

Let's begin by introducing the key MDM concepts and definitions and discussing why we believe that mastering your customer and vendor records is so important.

1   Introducing MDM — Concepts and Definitions

This chapter introduces the key Master Data Management (MDM) concepts and definitions. We begin to describe the business issues caused by master data "silos" within a company and the benefits of the Dun & Bradstreet services, including the D&B D-U-N-S® Number and D&B Corporate Linkage and Entity Matching. We discuss the MDM role as a company's "yellow pages" and also the importance of MDM data quality. Finally, we define the master data objects, including business partners, vendors and customers, and natural persons.

1.1   Introduction

During an IT course a few years ago, we spent three days discussing what a fact is, what an opinion is, and what a belief is. The challenge introduced in that course and that you are faced with here is to always try to gather the relevant facts before forming your opinions, which in turn will then form the beliefs that you are passionate about and that become a part of you. It was an excellent course and has influenced me several years later to always try to gather the relevant facts before forming an opinion.

With that in mind, read the following paragraph, which describes the business problem that we will focus on throughout this book:

> "Customer and vendor master data records in most companies are typically created in multiple systems, spreadsheets, and applications. As long as the master data resides in these silos, it will continue to evolve independently and often

in conflict. Decisions and processes based on inconsistent master data lead to greater business risk, inaccuracies, compliance issues, greater waste, and greater customer and vendor dissatisfaction. However, key business and IT stakeholders have not understood the significance of how poorly maintained business partner master data impacts their company's performance."

Now, let's examine each of these sentences in turn and test them as a fact, an opinion, or a belief:

Statement 1: "Customer and vendor master data records in most companies are typically created in multiple systems, spreadsheets, and applications."

This is an opinion. We started off by thinking this was a fact, but we don't know how most companies manage their customer and vendor master data records. Of the companies we have talked to, we think it's a valid opinion based on the facts that we have discovered so far.

Statement 2: "As long as the master data resides in these silos, it will continue to evolve independently and often in conflict."

This is another opinion, again based on the facts from the companies and business applications we have seen. We will discuss in detail the business issues caused by managing master data in silos to present the facts that support our opinion.

Statement 3: "Decisions and processes based on inconsistent master data lead to greater business risk, inaccuracies, compliance issues, greater waste, and greater customer and vendor dissatisfaction."

This is a belief. We will discuss the MDM business case and the benefits of using Dun & Bradstreet's services to provide accurate, consistent and up-to-date business partner master data.

Statement 4: "However, key business and IT stakeholders have not understood the significance of how poorly maintained business partner master data impacts their company's performance."

Another belief and possibly the most important one! We could have written this more simply: *"People don't get it,"* or *"People don't get MDM."* In this book, we intend to present you with the relevant facts so that you understand why we believe MDM to be so important for maintaining your customer and vendor records.

1.1.1 Understanding MDM and Asking the Right Questions

Unfortunately, most people in your organization probably do not understand the real business value and importance of accurate customer and vendor data to your company. This opinion is supported by the fact that current business processes often result in the creation of incomplete, partial, or inaccurate master data records.

A key issue for MDM programs is that many people in your company will not initially recognize the importance of your work. Typically, you will only update two SAP tables (Tables LFA1 [vendor] and KNA1 [customer]) — that's it! You won't even reproduce the functionality of the maintain customer and vendor SAP transactions (XD01 – Create Customer, XD02 – Change Customer, XD03 – Display Customer, and XK01 – Create Vendor, XK02 – Change Vendor, and XK03 – Display Vendor for SAP ERP 6.0users) because you'll just be maintaining the global attributes. People outside of the MDM program see all of this effort to update just two of the several thousands of SAP tables and wonder what all of the MDM hype is about.

Master Data Management of customer and vendor records is much more than hype. But are we asking the relevant questions? Let's start by considering a series of questions your business leaders may ask regarding your dealings with your suppliers:

▶ What is my total expenditure with a vendor?

▶ Am I leveraging the scale of my company by understanding the global overview of my dealings with a vendor?

▶ What is the financial and trading risk information of a vendor?

▶ Is there a risk that the vendor will go bankrupt?

▶ Am I trading with a "legitimate" vendor that I have authenticated?

▶ Do I understand who I am dealing with and their financial health?

▶ What are the potential strengths (and weaknesses) within the supply chain?

▶ Do I understand the implications of joint ventures?

▶ Have I implemented purchasing controls?

▶ Can I track issues such as health and safety status, and diversity and inclusion?

Next, consider the questions to ask concerning your customers:

▸ Who are my most profitable customers?

▸ How do I increase my revenue from my existing customers?

▸ How do I improve my operational efficiency when dealing with a customer?

▸ What is my credit risk with a customer?

Before these questions can be answered, however, you need to accurately identify a customer and a vendor across each of your business applications or master data silos. Organizations may have tens if not hundreds of silos of master data managed using different systems. Each master data silo is likely to have its own business partner create, maintain, and delete processes, and each master data silo may contain inaccurate data (incomplete, duplicate, or out-of-date records).

In the absence of an MDM program, accountability for master data quality is unclear. Financial reporting will differ from business unit to business unit based on master data definitions, and reconciling numbers takes a long time with considerable business effort spent in linking the data across the systems rather than actually analyzing the data. Obtaining business reports often requires specialist skills and reconciliation from your IT and accounting departments.

In the next three chapters, we'll explain why accurately maintaining your customer and vendor master data is so important to you and is a prerequisite to answering these key management reporting questions.

In **Chapter 2**, two detailed Case Studies illustrate the issues faced by a fictional Company CO1 whose master data is maintained in several silos using multiple business applications. The examples show Company CO1's current processes for handling customer and vendor master data are not robust, resulting induplicate, out-of-date, and inactive records that cannot be matched across the various systems. We'll assess the impacts of business mergers and acquisitions and also how the issues are then further compounded for large organizations.

Our conclusion from these Case Studies is that for Company CO1, the answer to these key business partner performance measurement questions is "Don't know." *How similar are your company's master data issues to Company CO1? What are the implications?* If "Don't know" is also the answer for your company, this is not usually the response your business leaders are looking for!

In an effort to improve the management and reporting of business partner information, companies often invest in new IT programs and initiatives. If an organization requires better vendor information, they will implement a new Supply Chain Management (SCM) system or a Supplier Relationship Management (SRM) or initiate a supplier reconciliation reporting exercise. Similarly for customers, the approach will be to deploy a new Customer Relationship Management (CRM) system or a Sales and Distribution (SD) system. If improved reporting is required, then an SAP NetWeaver Business Intelligence (SAP NetWeaver BI) warehouse solution is implemented to enable users to drill down and slice and dice the data.

Unfortunately, these initiatives often fail to address the root causes of the master data quality problems, and by adding more systems, they actually create more issues. There are now even more master data silos where customer and vendor records must be maintained, which results in more duplicate, out-of-date, inactive records that you can't match across systems. It's a vicious circle! And your business leaders are then disappointed that the initiatives didn't deliver the promised benefits.

MDM has been unfashionable for a long time, and in many ways, the name "Master Data Management" has been a cause of this. It conjures up phrases such as "data models" and "entity relationship diagrams," which tend to be the niche areas for a few specialist data experts. Recently, however MDM has become more important as business and technical leaders realize the true business value of MDM to their organizations.

MDM can be condensed to three key words: *people*, *processes*, and *data quality*. If in every system that contains customer or vendor records, you ensure that they are accurate, complete, up to date, unique (without duplicates), and active, you can answer your business leaders key questions every day without reconciliation exercises! And, you'll increase the value of your investments in each of your CRM, SD, SRM, SCM, and BI warehouse deployments. It's so much more than just those two SAP Tables LFA1 and KNA1, which this book will demonstrate to you.

Chapter 3 examines the MDM business case, highlighting the key benefits of uniform, consistent data, and lifecycle management processes. We'll show a way to quantify the business benefits and to present an overwhelming business case for implementing the MDM business procedures and applications to manage your customer and vendor master data.

We explore the financial and legal compliance implications, including the Sarbanes-Oxley Act. We examine the business case and the business process benefits through the lenses of SCM, CRM, Financial Accounting, and Management Information users. We also discuss the barriers to MDM adoption and consider how to set up MDM Governance and planning processes and the MDM Stakeholder map. Finally, we introduce the business partner master scorecard as a tool to monitor MDM progress to achieving the business case value.

> **Introducing Dun & Bradstreet**
>
> Being able to compare your company's master data against industry business standards is important. Dun & Bradstreet (D&B) maintains the world's largest business database containing information on more than 132 million businesses worldwide. D&B is by far the leading provider of business information for credit, marketing, and purchasing decisions worldwide.
>
> Today, more than 150,000 companies of all sizes rely on D&B to provide the insight they need to build profitable business relationships with their customers, suppliers, and business partners.

Chapter 4 covers the D&B services and the importance of the D&B D-U-N-S® Number. We introduce the D&B Worldbase database, D&B Corporate Linkage, D&B Entity Matching, and D&B Lifecycle management processes. We discuss the importance of authenticating your business partners for Sarbanes-Oxley compliance and analyze the SAP NetWeaver MDM D&B Enrichment adapter. We consider the implications of introducing external D&B services to a company. We then show how the SAP NetWeaver MDM solution can be applied to Company CO1 by revisiting Case Study 1 to link multiple business application with the unique D&B D-U-N-S Number.

Chapter 5 tackles the people issues. Changing the hearts and minds, attitudes, and awareness of your key stakeholders, your business people, and your IT people will take dedicated effort. We consider how to mobilize an MDM program and set up the appropriate data governance and standards and how to create a realistic MDM roadmap.

In **PART 2** of this book, we move on to describe SAP NetWeaver MDM, which enables you to consolidate and maintain master data from many different systems into a centralized repository. Because it can be integrated with any type of data source, users can continue to leverage their existing systems and applications (both SAP and non-SAP). SAP NetWeaver MDM enables you to improve your business processes and decision-making capability by aggregating and improving the reliability of your master data. By using SAP NetWeaver MDM linked to D&B to provide a central view of strategic master data, companies can significantly improve their business processes and performance.

Chapter 6 investigates the key SAP NetWeaver MDM architectural design principles and considers how to design a Technical Framework. We consider the roles of the SAP NetWeaver MDM Technical Design Authority and Solution Architects. We discuss the constraints of an organization's existing systems landscapes, such as multiple consuming systems and repository design principles. The chapter also covers instance strategies, SAP NetWeaver architectures, workflow and hierarchies, and D&B enrichment.

In this chapter, we design an SAP NetWeaver MDM architecture to get a unified view of the single source of truth. We provide business solution illustrations for designing a data model to achieve a unified view that can be exposed to Web Services cleanly and with security compliance.

Chapter 7 describes the best-in-class approaches to cleansing, migrating, and maintaining master data, as well as the various design options available for doing this using SAP NetWeaver MDM. We discuss data cleansing, including organizational data quality metrics and standards and how to investigate source system data and validate the results. We describe how to align source and target data and how to monitor the migration process, including the analysis and resolution of data quality errors.

We consider the ongoing data maintenance, including the SAP NetWeaver MDM Data Enrichment Architecture and how to drive data integrity through the use of workflows. We also discuss lifecycle management, data matching strategies, and data distribution and reporting. The SAP NetWeaver MDM technical landscape will reflect the capability to implement a master data management solution for different objects in different timeframes, while keeping the integrity and uniqueness of data intact.

Chapter 8 explores the SAP NetWeaver MDM landscape, including the technical landscape design and data modeling. We describe the use of features in SAP NetWeaver MDM Console, including repository design, main tables, lookup tables, hierarchies and taxonomy, qualified lookup tables, and configurations. We then describe the key functionality of the SAP NetWeaver MDM Data Manager and the workflow design, including how business users can handle workflow maintenance.

Chapter 9 explains the technical delivery of the SAP NetWeaver MDM data integration and enrichment processes. Using detailed examples, we describe the use of the SAP NetWeaver MDM Import Manager, Syndicator, and the D&B enrichment architecture.

Chapter 10 discusses integrating SAP NetWeaver MDM with the wider SAP NetWeaver components. Building a best-of-breed solution involves mapping business requirements for master data maintenance and leveraging technical components built in the SAP NetWeaver solution stack.

We describe how SAP NetWeaver Portal development provides robust end-user interfaces and explores SAP NetWeaver Process Integration (SAP NetWeaver PI). We define solutions for SAP NetWeaver MDM data syndication to multiple consuming systems, including messaging architecture, monitoring, and error handling. We discuss using Adobe forms for the data capture of customer and vendor details and its integration with the SAP Netweaver Portal and SAP NetWeaver MDM.

Finally, **Chapter 11** discusses how an SAP NetWeaver MDM solution is developed using a combination of the SAP Netweaver MDM Java API and web services. We also consider the deployment of advanced technical features, including latest versions, service packs, and upgrades to the SAP NetWeaver MDM landscape.

Target Audience

The book is written for organizations considering how to integrate master data management into their companies. Our target readers include business leaders (e.g., CEOs, CIOs) and business users of business partner data such as supply chain specialists, customer relationship managers, and data management teams, including data stewards. Business readers will gain an understanding of the implications of deploying a master data management program across an organization.

Technical specialists — IT enterprise, functional, and technical architects; SAP NetWeaver technical delivery experts; and SAP ERP deployment teams particularly with SAP experience — will understand how the SAP NetWeaver MDM toolkit can be developed to meet key business requirements.

Why It Is Important

MDM is an emerging growth industry with many organizations now actively considering the implications of master data and the best ways to progress. By linking the Dun & Bradstreet services and SAP NetWeaver MDM, we describe an approach worthy of consideration by many companies.

We've considered a wide range of inputs from our SAP NetWeaver MDM networks. We've met people from many companies and have attended and presented at several large MDM and SAP conferences. In this book, we discuss in detail many of the questions raised at those forums.

In short, this book describes the MDM processes and benefits of integrating customer and vendor information across an enterprise. This practical guide shows you how to introduce the Dun & Bradstreet business services into an organization and how to implement the key technical features of SAP NetWeaver MDM.

Let's now move on to discuss the key MDM concepts.

1.2   MDM Concepts

Master data is the core data of an enterprise — its customers, vendors, products, and employees. MDM is the collection of applications and processes to provide your company with the capability to integrate and measure master data usage across your enterprise. The need to integrate master data throughout your organization is driven by improving your business processes, complying with regulatory demands, creating financial reports, and providing accurate and informative business management reports.

Let's break down the definition further:

1. MDM is a combination of data governance, business processes, data quality, data enrichment, and a technical solution.

2. MDM is an enterprise-wide program that requires the cooperation of a company's business units and includes policies and responsibilities for managing master data.

3. MDM is a key business process requiring joint efforts from different business areas as well as overall organizational rules and processes.

4. MDM must ensure the availability of accurate and up-to-date master data that is of good and trusted quality.

To support the MDM business process, MDM requires a technology that includes the definition of processes and responsibilities for master data maintenance. MDM needs to support the synchronization of master data from records of origin to the distributed systems across the enterprise. SAP NetWeaver MDM provides this technical solution.

To help you grasp these MDM concepts, we will introduce several analogies for you in this book. The first is as follows.

Comparing MDM and Physical Fitness Analogy
An unusual analogy is to compare the quality of your company's customer and vendor records with a person's physical fitness.
Your records are "obese" if there are too many of them. Obesity is caused by duplicate records and by inactivity over a number of years, when you fail to delete records that have not been used. Your records may be "slightly overweight" if you have a relatively small number of inaccurate records. Ideally, your records are "lean" and current. We'll define metrics to enable you to measure and assess the "system indexes" (similar to "body mass indexes") of your current vendor, customer, or business partner.
To keep your records accurate and up to date, you'll need lifecycle ("lifestyle") management. You need data standards in the way you control your calorie intake; that is, follow certain rules and you will keep the records healthy.
Finally, you can't become physically fit in one day; it requires months and years of dedicated effort and control. Every day, however, you can improve your master data by following the rules (don't eat candy), searching before you create to avoid duplicates (exercise right), filling in full details (eat well), and keeping all of your data up to date (work out your whole body).

We can create metrics to measure your business partner or vendor or customer system index in a similar way that you can measure your body mass index (BMI).

Let's consider the following definition for vendors:

Vendor System Index (VSI) = ([Number of Available Vendor Records/ Number of Unique Active Vendor Records] – 1) × 100

- ▶ **Number of Available Vendor Records** is the number of vendor records currently set up in a system that are not blocked or end dated.

- ▶ **Number of Unique, Active Vendor Records** is the number of unique vendor records as matched with the D&B D-U-N-S Number that has been used in a transaction in the system in the past three years. (You can count a D&B D-U-N-S Number only once. Be sure to exclude duplicates.)

The **Vendor System Index** (VSI), (or the similar **Customer System Index** (CSI), or the **Business Partner System Index** (BPSI)) can be applied to each of your business applications where customer or vendor records are maintained. They give you a view of the health of your master data records.

A VSI score of 10% or below for a system shows that you have your "lean" data under tight control. You have very few duplicates or inactive records left hanging in the system. For example, if you have 1,100 vendor records in your system, this means at least 1,000 unique records as matched to D&B have been used in the past three years.

A VSI score of between 10% and 50% indicates that your data is "overweight" and is not being subjected to tight master data management control. For example, if you have 1,100 records in your system, this means you have between 733 and 1,000 unique records as matched to D&B and used in the past three years.

A VSI score in excess of 50% would imply that your data is "obese." For example, if you have 1,100 records in your system and 275 unique records as matched to D&B and used in the past three years, then your VSI will equal 300%.

If your system is a few years old, don't be surprised if your initial VSI is 300% to 400%, or even more! Initial data loads, mergers and acquisitions, and changes in procurement strategy all contribute to the fact that the number of vendor records currently set up in your system greatly exceeds the vendors that you'll actually procure from this year.

MDM – Program versus Daily Event

One of the misunderstandings of MDM is that it is a huge program of work that will last for several years. Maintaining accurate master data is also an event that happens several times every day. Each time you set up or change a customer or a vendor record in a business application, you need to do it well. In a world with MDM, you must follow your company data standards and complete full and accurate records details.

You must search across all of your company records to see if you're already dealing with that business partner. One of the key functions of SAP NetWeaver MDM is to accurately inform you which customers and vendors are already being used in business applications across your organization. This provides you with useful insights and opportunities to leverage your organization's scale.

As the companies you transact with change, you need to update your master data record details to reflect mergers and acquisitions. If you haven't interacted with a customer or a vendor in a number of years, it should be archived from your business applications. Chances are that the company will have changed in that period and that your records are now out-of-date. A good rule to follow is that if you aren't going to use the record this year, remove it.

It may take years to change your key stakeholders' attitudes concerning how they treat and respect your customer and vendor master records. The silos that you've already built up need to be cleansed and made current, and duplicate records need to be deleted.

You must repeat the MDM messages to your key stakeholders within your company consistently because outwardly, the business processes may look just fine without MDM. After all, orders are being processed, and invoices are being paid. You'll meet resistance in the form of statements such as the following:

▶ So why does a new project have to follow the MDM rules? It's quicker to load the data without the additional rules, and my part of the organization stands alone (an island!).

▶ If I integrate with another system (MDM), it introduces a project risk and extra costs.

These are the attitudes that you are constantly going to need to overcome. Projects will come and go and so too will business applications. It's your customer and vendor master data and the MDM processes that will persist over the long term.

Let's now consider some of the key MDM terminology that we will be using throughout this book.

1.2.1 MDM Terminology

We'll begin by considering the MDM consolidated, harmonized, and centralized models.

Consolidated Model

In the consolidated model, MDM is used to collect master data from several systems and to store the details in the central SAP NetWeaver MDM business partner repository. Consolidation allows you to detect and clean up duplicate and identical records and update the consuming systems key fields for cross-system key mapping linkage.

As an example of a consolidation scenario, you may decide to tag the key identifier of the D&B D-U-N-S Number onto each of the consuming systems records. This will be the only SAP NetWeaver MDM attribute stored in the consuming system.

Harmonized Model

In the harmonized model scenario, SAP NetWeaver MDM enhances the consolidation model by also providing other global master data attributes that are stored in the consuming systems. This enables you to synchronize globally relevant attributes across your company's landscape. The number of global attributes to be harmonized needs to be carefully considered and may, for example, include legal names and addresses.

Centralized Model

The tightest form of MDM integration is the "centralized" model. In this scenario, SAP NetWeaver MDM is the "master" system, and the consuming systems are the "slaves." Whereas the emphasis in the consolidation scenario is on local data maintenance, the centralized scenario focuses on creating and maintaining the global data in the central SAP NetWeaver MDM repository. SAP NetWeaver MDM then distributes the record with the global data attributes to the consuming systems, where the local attributes can then be added.

In a centralized model, you can't create a vendor or a customer record directly in a consuming system; the record must first be created in SAP NetWeaver MDM and then distributed. This is the cleanest, purest approach and achieves all of the MDM primary business benefits.

Hybrid Solutions

When considering which model to use, there isn't a right or wrong answer. You can also have a hybrid solution where some of your consuming systems follow the consolidated model and others the centralized approach.

Several factors impact the design decision, including the importance of the consuming system (based on its scale and the number of vendor and customer records) and its expected life span.

For instance, is the consuming system a short-term legacy system where a consolidated model can be pragmatically applied, or is it a long-term strategic application where a centralized model will be introduced? New deployments are typically good candidates for a centralized MDM model.

Figure 1.1 shows how the SAP NetWeaver MDM repositories can be designed in a hybrid solution.

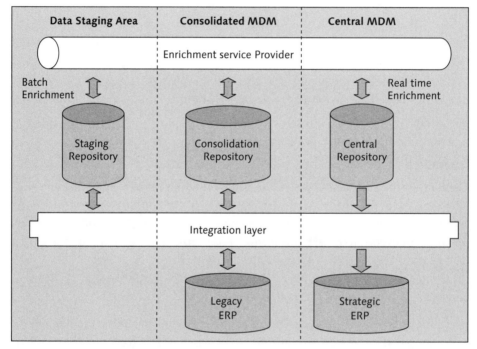

Figure 1.1 Data Staging, Consolidated, and Centralized MDM Repositories in a Hybrid Architecture

You are also likely to create an SAP NetWeaver MDM data-staging repository where your existing customer and vendor records are cleansed, matched, and de-duplicated. One of the peculiarities of an SAP NetWeaver MDM implementation is that each of your business applications will continue after the go-live and the customer and vendor records are already set up. The existing live operational data needs to cleansed and then moved to either a consolidated or a centralized repository. In Chapter 6, we describe the options for developing your SAP NetWeaver MDM architecture for an enterprise.

1.2.2   Scope of This Book

This book focuses on the MDM business benefits of integrating business partner master data processes across an enterprise. We'll discuss the Dun & Bradstreet services, including the D&B D-U-N-S Number and Corporate Linkage. You'll see how to integrate SAP NetWeaver MDM into an organization, including data governance, enterprise data services, and data stewardship.

We'll describe SAP NetWeaver MDM architectures, including centralized, harmonized, and consolidated models, and global and local attributes. We'll consider the SAP NetWeaver MDM technical delivery, including how to use key features such as the enrichment adapter, hierarchy management, and workflow to link multiple distributed systems.

MDM is currently a "hot topic" in the IT world. Several new software vendors have recently emerged with new MDM tools, and acronyms such as CDI (Customer Data Integration) or PIM (Product Information Management) are being used. As a result, several alternative architectures and approaches to MDM can be taken. This book focuses only on the SAP NetWeaver MDM product working within the SAP NetWeaver stack.

1.2.3   Introducing the Master Data Silos

Business partner master data is typically managed and maintained in several different systems applications and spreadsheets throughout a company. Often several different views of master data exist within a company as different specialist areas (e.g., SCM, CRM, SD, financial accounting, and business information reporting) each create their own individual versions of a master data record, that is, their own versions of the truth.

It's difficult to understand when we are trading with the same vendor, or branches of the same vendor. A master data silo is likely to be maintained using a different system with its own data model and field sizes. In each silo, there are different definitions of customers and suppliers. The format, content, and data quality of master data fields varies across the business applications.

Within each application or master data silo, there's a likelihood of inaccurate business partner master data. We define inaccurate business partner master data to be *incomplete data* in cases where only partial details are entered such as addresses missing a ZIP code, street, city, or country details. *Out-of-date data* has not been updated to reflect changes in a business partner's name and address details (when companies move) and corporate linkage (when companies merge or acquire other companies). *Duplicate data* occurs when two or more active records exist in a system for the same business partner.

There are several reasons for inaccurate records in each of the master data silos. The Create User Request Form is incomplete, such as including only the bank details necessary to pay an invoice with the address fields missing. Matching business partner names and addresses without a key is difficult and as you can't easily determine whether a business partner record already exists in a system, duplicates are created. Various company relationships such as ordering addresses and payment addresses further complicate the company search process.

The business partner data is maintained to different standards by the different business teams across the organization. Service levels vary and do not necessarily involve data accuracy as a performance metric. Applications are not integrated, so, for example, incomplete vendor records are created directly in the financial accounting system so that invoices can be paid.

Large organizations may have several hundred applications where business partner master data is maintained. Global companies operate in many countries and local systems may be needed for legislative reasons or decentralized reasons (each local business unit is accountable for their own profits and losses so build their own IT strategies). Mergers and acquisitions also result in multiple customer and vendor data capture processes and systems.

Market segments within the same organization may target the same companies with multiple product offerings, which can result in duplicate customer records. Your SAP ERP 6.0 instance strategies may result in multiple environments to facilitate various business offers and organizational setups, again causing duplicate records.

Business partner data in each of these applications are usually maintained by different teams, which may be either internal or external to the organization. Each of these teams may view accurately maintaining vendor and customer records as a lower priority than their other business activities. For example, your accounts payable and accounts receivable teams will view managing the payments of invoices as a top priority because their service level agreements depend on it. Likewise, your customer services team will value the correct order details and accurate customer pricing ahead of the customer record itself.

In SAP deployments, it will be more important for your data conversion team to transfer all of the accounts receivable and accounts payable open items than it will be to load accurate, unique, and active customer and vendor records. If you are managing a company merger or acquisition, the priority will be to copy all of the existing customer and vendor records (and open transactions) to the chosen financial system, rather than to remove the duplicate records.

> **Persuading Key Stakeholders to Value Accurately Maintained Customer and Vendor Records**
>
> Accurately maintaining customer and vendor records is critically important because they are among the most important data records in your entire company, which makes persuading key stakeholders to change their minds and processes a number one critical success factor to your MDM program. It's the time that it takes to convince the business users to change their process that can make MDM a long-running initiative. You'll need to change people's minds and then to change the core business processes that have often been running in the same way for years.

Let's now consider how Dun & Bradstreet can help you with the master data issues.

1.2.4   Introducing the Dun & Bradstreet Concepts

The D&B data services can help you manage your master data across the silos. A major aim of MDM is to provide a consistent, adequate, and accurate data view of the company's core business entities. Without a unique identification and reconciliation of master data, enterprise initiatives are unable to do this.

The D&B D-U-N-S Number is a unique, nine-digit; nonindicative identification number assigned to every business entity (currently more than 132 million) in D&B's Worldbase database. It serves an important key that enables a company to accurately link its operational systems.

No other numbering system is as established, recognized, and globally accepted. A D&B D-U-N-S Number is not assigned until multiple data sources confirm that a business exists — this enables authentication., This is key to meeting Sarbanes-Oxley Act requirements, which introduces a legal and regulatory focus on internal controls, including the timely ability to access and analyze information with respect to your company's finances and operations Global policies around D&B D-U-N-S Number assignment provide for consistency in site identification. It acts as an industry standard for business identification and is recommended by the United Nations, the European Commission, and more than 50 industry groups.

A D&B D-U-N-S Number is retained for the life of a business. No two businesses ever receive the same D&B D-U-N-S Number, and the numbers are never recycled. The number is retained when a company moves anywhere within the same country and follows a business through every phase of its life, including bankruptcy. This helps companies easily collect consistent information, such as the business address, demographics, financial information and reference, and diversity status.

D&B puts a huge effort into maintaining its Worldbase database through a company's lifecycle of changes, such as changes of name and address, as well as mergers and acquisitions. D&B's business model includes providing services of up-to-data credit and risk information, which requires accurate business partner details and corporate linkage. This business model is a strong motivation for D&B to keep its company data accurate and up to date.

D&B uses numerous sources to collect information, including business owners, government sources, public records, customer files, and third parties. This multiple source approach helps to confirm the accuracy of the data collected and to identify new companies as they are set up around the world.

D&B Entity Matching

D&B Entity Matching is the process by which you can search the D&B Worldbase database to match the appropriate D&B D-U-N-S Number to each of your customer and vendor records. This ensures that you aren't reporting duplicate information on your business partners. You provide D&B with the company name and address details, and the D&B Entity Matching ensures that disparate data elements are associated with the right business. The matching process is based on some sophisticated algorithms. If you provide accurate and complete names and addresses, the success rate of the matching improves.

In "simple" organizations, such as companies where the legal entity, the purchasing address, and the accounting address are in the same place, this can easily result in a D&B D-U-N-S Number match. However, if your business application also stores purchasing, ordering, or ship to addresses, the matching can be more difficult when you deal with more complex business partners. Several iterations of D&B Entity Matching are needed in these situations.

D&B Corporate Linkage

D&B Corporate Linkage is the relationship between different companies within a corporate family (see Figure 1.2). Linkage occurs in the D&B database when one business entity "controls" another business entity because it has financial or legal responsibility for another business, creating a Headquarters/Branch or Parent/Subsidiary relationship. Corporate linkages are updated monthly and reflect mergers, acquisitions, openings, and closings through the update.

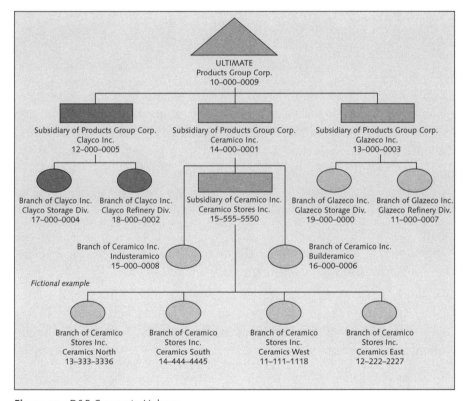

Figure 1.2 D&B Corporate Linkage

D&B Corporate Linkage can reveal relationships between your suppliers and customers that you otherwise would not be aware of. You can see where your specific customers and suppliers fit within larger corporate hierarchies and identify how much they are spending with your vendors, to better understand your total risk exposure in the supplier portfolio.

D&B provides linkages for Branch to Headquarter, Subsidiary to Parent, to Domestic Ultimate, and to Global Ultimate companies. The hierarchy entities are defined here:

▶ **Global Ultimate**
The top most responsible entity within the corporate family tree.

▶ **Domestic Ultimate**
A subsidiary within the global family tree that is the highest-ranking member within a specific country.

▶ **Headquarters**
A family member that has branches or divisions reporting to it and is financially responsible for those branches or divisions. If headquarters is more than 50% owned by another corporation, it's also a subsidiary. If it owns more than 50% of another corporation, it's also a parent.

▶ **Branch**
A secondary location of its headquarters. It has no legal responsibility for its debts, even though bills may be paid from the branch location.

▶ **Parent**
Corporation that owns more than 50% of another corporation. A parent can also be a headquarters if it owns branches.

▶ **Subsidiary**
A corporation that is more than 50% owned by another corporation and has a different legal business name from its parent company. There are also single location subsidiaries where the subsidiary does not have anything reporting to it.

▶ **Affiliated companies**
Related to a business through common ownership by the direct parent company. All of them share the same parent company. A direct parent company is a corporation that owns more than 50% of another corporation's capital stock.

Let's now consider how the D&B D-U-N-S Number and MDM help to reconcile the master data silos.

1.2.5   Reconciling the Master Data Silos with the D&B D-U-N-S Number

The D&B D-U-N-S Number and MDM act as the "glue" to link the various master data silos together in a coherent way. By applying the D&B Entity Matching process to your business applications, you can now match each of your customer and vendor records to a D&B D-U-N-S Number. This approach will take a few iterations and some data cleanup activities.

You can now address how many customers and vendors you have much more accurately and with certainty. As you establish the common D&B D-U-N-S Number across each system, you can identify the number of vendors shared across the SCM system, the Financial Accounting system, and the Business Intelligence warehouse.

By establishing the MDM processes as part of the create customer and vendor processes in each of your business applications, you can guarantee that each new record gets a D&B D-U-N-S Number. By refreshing the data from D&B, you ensure that the company name and address and the D&B Corporate Linkage data is kept up to date throughout a company's lifecycle.

When MDM is established as a repeatable process, you can also address how many customers and vendors you have next month as well. Reports of your current customer and vendor details can be produced automatically without the need for an intensive manual reconciliation exercise.

With regard to the Business Information warehouse SAP reporting, you also have the D&B Corporate Linkage available in SAP NetWeaver MDM. You can provide the business partner hierarchy details to enable customer vendor reporting not just at the individual company level but also aggregated to group and country level (Global Ultimate and Domestic Ultimate levels). You can also see the relationships across entire company structures, which is a huge step forward!

1.2.6   Records of Reference, Records of Origin, and Consuming Systems

In Chapter 2, we'll introduce Company CO1's business applications: a Customer Relationship Management system (CRM1), Supply Chain Management system (SCM1), Sales and Distribution system (SD1), Financial Accounting system (FI1), and Business Intelligence (BI1).

Figure 1.3 shows how the record of origin, the record of reference and the consuming systems will be integrated for Company CO1.

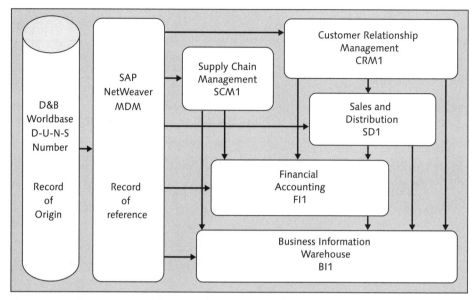

Figure 1.3 Linking the Record of Origin, the Record of Reference, and the Consuming Systems for Company CO1

You can think of SAP NetWeaver MDM as a middleware or a hub for data; it sits between the records of origin and the consuming systems and stores all of the connections.

Record of Origin

The *record of origin* is the original source of master data records for your organization. The *system of origin* is the system where the record of origin is maintained. Throughout this book, we will be considering the D&B Worldbase database as the system of origin, which provides the records of origin. The unique key of the record of origin will be the D&B D-U-N-S Number.

Record of Reference

The *record of reference* represents the sole and single version of the truth for your operational data across the company. The *system of reference* is the system where the record of origin is maintained. In this book, SAP NetWeaver MDM is the system of reference providing the record of reference. An important key of the record of reference is the D&B D-U-N-S Number. You'll store the record of reference for your business partners (customers and vendors) in an SAP *NetWeaver MDM business partner repository*.

Consuming System

A *consuming system* is a business application that uses a master data record. A key requirement for your SAP NetWeaver MDM system is to register and keep up to date all applications that consume your records and their key mappings, such as the customer number or vendor number in the business application).

Lifecycle Management processes need to be established so that when your business partner's details change, your master data records are updated. Companies are dynamic and as they change names and addresses, through relocation and mergers and acquisitions, this must be reflected in your business systems. Unless master data is maintained consistently across applications, comparisons and reconciliations across the applications will be inaccurate.

Let's now consider another analogy, this time that SAP NetWeaver MDM acts as the "yellow pages" for your corporation where all customer and vendor records can be looked up.

1.2.7 The "Yellow Pages" of a Corporation

A key MDM principle is that the MDM record of reference will represent the sole and single version of the truth for operational data across the company. This implies that business processes need to be established so that MDM does in fact uniquely identify each and every customer and vendor record that your organization deals with.

Currently, business users only search individual master data silos when they need to set up a new record. When they receive a create user request form, such as a Word document, a web form, or an email, business users typically search only the individual system to see if the customer or vendor record exists and then create the record if the search is unsuccessful.

By introducing SAP NetWeaver MDM to a company, this implies that the business users for each system will now need to initially search in SAP NetWeaver MDM to see if the business partner record exists. The new business procedure is:

▶ The data steward receives a request to create a new vendor or customer in a request form such as a Word document, a web form, or an email.

▶ Search the SAP NetWeaver MDM business partner repository.

▶ If the record is not found in the repository, then create a request for a new business partner record.

▶ The business partner record is then created in SAP NetWeaver MDM and distributed to the business application.

▶ The local business user updates the business partner record by adding the local attributes.

There are similarities between MDM and the yellow pages phone book services. MDM is the place where all business users should try to find the relevant business partner details. MDM is the single point of reference for business partners in a company, and searching MDM as part of the creation of a new business partner record is required to become part of the business process.

Given these requirements, it's important that MDM provides fast and informative business partner search functionality, such as by deploying Web Services with quick response times. We describe the creation of web services in Chapter 11. If the SAP NetWeaver MDM business partner search process is unsatisfactory, business users will resist the introduction of SAP NetWeaver MDM into the business partner setup.

1.2.8 The Importance of MDM Data Quality

If SAP NetWeaver MDM is the 500th system where business partner master data is maintained in your organization, then it must be demonstrably the "best" source of master data. You need to establish good operational procedures to ensure that the data is kept up to date, with frequent refreshes of data from both D&B and your consuming systems. You need to employ good SAP NetWeaver MDM data stewards and ensure that they are fully trained.

You must create good key performance indicators that measure the number of SAP NetWeaver MDM records, the number of unique D&B D-U-N-S Numbers keys, and the number of SAP NetWeaver MDM business partner updates (with refresh processes).

Be careful when you take on new SAP NetWeaver MDM projects and with the initial uploads of data into SAP NetWeaver MDM. Rigorous ongoing processes where requests are keyed online and validated through workflow processes will be bypassed during the batch migration of legacy systems records to SAP NetWeaver MDM. It's important to ensure that the legacy data is cleansed and complies with the SAP NetWeaver MDM data standards before loading.

Users must keep in mind that it should be a priority to protect the integrity of the unique key and avoid duplicate records at all costs. The MDM reputation is damaged if business users reveal inaccurate or duplicate data when searching the MDM data. The D&B D-U-N-S Number key should be mandated. Poor quality MDM data can result in the failure and the withdrawal of management support for your MDM program.

1.3   MDM Definitions

Business partners, materials, and employees are typically a company's most important master data objects. A *business partner* is either a customer or a vendor (otherwise known as a supplier). SAP NetWeaver MDM is applied to these objects primarily because there is an immediate and significant business benefit to be gained in driving revenue, streamlining costs, and ensuring compliance. In this book, we've restricted the scope just to business partners, because of its business importance and value.

Grouping a set of master data objects and attempting to treat them in the same way because of their frequency of update is a strange "techie" kind of thing to do. Although there are common features to updating a table, such as search before creating a duplicate, key fields and mandatory attributes, and create, update, and delete functionality, there are also significant differences in the business rules, processes, and business value for managing each of the different master data objects. The most important objects are customers and vendors, which is supported by the business case described in Chapter 3.

1.3.1 Master Data Objects

Let's now briefly discuss the Employee, Material, and Financial Accounting master data objects.

Employee Master Data

Employee data is a valuable master data object. Your company will invest considerable effort into maintaining this; unfortunately, they won't pay you twice, so duplicate records are strictly forbidden. There are many rules to be followed, including data protection, works councils, and national legislation. Protecting your identity is a key requirement.

Comparing business partner and employee master data processes is helpful. There are several potential employee keys: employee numbers, personal identifiers, and tax numbers such as the US Social Security Number and the UK National Insurance Number. The D&B D-U-N-S Number by comparison has the major advantage of being a global identifier.

Currently, there are many more rules to follow with maintaining personal data as compared to company data. Over time, this is likely to change due to acts such as Sarbanes-Oxley.

Material Master Data

Material master data is another important master data area. This covers both the products you purchase from vendors (or indirect materials) and those you sell to customers (direct materials).

One of the reasons we didn't cover this topic is that materials vary from company to company and industry to industry. You also don't have the helpful D&B D-U-N-S Number to use as a unique key; instead, your materials need to be subdivided into classes, subclasses, and classifications. Manufacturer's part numbers help but also create additional complexity as it's difficult to know for sure if two similar parts produced by different manufactures are in fact the same material. You will need to decide whether to store one or two records of reference in SAP NetWeaver MDM in these situations.

Financial Master Data

Financial data, such as cost center, profit center, and chart of accounts, will also be managed once by your organization. Rather than using SAP NetWeaver MDM, financial data is best managed in an SAP ERP 6.0 environment, which has the pre-built rules already developed.

1.3.2 Business Partners

Often, companies may buy from and sell to the same companies. A *business partner* is a company you either buy materials or services from (vendor) or sell products or services to (customer).

The company structures of your business partners won't actually change depending on your relationship with them. Also you can trade with legal entities throughout a Corporate Linkage. You may sell services to a Global Ultimate company, procure services from a Domestic Ultimate company, procure materials from a Parent company, and sell products to a Subsidiary company. With complex large organizations, you may be trading with up to 15 levels of hierarchical data.

The fundamental question of what a business partner is can be answered by considering all of the nodes on the D&B Corporate Linkage where you transact with a company, from the legal entity you deal with up to the top Global Ultimate level. This allows you to answer the following key business questions:

▶ Am I leveraging the scale of my company by understanding the global overview of my dealings with a business partner?

▶ What is the financial and trading risk information of a business partner?

▶ Is there a risk that the business partner will be made bankrupt?

If you restrict yourself to just considering the legal entities you are actually transacting with, then aggregating your spend and sales (and risks) across a corporation would be impossible.

At the levels you do trade with, it's possible to have several different relationships with your business partners. Figure 1.4 shows an example where a company is both buying and selling from the Subsidiary S Co. On the vendor management side, there is an ordering address and a payment address to set up. On the customer management side, there is a ship to, a bill to, and a payment address to establish.

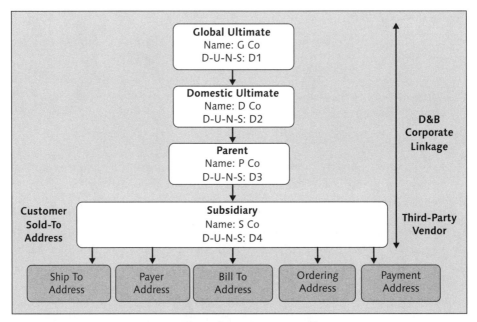

Figure 1.4 Business Partner Master Data and D&B Corporate Linkage

Consider your business partner by the D&B Corporate Linkage structure. There will be one structure that is the "trunk" of the organization you deal with. The customers and vendors you deal with exist as "branches" of the tree.

The business partner relationships can be set up once in SAP NetWeaver MDM. A one-to-one relationship exists between the D-U-N-S Number and the D&B Corporate Linkage. However, you need to set up separate customer and vendor relationships because these are set up in different tables with differing rules in your consuming systems.

1.3.3 Vendor Definitions

Vendor master data is the master data information of companies you purchase materials or services from.

You can procure materials and services with legal entities throughout a Corporate Linkage from the Global Ultimate and the Domestic Ultimate companies down to the Parent and Subsidiaries. With complex large organizations, you may be purchasing from several levels of a company hierarchy.

▸ Your business leaders are keen to understand the total spending with a vendor and whether it is a "legitimate" vendor that has been authenticated. This will enable you to leverage the scale of your company by understanding the global overview of the dealings with a vendor and the potential strengths (and weaknesses) within your supply chain.

ISAP NetWeaver MDM and the D&B Corporate Linkage help you to understand the company structures of your vendors. This helps you to address who your vendors are, where they are located, what their capabilities are, whether or not they are stable, and if you should be trading with them.

In the vendor example in Figure 1.5, D&B provide a Corporate Linkage of four legal entities. The Subsidiary S Co is linked to two partner records: an ordering address and a payment address. The Subsidiary, the ordering address, and the payment address are each linked to the same D&B D-U-N-S Number (D4).

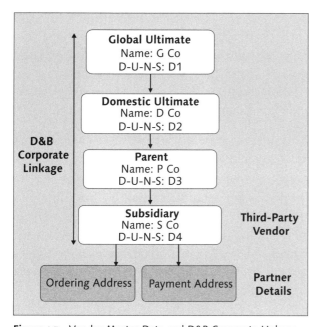

Figure 1.5 Vendor Master Data and D&B Corporate Linkage

SAP ERP 6.0 Vendor Management

In SAP ERP 6.0, business transactions are posted to accounts and managed using those accounts. Business users must create a *vendor master record* for each account that is required, which controls how business transactions are recorded and processed by the system.

Specifications made in the vendor master records include the default values when you post items to the account such as the terms of payment. The vendor master record also stores the attributes needed for processing business transactions such as bank details and payment methods (e.g., check or bank transfer) for automatic payments.

A vendor master record is required to allow financial transactions to be entered against the vendor. For purchasing documents to be created for a vendor; the master record must be extended to the relevant company code.

A *vendor account* is used to represent and control a vendor, and a *vendor account group* is a subdivision of suppliers that controls the functionality available to the vendor account. Partner functions include the ordering address, which is the address a purchase order is raised against, and a payment address, which is the address to which an invoice is sent.

The LFA1 vendor table is an important table in SAP ERP 6.0. This is supported by the number of SAP tables that are linked to it. Typically, LFA1 has more than 30 parent tables and more than 700 child tables in the data model. Invalid or duplicate record details in your LFA1 table will impact many other tables, data records, and functionality in SAP ERP 6.0.

1.3.4 Customers

Customer master data refers to the master data information of companies you sell to. Similarly to vendors, you can sell products and services with legal entities throughout a Corporate Linkage from the Global Ultimate and the Domestic Ultimate companies down to the Parent and Subsidiaries. With complex large organizations, you may be selling to several levels of a company hierarchy. Let's consider some of the key management reporting questions of your business leaders:

- ▶ Who are my most profitable customers?
- ▶ How do I increase my revenue from my existing customers?
- ▶ How do I improve my operational efficiency when dealing with a customer?
- ▶ What is my credit risk with a customer?

In the customer example in Figure 1.6, D&B provides a Corporate Linkage of four legal entities. The Subsidiary S Co is a sold-to address and is linked to three customer records: a ship to address, a bill to address, and a payer address. The sold to, ship to, bill to, and payer addresses are each linked to the same D&B D-U-N-S Number (D4).

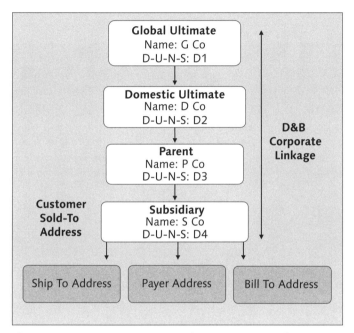

Figure 1.6   Customer Master Data and D&B Corporate Linkage

SAP ERP 6.0 Customer Management

In an SAP ERP 6.0 application, all business transactions are posted to and managed in accounts. Users must create a *customer master record* for each required account containing the data that controls how business transactions are recorded and processed by the system. It also includes information about a customer that is needed to conduct business.

Both the accounting (FI-AR) and the sales (SD) modules use the customer master records. The Sales and Distribution (SD) application component is used to enter and process customer master records for order processing, shipping, and billing.

Specifications in SAP customer master records are used as default values when you post items to the account such as the terms of payment. For processing business transactions, you set up account control data, such as the number of the General Ledger (GL) reconciliation account and the dunning procedure, the date of the last dunning notice, and the address required for the automatic dunning process. For communication with the customer, you set up the relevant ship to, bill to, sold to, and payer details.

The SAP KNA1 and LFA1 Tables

Similarly to the LFA1 vendor table, the KNA1 customer table is an extremely important master data table in SAP ERP 6.0. You can find evidence to support this if you examine the SAP ERP 6.0 data model and consider the number of tables that have relationships to both KNA1 and LFA1.

You will typically find that the KNA1 customer table has relationships to more than 60 parent tables and more than 950 child tables depending on your implementation. Similarly, the LFA1 vendor table typically has relationships to more than 30 parent tables and 700 child tables.

Invalid or duplicate record details in both your KNA1 and LFA1 table also impacts many associated SAP data tables, records, and functionalities.

Maintaining customer and vendor data through MDM is really not just updating a couple of SAP tables both from a business and a technical view. There is much more to it than that!

1.3.5 Natural Persons

Natural persons are individuals a company either purchases from or sells to. Customers represent the B2C (business-to-consumer channel) as opposed to the B2B (business-to-business channel) we have so far considered.

Although we don't cover the management of natural persons data in this book, the following points are worthy of consideration. First, decide whether the natural persons are truly global data by identifying how many records are shared across multiple business applications. There is no similar concept to the D&B Corporate Linkage for natural persons so each individual is a standalone record.

You should separate your natural person's data from business partner data in MDM by maintaining the data in a separate repository, and you shouldn't attempt to link the data with the D&B D-U-N-S Number. Natural person's data is subject to data protection and data privacy laws that vary from country to country. Creating a single MDM natural persons repository is likely to require legal agreements for large companies that span many regions. A unique key will help you identify natural persons, but be careful in how you design and maintain any personal identifier and consider the identity rules and the consequences of identity theft.

Performing a mini business case exercise assessing the benefits of maintaining natural persons in MDM is recommended.

1.4   Summary

Chapter 1 introduced the key MDM concepts and definitions. We discussed the business issues caused by master data silos within a company and also introduced the Dun & Bradstreet services, including the D&B D-U-N-S Number, D&B Corporate Linkage, and Entity Matching. The MDM role was deemed the company's "yellow pages," and we explained the importance of MDM data quality and the need to be the best, most complete, accurate and up-to-date source of business partner data in your organization. Finally, we provided some definitions of the master data objects, including business partners, vendors, and customers.

Let's now investigate in detail the issues faced by a fictional Company CO1, which uses multiple business applications to maintain its customer and vendor master data in the absence of MDM.

Let's now consider the issues faced by companies that maintain customer and vendor records in multiple business applications in the absence of MDM and data governance and standards.

2   Why MDM Is Needed: Master Data Silos Issues

This chapter considers how organizations with multiple business applications manage their master data without MDM. We'll analyze the business issues that are caused when these applications and master data "silos" are maintained by different organizational teams. We'll discuss two detailed case studies and also consider the implications of business mergers and acquisitions. Finally, we'll describe how the issues of master data silos are further compounded for large organizations.

Typically in many companies today, master data is created in multiple systems and spreadsheets. As long as the data resides in these multiple silos, it continues to evolve independently and often provides conflicting information. Business decisions and processes based on inconsistent master data will than lead to inaccuracies, greater waste and customer dissatisfaction, and increased business risk with potential financial and compliance issues. The problem of inconsistent information is compounded when your company then needs to share and publish its master data with your business partners or across your organization.

Two case studies in this chapter illustrate the current customer and vendor maintenance processes in an organization and the related issues. In Case Study 1, we consider the issues faced by a fictional Company C1 with a relatively "simple" architecture. In Case Study 2, we move on to discuss the additional complexity caused when company C1 then merges with company C2 and acquires another set of business processes and applications.

Let's first introduce an analogy.

> **The Importance of Sharing Master Data — Boys and Toys**
>
> Young children often fight for their favorite toy, and they refuse to share with their siblings or best friends.
>
> As they grow up and become business leaders, they will have new toys — marketing divisions, customer services divisions, and financial accounting departments. They will each look to control their piece of the organization and will be the system owners of the Customer Relationship Management application, the Sales and Distribution application, and the Financial Accounting application.
>
> Unfortunately, they still need to share because the management of customer records and order taking, invoicing, and payment processes span the entire organization. Sharing master data and integrating business processes across the applications is a critical success factor to enable them to "play happily" in a successful company.
>
> There is a significant business investment in deploying an SAP CRM, SAP SCM, and SAP NetWeaver BI business application. Shared customer and vendor master data enabled by SAP NetWeaver MDM is a prerequisite to maximize the business value from these investments.

Let's now move on to Case Study 1, where we will describe the Company CO1, which unfortunately hasn't understood the importance of sharing or the value of maintaining its customer and vendor records.

2.1   Case Study 1 — Master Data Silos

The case study highlights the issues caused by maintaining business partner master data in multiple systems across an organization. Let's imagine that you are a senior business leader for the fictional Company CO1. You are interested in understanding more about your company's profitability and your total expenditure with your leading customers and vendors.

▶ You'll consider who are your most profitable customers and how you can improve your revenue and operational efficiency when dealing with a customer. Similarly you will consider your spending with a vendor and whether you are leveraging the scale of your company, by understanding the global overview of dealings throughout the vendor's corporate structure.

Company CO1 currently has five systems where business partner master records are maintained. Figure 2.1 shows the overall applications architecture. We can see from the diagram how the five business systems are linked together and also that the information stored on the customer and vendor records varies by application.

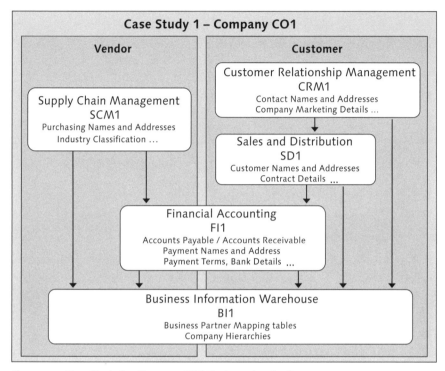

Figure 2.1 Case Study 1 – Company CO1 Business Applications

We'll consider how the customer and vendor master data records are maintained in each of these business applications. Let's now discuss the Financial Accounting application FI1 and the processes for creating vendor records.

2.1.1 Financial Accounting Application (FI1) — Vendors and Accounts Payable

In Company CO1, the system owner for the Financial Accounting (FI) application is the Chief Financial Officer (CFO), and the business users are the Accounts Payable (AP) and Accounts Receivable (AR) teams. In our example, Company CO1 has outsourced its financial accounting operational processes to a third party.

Let's consider the various ways in which the vendor records are created in the FI application. The AP team may need to create a new vendor as part of the process to manage a request for an invoice payment or a request to raise a purchase order. The AP team may receive a create vendor request form. Many of the FI1 vendor records were created in the SAP FI CO application as part of a data conversion exercise. Mergers and acquisitions also provide a source of new vendor records.

The following are the create vendor processes:

1. A vendor raises an invoice that requires payment.

2. The procurement team raises a purchase order request.

3. A vendor request form is completed.

4. Vendor records are created as part of a data migration exercise.

5. A merger or acquisition creates a batch of new vendor records.

Each of these processes are discussed in the following subsections.

1. A Vendor Raises an Invoice That Requires Payment

You may have assumed that to pay an invoice, a purchase order would previously have been raised in the FI application. However, because the CO1 business processes and systems are not integrated, in this scenario, the first time the AP team is made aware of a purchase is when the vendor sends an invoice that needs to be paid. The invoice includes the vendor's payment name and address details, payment instructions, and payment date.

The AP team contacts the relevant person in your organization to authorize payment. This can take time and impact the Service Level Agreement, which has a measure based on managing the payment process in a defined number of days.

After authorization has been agreed upon, the AP user then searches the SAP database to see if he can find the vendor. If the record cannot be matched based on the name and address details provided on the invoice, then he creates a new vendor record in the FI1 application.

In these situations, creating the vendor record is an additional, unplanned step in the invoice payment process. In this scenario in Company CO1, limited data quality checks are carried out; if the invoice contains incomplete vendor information, these will nevertheless be entered into your FI1 application. The main business driver is to arrange the payment of the invoice to the correct bank account, with the quality of the vendor master data record of secondary importance.

The vendor data attributes entered relate to the accounting view of the vendor: the payment name and address, the bank details, and the payment terms.

2. The Procurement Team Raises a Purchase Order Request

Company CO1 has a rule that all invoices exceeding $10,000 must also have a corresponding purchase order raised in the FI application. Your procurement team currently raises a purchase order request by sending an email to the AP team using a standard template.

Once again, the AP user searches the SAP database to see if he can find the vendor. If the record cannot be matched using the name and address supplied on the purchase order, then a new vendor record will be created in the FI1 application with the base details provided on the purchase order. In this scenario, the creation of the vendor record is an additional step in the create purchase order process.

3. A Vendor Request Form Is Completed

In Company CO1, there is a vendor request form for the setup of new vendor records in the FI application. The AP team has created the template for the form, but it is rarely used. The form includes the data attributes required for the accounting view of the vendor, including payment names and addresses, bank details, and payment terms.

Customer and Vendor Master Data Forms

It's important for your MDM program to design a suitable customer and vendor maintenance form that captures the relevant details for the whole of your organization and not just a subset, such as for the AP and AR teams. A clear and comprehensive master data entry form is an excellent way to enforce data standards, and to mandate and validate relevant data attributes.

A good question to ask is how many customer and vendor master data forms currently exist across your organization. Is there one per application? What are the mandatory attributes? What data validation is carried out? Is the completion of the form mandatory?

Later, we'll discuss how implementing an SAP Interactive Forms by Adobe solution can improve your customer and vendor master data capture processes. The user interface is slick and flexible; you can also enforce mandatory attributes and allow look-ups with dropdown screens. The Adobe forms are integrated with the SAP NetWeaver Portal so that the details can be automatically uploaded without rekeying the details. This is excellent functionality that we'll discuss further in Part 2 of this book.

---

4. A Vendor Record Was Created During a Previous Data Migration

Company CO1 previously used a non-SAP FI application but migrated to the SAP FI CO solution two years ago. The deployment team's major focus was to ensure that all outstanding transactions and AP open items were migrated to the new FI1 application. The critical success factor was to match the opening and closing balances and to provide an audit trail to support this.

However, the previous non-SAP FI vendor master data records had been poorly maintained. The system had limited functionality, which meant that duplicate vendor records were created to handle situations such as companies with multiple payment terms or bank details. It was also difficult to search the previous application, so duplicate records were created. The non-SAP data model was limited, and when converted to the SAP model, this created yet further duplicate records. The legacy systems data attributes were a subset of the SAP attributes.

To meet the deployments schedule and critical success factor, the data conversion team decided to copy all vendor records, including duplicates, to the SAP FICO application. This also meant that records for inactive vendors that had not been used for several years were also created in the new system.

Because only partial vendor details were migrated during the data conversion to the FI1 application, this made these records difficult to retrieve as part of the ongoing search processes. As a result, further duplicate records have subsequently been created in the FI1 application.

SAP NetWeaver MDM and Data Conversions

Your SAP NetWeaver MDM program needs to be closely involved with each of your company's major implementation projects to influence their data conversion processes. The master data standards that you'll mandate on all new vendors and customers records also apply to the records that already exist in your business applications.

You should avoid copying incomplete, inaccurate, and duplicate vendor master data records from an old system to a new system. Make every effort to prevent GIGO (Garbage IN – Garbage OUT) with any future deployments of business applications.

---

5. A Merger or Acquisition Creates a Batch of New Vendor Records

A merger or acquisition is another way vendor records can be created in your FI application. This is a similar process to a data conversion process and involves loading a batch file of records into FI1. Again, a primary business driver is ensuring that all AP open items are migrated to your FI application.

If a vendor record already exists in your FI1 application, this will result in a duplicate record being created. If the company you are acquiring has a different data model with varying data attributes, this can cause data conversion issues. The implications of mergers and acquisitions are discussed later in this chapter, in Case Study 2.

Let's now move on to consider the processes by which customer records are created in your FI1 application.

2.1.2 Financial Accounting Application (FI1) — Customers and Accounts Receivables

In Company CO1, your AR processes are also outsourced, and there are also multiple ways in which a customer record can be created:

1. The sales team raises a manual invoice for a new customer.
2. An invoice is raised in the Sales and Distribution application SD1 for a new customer payment address, which automatically creates a new customer record in FI1.
3. A create customer request form is completed.
4. Customer records are created as part of a data migration exercise.
5. A merger or acquisition loads a batch of new customer records.

Each of these processes is discussed in the following subsections.

1. The Sales Team Raises a Manual Invoice for a New Customer

Unfortunately, your non-SAP Sales and Distribution application (SD1) has limited functionality and isn't suitable for maintaining the complex contracts and agreements that your sales representatives have recently negotiated with several of your customers. Their innovative new offer attracts a lot of interest with new customers and is managed outside the current systems in spreadsheets.

The customer services team sends the invoice to the AR team for manual entry into the FI1 application. This contains the customer's payment name and address details. The AR user searches the SAP FI1 application to see if he can find the customer. If the record cannot be matched based on the name and address details provided on the invoice, then a new customer record is created.

2. An Invoice Is Raised in the Sales and Distribution Application SD1 for a New Customer Payment Address, which Automatically Creates a New Customer Record in FI1

In Company CO1, established customer interfaces exist between the SD1 and FI1 applications. The SD1 application maintains the majority of your customer details, including the legal entity details (or the equivalent to the SAP sold-to record) and the delivery, invoice, and payment address details.

The SD1 legal entity and the payer details are interfaced to the FI1 application and stored as sold-to and payer records. A minimal attribute set is interfaced to the FI1 application, including the SD1 system key. The SD1 application currently contains duplicate records that are transferred into FI1.

3. A Create Customer Request Form Is Completed

A create customer request form provides the details to set up a new customer in the FI1 application. The AR team created the template, but as with the vendor request form, this is rarely used. The form includes the data attributes required for the accounting view of the customer, including the payment names and addresses, the bank details, and the payment terms.

4. A Customer Record Is Created During a Data Migration Exercise

As with the vendor records, at the time of the FI1 go-live, the data conversion team copied all of the customer records, including duplicate records, from the legacy system to the FI1 application. These records included customers who had been inactive for several years and were of poor quality, with missing address details.

Because incomplete customer name and address details were migrated to the FI1 application, these original converted customer records are difficult to retrieve as part of the ongoing search processes. This has been a cause of further duplicate customer records over time.

5. A Merger or Acquisition Creates a Batch of New Customer Records

A merger or acquisition is another way for customer records to be created in your FI1 application. Again, the primary driver at the time of the merger is to ensure that all AR open items are migrated to the new system so as a result all customers are transferred.

If the customer record already exists in your FI1 application, this results in a duplicate record being created. Also, if the company you are acquiring has a different customer data model with varying data attributes, this causes issues.

Let's now switch applications and consider how customer master records are created in your CRM application.

2.1.3 Customer Relationship Management Application (CRM1)

Your CRM1 business application provides the functionality to cover many customer interaction activities, including marketing, sales, and customer retention. CRM1 supports communication with customers via a number of channels, including the Internet, contact centers and mobile clients. Sales representatives can access data and functions contained in CRM1 via offline applications, which are then synchronized.

The advantages of the CRM1 application include providing a global overview of your customer data and understanding who your customers are and their contribution to sales. This overview helps you identify the potential strengths (and weaknesses) in your customer relationships and helps you better understand the people and accounts you are dealing with. You can also reach out to customers with better contact information details.

Your CRM1 application stores a lot of detailed information regarding your customers, including contact names, account details, channels of trade details, and complaint management information.

In Company CO1, the CRM1 application owner is the marketing director and the business users are the marketing team, the sales representatives, and the customer services division. Unfortunately, in Company CO1, however, data standards are not enforced when entering new customers in the CRM1 application. The sales representatives in particular have insufficient time to complete the administrative tasks.

Many of the customer record details were originally migrated into CRM1 from the Sales and Distribution application (SD1). At that time, all records were uploaded, including the inactive records and the duplicates. The SD1 and CRM1 data models are quite different, and only a small number of data attributes were initially transferred.

Two years ago, the marketing team purchased a list of prospects for a new market segment that was then being targeted. These were uploaded as a batch file into the CRM1 application, but unfortunately, the business idea did not materialize. The prospect list is now out of date, and these prospects are unlikely to be converted into new actual customers. However, there are no archiving procedures implemented with the CRM1 application, so these records continue to appear when users attempt to search and retrieve details. This data quality issue has caused negative feedback, and several more duplicate records have subsequently been created.

There are no operational interfaces from the CRM1 application to either the SD1 or the FI1 applications. Customer orders are placed in the SD1 application because of the requirements of the stock availability functionality. Unfortunately, the CRM1 application does not show the current financial transaction details with customers, which reduces the value of the functionality.

> **SAP NetWeaver MDM and CRM**
>
> In Case Study 1, we describe a situation where Company CO1 isn't getting good value from its CRM program. The root causes are that the CRM program hasn't appreciated the importance of sharing its customer data and processes across the CO1 organization and also the difficulties of integrating "best of breed" applications.
>
> Dividing processes such as customer management, order taking, and invoicing across multiple, disparate business applications introduces risk and needs careful process and data design consideration. For the CRM program to be successful, it requires consistent, shared customer data with the SD1 and the FI1 applications. SAP NetWeaver MDM is the tool to provide this and to "glue" these applications together.
>
> We won't be so bold as to suggest that by implementing MDM with CRM you will get a successful CRM program. However, MDM is an important building block for CRM that will help to overcome some of the obstacles by enabling customer data to be shared across the organization.

The process of converting a prospect record to a customer record is an important one for SAP NetWeaver MDM. At this point, duplicate records can be created, or incomplete data may be entered. If these prospects to customer processes are driven from the CRM1 application for Company CO1, then SAP NetWeaver MDM is required to be tightly integrated with CRM1.

2.1.4 Sales and Distribution Application (SD1)

The Sales and Distribution (SD1) application provides functionality to manage the customer sales, delivery, and billing tasks in Company CO1. Key elements include customer quotation processing, contract management, sales order processing, delivery processing, and billing and sales information details. The application owner is the customer services division manager, and the customer services division team members are the application users.

In SAP, the SD component allows users to manage sales and distribution activities. The business processes include scenarios for sales, shipping, billing, sales support, and sales information.

However, the SAP solution is not used in Company CO1, which chose instead to implement a non-SAP package solution several years ago. In the subsequent years, the company has tailored the solution to meet its specific needs. The original package provider no longer supports the application.

The SD1 application provides a lot of the customer management processing for Company CO1. Customers and contracts are created, orders are placed, and invoices are produced and sent both to customers and to the FI1 application for payment. However, in an increasing number of cases, invoices are now created in spreadsheets and sent directly to customers. Manual invoicing is now required because the types of contracts currently being negotiated are too complex for the SD1 contracts application. The manual invoices are processed in the FI1 application.

The customer records in the SD1 application are not in a healthy state. The original data migration process did make some attempt to cleanse the data, but the records have been poorly maintained in the intervening years. Archiving processes have not been implemented, and customer records are updated haphazardly, without formal data standards. The business users have moved their attention to the maintenance of the spreadsheets to manage the complex contracts, and there is little confidence in the quality of the customer records in SD1.

SD1 is now a "tired" application that has seen little business or IT investment in recent years. The operational support team has been reduced to a minimal level to save costs, and all of the team members who tailored the original solution have now moved elsewhere. Most of Company CO1's recent IT spend has been on the CRM1 and BI1 programs.

The Consolidated MDM Model and the Sales and Distribution Application

When Company CO1 decides to proceed with its MDM program, the SD1 application is a classical case where the consolidated MDM model can practically be applied.

SD1 now has a limited lifetime, and several business leaders are advocating that the application should now be replaced by SAP ERP 6.0 software. By following the consolidated model, the D&B D-U-N-S Number can be tagged to each of the SD1 customer records, and the key mapping can be stored in SAP NetWeaver MDM. Periodically, SD1 customer records will be extracted for comparison and to ensure consistency with MDM.

This provides the benefits of matching the SD1 customer records to the CRM1, FI1, and BI1 records without initially needing to change the SD1 processes to integrate with SAP NetWeaver MDM. This will be the quickest way to implement SAP NetWeaver MDM. The centralized model can then be designed as part of the SD1 replacement project.

We will now consider Company CO1's Supply Chain Management (SCM) application.

2.1.5   Supply Chain Management Application (SCM1)

The Supply Chain Management application (SCM1) provides the functionality to perform sourcing, procurement, and logistics management activities. It covers the movements and storage of materials, inventory, and finished goods. In global companies, sourcing may be managed on a global basis. The vendor master record details include the bidder details, and the sourcing and procurement contacts. The Head of Procurement is the SCM1 application owner, and the business users are the Supply Chain Management team members.

The quality of the vendor data in Company CO1 has been significantly improved in the past six months. The Head of Procurement recently joined the CO1 organization, and he has introduced some new ideas regarding the procurement strategies. As part of this initiative, many vendors have recently been blocked. However, the supply chain processes were severely impacted when a key supplier was suddenly made bankrupt. The Head of Procurement has seen the business value of SAP NetWeaver MDM for vendor management and is the initial MDM champion in the CO1 organization.

SAP NetWeaver MDM, Vendors, and Pilot Implementations

In many respects, establishing vendor master data management processes in SAP NetWeaver MDM is easier than for customers. Your procurement processes tend to have tighter controls with a defined set of rules that must be followed before company funds can be spent. Customer sales can be more entrepreneurial with marketing teams and sales representatives developing nonstandard innovative offers to generate new revenue.

Vendor data models also tend to be more straightforward as you will typically transact closely with the company's legal entity structures. Customer data models can be more complex with multiple ship-to and bill-to addresses to maintain.

For these reasons, vendor management is a good master data object to start your SAP NetWeaver MDM journey with in an initial pilot implementation.

Let's now consider how master data silos impact SAP NetWeaver Business Intelligence (BI1).

2.1.6   Business Intelligence (BI1)

The Business Intelligence Warehouse (BI1) provides the data and tools for analyzing, monitoring, and measuring your organization's key performance indicators. It gathers information from several applications (CRM1, FI1, SCM1, and SD1 in Case Study 1). Vendor and customer details are key data elements and business partner hierarchies also provide important business information, particularly for spend analytics and credit limit reporting. Typically, both vendor and customer names and addresses details are stored along with the company hierarchies. The BI1 application owner can vary, and in Company CO1, is jointly managed by the head of procurement and the customer services division manager. An operational performance team manages the BI Extract, Transform, and Load (ETL) processes to populate the data warehouse and to produce the standard management reports.

 The Business Intelligence Warehouse has been Company CO1's biggest recent IT investment. The business case was based on the benefits of aggregating the data in one place to enable a better understanding of the total company spend and profitability. The BI1 solution also provides the functionality to drill down into hierarchical data to explore areas of business interest.

The BI1 application is required to provide reliable information easily to the people who need it, when they need it. It should facilitate speedier, informed decision making so that you can find the information you need quickly and with certainty.

Accurate and accessible information is needed to support management processes, which include setting customer and vendor plans and targets, monitoring operations, analyzing outcomes, and reporting the results to your key stakeholders.

Unfortunately, the poor quality of the underlying customer and vendor master data records in Company CO1 is a major barrier to the success of the Business Intelligence Warehouse. As we've described, inconsistent master data exists across the organization, with duplicate records, partial records, and out-of date records to analyze and no single source of truth. There is also redundant data, and the data models differ across the business applications.

The BI1 ETL processes attempt to develop some rules and logic to improve on this situation, but in the end, your application programmers cannot create system-matching rules when the core master data maintenance rules are not in place. Attempting to match company records across systems by using matching algorithms and phonetic matching techniques cannot overcome duplicate, incomplete and out-of-date records in the source systems.

Unfortunately, the BI1 reports now provide limited value. It's not possible to accurately identify some of your customers and vendors, and in the absence of the D&B Corporate Linkage, you can't aggregate spend and sales up to the Global Ultimate level. The BI1 application is unfortunately a victim of the Garbage in — Garbage Out problem that we described earlier. The Business Information warehouse reports the CO1 Company had hoped would add so much value are hardly used. The misleading information provided by partial spend and sales aggregation reports are in many ways worse than no information because invalid business decisions based on the incomplete and inaccurate BI1 data can prove to be costly.

SAP NetWeaver MDM and Business Intelligence BI

Not surprisingly, MDM programs are sometimes led by a Business Intelligence program initiative. Accurate customer and vendor records are an essential prerequisite for a successful BI program to deliver valuable business information.

However, if you are considering combining your SAP NetWeaver MDM and BI programs, then you should take care to fully consider your objectives. Ideally, your SAP NetWeaver MDM processes will be integral to the creation of the vendor and customer records in your consuming systems. These need to be established as *frontend* processes, to avoid the creation of duplicate records and to authenticate your business partners ahead of any transactional processing.

SAP NetWeaver MDM and Business Intelligence BI (Cont.)
However, BI reporting is a *backend* process; that is, it captures the transactional data from the various business applications and provides analysis tools to assess the data. It's important not to confuse the SAP NetWeaver MDM and BI objectives in these BI-led initiatives because the frontend and backend processes are very different.

To summarize Case Study 1, vendor master data is maintained in two applications: SCM1 and FI1 (AP data). Customer master data is maintained in three applications: CRM1, SD1, and FI1 (AR data). Finally, both vendor and customer data are maintained and analyzed in BI1. The system, the master data attributes, and the organizational users are shown in Table 2.1.

Application	Master Data Attributes	CO1 Application	CO1 Organization	Internal/ External
SCM1 – Supply Chain Management application	Vendor purchasing names and addresses; supply chain relationships details	Non-SAP	Supply chain management team	Internally maintained by employees
FI1 – Financial Accounting application	Vendor payment names and addresses, payment terms, and bank details	SAP FI CO component (CO1 instance)	Financials AP team	Outsourced to an external third-party service provider
CRM1 – Customer Relationship Management application	Customer contact names and addresses, marketing and relationships details	Non-SAP	Marketing and sales representatives and customer services division	Internally maintained by employees
SD1 – Sales and Distribution application	Customer names and addresses, contract details, invoicing details	Non-SAP	Customer services division	Internally maintained by employees

Table 2.1 Company CO1 Applications and Organizational Teams

Application	Master Data Attributes	CO1 Application	CO1 Organization	Internal/ External
FI1 – Financial Accounting application	Customer payment names and addresses; Financial Accounting details, e.g., payment terms and bank details	SAP FI CO component (CO1 instance)	Financials AR team	Outsourced to an external third-party service provider.
BI1 – Business Intelligence	Business partner mapping tables; company hierarchy structures	Non-SAP	Operational performance team	Internally maintained by employees

Table 2.1 Company CO1 Applications and Organizational Teams (Cont.)

The next section summarizes the issues that you'll encounter when you maintain customer and vendor master data across multiple business applications.

2.2 Maintaining Master Data Across the Silos

Earlier we described MDM as a business application sitting between the record of origin and your consuming systems. Linking the record of reference to the record of origin is relatively straightforward. There is a 1:1 relationship with the D&B D-U-N-S Number as the unique key.

However, the complexity of the consuming systems provides many of the challenges for your SAP NetWeaver MDM program. Each business application has a different data model and data attributes and is maintained using different processes by different teams. The data quality will vary depending on both its current and historical treatment. This includes the initial data conversion, the operational maintenance of the customer and vendor records, the system interfaces, and the batch import of records during mergers and acquisitions.

Your SAP NetWeaver MDM program will need to persuade each of the consuming systems owners and business users to both change their current processes and cleanse the existing data. They each must be willing to share the common key —

the D&B D-U-N-S Number — and to follow the new data standards to incorporate SAP NetWeaver MDM into the operational business procedures.

2.2.1 Business Data Varies by Application

The business application, its data model, and its functionality drive the stored customer and vendor data. For example, the Financial Accounting application stores financial data and the important attributes such as bank details and payment terms. The names and address details are typically for legal entities and payer addresses.

A best practice for companies is to establish standard processes and controls both for supplier and customer registration. For vendors, information such as company search by name, identifier, location, company identification and contact information, demographics information, financial information and references, supplier diversity information, insurance, federal tax, and certification information are all relevant.

Following are the key questions that you need to address for your SAP NetWeaver MDM program (we'll consider these design considerations further in Chapter 6):

▶ Which of these attributes are your global attributes to be shared across all of your business applications?

▶ Which attributes are best maintained locally in the business applications?

▶ Will your customer and vendor master data be captured in one request form and then subsequently be keyed or uploaded into the relevant business applications?

2.2.2 Different Teams and Organizations

In Case Study 1, we defined a situation in Company CO1 where the marketing team, the supply chain management team, the customer facing team, and the financial accounting team each acted independently, and company-wide data standards were not established. The quality of data entry was variable and based on the business unit's operational procedures, the individuals involved, and their line management.

Let's not forget that the data conversion team who created the original master data records, the IT division who created applications interfaces, and the mergers and acquisition teams who uploaded a batch of records have all impacted the quality of your master data. These batch processes and interfaces need to be subjected to the same rigor and data standards as your day-to-day operational procedures.

Over time, the people and teams who maintain your master data will change. Individuals move on to new roles and pass on their accountabilities to new team members. In Case Study 1, the handover of the customer and vendor maintenance processes is likely to be a brief one because there is little formal documentation and few operational procedures. There will be a handover process and some limited training, but it is unlikely that the new business users will exactly follow the same processes as their predecessors. Attributes such as search terms may be treated differently, and attributes that are nonmandatory may be omitted. Duplicate records will be created if the new business users do not understand the previous search processes and the historical maintenance procedures. The new users also may not understand the value of the customer and vendor record to the company because the training didn't cover this.

Also, organizational units will change over time. Companies reorganize, and the customer and vendor record maintenance teams may centralize and then decentralize over time. Each time there is an organizational change and new users take over, this can again introduce new business processes for maintaining your master data.

2.2.3   Impacts of Outsourcing

Potentially each of these maintenance processes can be outsourced to an external third-party service provider, which adds yet one more team and one more company into the process. In Case Study 1, the Financial Accounting processes have been outsourced.

There is an old adage that you should "never outsource a problem," and currently there is a problem with the maintenance of master data in Company CO1. The lack of data standards and unclear operational procedures resulted in many duplicate and out-of-date records in the FI1 application before it was handed over to the outsource company to maintain.

Outsourcing a data entry process to an offshore company introduces complexity because the new users won't necessarily know local name and address standards. This issue is particularly relevant for global companies with global systems. Over time, a changing workforce may not fully understand the previous processes and the historical usage of business partner master data attributes. Inconsistent application of customer and vendor record entry over time causes confusion and data quality issues.

The service levels you agree on with your outsourced partner may not include the data quality of your master data records as a key metric. The Service Level Agreement may actually discourage accurate master data with other metrics such as all invoice payments to be made within x days acting as a disincentive. For example, if a customer or vendor request form is inaccurate or incomplete and needs to be returned and queried with the requestor, this will slow down the payment process and jeopardize the SLA. In these cases, incomplete master records may be created so that invoice payments can be made. Future searches of the incomplete data will not match accurately, and the data won't be maintained appropriately and duplicates will be created.

Carrying out rigorous searches of existing data to see if the business partner is already set up takes time and effort. After your business partner master data quality is compromised with incomplete or inaccurate names and address details, the duplicate record setup increases, and searching for existing companies is less likely to be carried out.

These basic search and maintenance issues need to be resolved, which involves people from the outsourced team cleansing and removing duplicate master records. You need to establish change management procedures to mandate the new SAP NetWeaver MDM processes as part of the customer and vendor record creation processes.

SAP NetWeaver MDM and Outsourcing

Eventually the SAP NetWeaver MDM program's operational processes will become a good candidate for outsourcing. The D&B Entity Matching processes, the SAP NetWeaver MDM Company Search processes, and the maintenance processes are core services that can be externally sourced with appropriate Service Level Agreements.

However, you should leave outsourcing until your SAP NetWeaver MDM solution has scaled and you are close to the end of the SAP NetWeaver MDM Phase 2. A lot of "value add" project work and data discovery with consuming systems needs to be done before you consider "commoditizing" SAP NetWeaver MDM and outsourcing the SAP NetWeaver MDM services as your organization's way forward.

2.2.4 Features of Unlinked Systems

Multiple business applications linked in the way we described in Case Study 1 have the following properties. Vendors and customers are set up several times in various pockets with different parts of your organization performing their business processes in isolation. The business applications data models and business rules vary and are not integrated. Invoices can be paid by creating supplier records in the Financial Accounting system.

Even when companies use an integrated solution such as SAP provides, they sometimes choose to implement only parts of the solution such as the Financial Accounting functions, while preferring to use specialist supply chain applications and CRM applications alongside them. This is the situation described in Case Study 1.

Your purchasing organization is unable to leverage its spend with business partners and cannot scale its transactions to benefit from volume discounts because each organizational unit generates its transactions in unconnected systems. A vendor may understand its sales to a large organization better than the organization itself if its systems are connected and its master data processes are established. This additional knowledge can help the vendor to negotiate a better deal.

Credit management is problematic because the sales organizations do not understand their overall exposure positions. In the case of a failure of a very large business partner, it could take some time to understand the full implications to a company. This is one of the reasons for the Sarbanes-Oxley legislation and the real-time disclosure clause.

Accounting and business intelligence reconciliation takes most of the business analysis effort rather than analyzing the corporate spend and leveraging global positions. Group financial and procurement organizations then trying to make sense of the master data run into difficulties. Instead of focusing on the overall business transactions carried out with a business partner company, considerable internal effort is spent in trying to reconcile inaccurate, incomplete, or out-of date customer and vendor information. This adds little business benefit and provides results that are inconsistent and need to be repeated frequently. We strongly advocate trying to fix the root cause of the problems once using SAP NetWeaver MDM, as opposed to repeatedly providing "quick fix" reconciliation reports. The root cause is to change the underlying business processes for the search, create, update, and deletion of your customer and vendor records in each of your business applications.

Lack of Standards — Mandating Legal Entities

New rules and standards are often unpopular with those who are impacted. A good example is the "No smoking in a public place" legislation, which has been introduced in an increasing number of countries and cities in recent years. For many years, it was accepted that going out to a restaurant or bar would also include and returning home with smoke fumes on their clothes. Within a few weeks of the legislation taking effect, people became used to the new rule. Now, after getting used to the smoke-free environment, most people find it very noticeable, if not difficult, to acclimate to cities and counties who allow smoking in public places.

The good thing about the "no smoking in a public place" rule is that it's a clear rule to everyone, and the majority can see the benefits. There has been some debate about what constitutes a "public place," but these definitions have been clarified over time. Under this legislation, smoking is prohibited in many public places, including workplaces, commercial premises, educational institutions, and sports venues.

SAP NetWeaver MDM and the Master Data Silo Smoke Screen

Adopting a new company data standard mandating that "All customers and vendors must be authenticated with a D&B D-U-N-S Number and be maintained with MDM" may initially be unpopular as your organizational units will resist the change management process. However, the majority will soon see the benefits, and after it becomes part of your culture, it will become a standard process to follow. The new standard will remove the "smoke screen" of your current master data silos, and in the future, you will ask the following questions:

▶ How could you set up a new business partner without a D&B D-U-N-S Number?

▶ How would you authenticate that a company is who it says it is?

▶ How could you verify a company's credit status and risk?

▶ How could you search to see if the customer or vendor is already used in your company without it?

> **SAP NetWeaver MDM and the Master Data Silo Smoke Screen (Cont.)**
>
> Eventually, the rule will become as obvious as the "no smoking in a public place" rule. The data standard is clear, concise, measurable, and enforceable. You have either tagged a customer or vendor record with a D&B D-U-N-S Number or you haven't — it's true or false. Similarly, your SAP NetWeaver MDM repository either holds the key mapping to the business application record or it doesn't.

Data standards are extremely important to your SAP NetWeaver MDM program. If you can convince your business leaders to adopt this kind of rule early on, then you can dramatically speed up the SAP NetWeaver MDM adoption process. By mandating the new standard, people who were used to behaving in one way now must act differently.

Instead of trying to persuade each individual organizational unit, you will be in a position to mandate compliance with the SAP NetWeaver MDM initiative and put the onus on them. SAP NetWeaver MDM is fundamentally a "people and process" issue — if you can convince the people, you can drive through the process changes to achieve success more easily.

2.2.5   Maintaining Data Silos — Business Process Issues

Let's now consider the current search, create, update, and delete issues faced when business users in Company CO1 attempt to maintain business partner data across the five systems and see how the new data standard can help the situation.

1. Company Search Processes

Matching business partner names and addresses without a unique key is difficult. You can't easily determine if a business partner record already exists in a system. Company names and addresses are inexact, and comparisons of name and address fields require special algorithms and methods.

Company names may be partially keyed, and business names and trading names can cause confusion. Phonetic matching can help the process, but that requires good algorithms and human checking. Name fields in a business application may have insufficient characters to store a full legal entity name. Company addresses may be incomplete with the street, city, ZIP code, or country missing, invalid, or inaccurate.

Company relationships further complicate the company search process. For vendors, the data entered into the SCM1 application may be for an ordering party, but in the FI1 application, for a payment name and address. For customers, there are several relevant business records to be stored in the CRM1, SD1, and FI1 applications, including sold-to, ship-to, bill-to, and payer names and addresses.

In some applications, related addresses may be stored but not clearly differentiated. The business user requesting or entering the master data details may not know the underlying company structure of the business partner.

However, if the rule "All customers and vendors must be authenticated with a D&B D-U-N-S Number and be maintained with MDM" was mandated by your company, your company search processes would become much more accurate. For example, you will be able to search by Global Ultimate Parents, as well as by individual companies. If a D&B request returns a D-U-N-S Number that you already have in SAP NetWeaver MDM, you can distribute the existing record. The unique D-U-N-S Number means you can avoid creating a duplicate record in your SAP NetWeaver MDM repository and therefore through to your consuming systems.

2. Company Create Processes

As we've already discussed, business partner data created in multiple systems have different business rules for each application, are maintained by different teams, and are captured using several forms. Each team collects the business partner master data using different forms and with varying standards and rules. Capturing business partner master data accurately and consistently at the source is a key requirement for a successful SAP NetWeaver MDM business partner management system.

▶ With this new rule mandated for Company CO1, SAP NetWeaver MDM will play an important role during the business process of converting a prospect into a customer. At the point where your sales team decides they want to do business with a new customer, they will go through a set of new operational business procedures. With a live SAP NetWeaver MDM operational environment in place, the create customer process in the CRM1 application will now include the following new information checks: Have you authenticated who the customer is? Have you matched the customer to the relevant D&B D-U-N-S Number?

▶ Have you checked where else the customer is being used across the organization? Have you reviewed the D&B Corporate Linkage and the total spend and sales across your organization?

▶ Is the customer new to your organization? Is it a record that is already set up somewhere else in your organization or even in the CRM1 system already? Have you checked the D&B D-U-N-S Number key mapping in SAP NetWeaver MDM?

▶ Have you validated that the customer is a company you should be doing business with?

▶ Have you checked the credit rating of both the customer and its Global Ultimate Company? Have you assessed your current credit exposure across the entire D&B Corporate Linkage?

Similarly, the new create vendor processes in the SCM1 application will now include the following information checks:

▶ Have you authenticated who the vendor is? Have you matched the vendor to the relevant D&B D-U-N-S Number?

▶ Have you checked where the vendor is being used across your organization? Have you reviewed the D&B Corporate Linkage and the total spend across your organization?

▶ Is the vendor new to your organization? Is it a record that is already set up somewhere else in your organization or even in the SCM1 application? Have you checked the D&B D-U-N-S Number key mapping in SAP NetWeaver MDM?

▶ Have you validated that the vendor is a company you should be doing business with? Does it fit in with your procurement strategy?

▶ Have you checked the credit worthiness of both the vendor and its Global Ultimate company? Is there a risk of bankruptcy?

3. Lifecycle Management Processes

Lifecycle Management processes need to be invoked when your business partners change and your master data records need to be maintained. Companies are dynamic in regards to changes to names, addresses, and mergers and acquisitions that must be managed. Unless each application — SCM1, FI1, CRM1, SD1, and BI1 — is maintained in a consistent manner, comparisons and reconciliations across the applications will be inaccurate.

Adopting the new rule in Company CO1 will be a significant help in keeping your records up to date. You will establish processes to periodically refresh your customer and vendor records with the very latest D&B Worldbase details, using the D&B services to provide the Lifecycle Management. SAP NetWeaver MDM will then distribute the relevant changes to your consuming systems so that each application is maintained consistently.

4. Deletion Processes

Deletion of old vendor records takes administrative effort with little apparent benefit to the organization. However, this is important, and we should consider why all of the business effort is spent in creating new customers and vendors as opposed to revisiting old records that have been created some years ago but have not been updated.

As we've discussed, your business partners are dynamic organizations. Over time, some previously legitimate companies may become "undesirable" companies that you no longer want to deal with such as if they now become bankrupt. Leaving old inaccurate business partner records in your company's business applications is a risk.

SAP NetWeaver MDM and the Census

By carrying out a census, you can validate periodically that your master data record details are accurate with your business partners. After you have entity-matched them with D&B, you can then consider emailing them and asking them to validate their details.

You can then store each response on the appropriate record in the SAP NetWeaver MDM repository to confirm that the record has been authenticated both by D&B and your business partner. This will help to resolve any long-term records that were created several years ago and need to be updated.

This could become an ongoing business process that is similar to a government census. If your SAP NetWeaver MDM business case is so compelling and your customers and vendors are so important to your organization, why not ask them every two or three years to verify their master data details?

SAP NetWeaver MDM and the Census (Cont.)

This is a good audit and compliance process that also provides a good measure of the data quality of your business partner master details. It is a straightforward and low-cost technical process that involves sending emails, repeating the messages in the case of no replies, and storing the responses.

Earlier, we compared your customer and vendor data with your physical fitness. Every couple of years, you may go to your doctor for a health check. Are your customer and vendor records also worthy of such a check periodically?

SAP NetWeaver MDM and the Data Fitness Analogy (Part 2)

Another approach to consider is to conduct a "How fit is your customer and vendor master data?" review. You could extract your master data from a consuming system and review when each active record was created, when it was last updated, and when it was last involved in a business transaction.

▶ How many records were originally loaded as part of the data conversion exercise?

▶ How many records were interfaced from another business application or were created as part of a mergers and acquisition process?

▶ How many records have not been updated in the past three years or have not had any invoices in that period?

This is a useful exercise particularly ahead of trying to measure your business performance with customers and vendors. Analyzing only the record counts of vendors and customers can provide you with misleading information, and it's good to understand the underlying state of your company's master data before producing management reports. This information also helps with service level agreement negotiation and to better understand revenue and expenditure reporting.

Let's now consider the types of analysis you as a business leader for Company CO1 want to carry out. For now, continue to assume that the SAP NetWeaver MDM and D&B solution is not yet introduced to Company CO1 and that the data silo issues remain.

2.2.6 Measuring Performance with Business Partners

Your senior business leaders (CEOs and CIOs) want to understand Company CO1's profitability and spend relationships with its leading business partners. They will ask the following questions regarding your customers and vendors:

- Who are my most profitable customers?
- How do I increase my revenue from my existing customers?
- How do I improve my operational efficiency when dealing with a customer?
- What is my credit risk with a customer?
- What is my total spending with a vendor?
- Am I leveraging the scale of our company by understanding the global overview of my dealings with a vendor?
- What is my financial and trading risk information of a vendor?
- Am I trading with a "legitimate" vendor that I have authenticated?
- Do I understand who I am dealing with and their financial health?
- What are my potential strengths (and weaknesses) within the supply chain?
- Do I understand joint ventures?
- Have I implemented purchasing controls?
- Can I track issues such as health and safety status and diversity and inclusion?

To answer each of these questions, you'll need accurate and accessible customer and vendor management information. However, for Company CO1, you know that this data is currently difficult to obtain.

You'll initially need to answer some more basic questions:

- How do I uniquely identify my customers and vendors?
- Is the customer and vendor data accurate, complete, and up-to-date?
- How many vendors and customers does my company have?
- What is the legal entity structure of the customers and vendors I am working with?

Let's now consider how many records are in each system while recognizing that this can provide you with misleading information depending on the underlying state of the business application's data.

Table 2.2 provides the vendor and customer record counts by business application for Company CO1.

Applications	CO1 Applications Name	Vendor Active Records	Transactions in the Past Two Years	Customer Active Records	Transactions in the Past Two Years
CRM1	Customer Relationship Management			3000	1200
SCM1	Supply Chain Management	4500	1000		
SD1	Sales and Distribution			2000	1100
FI1	Financial Accounting	6000	950	2500	975
BI1	Business Intelligence	9000	1200	6500	1300
Totals	Totals	19500	3150	14000	4575

Table 2.2 Company CO1 Vendor and Customer Record Counts

Let's now consider three fundamental questions:

1. How many vendors does company CO1 have?

2. How many customers does company CO1 have?

3. How many business partners does company CO1 contract with (i.e., a business partner you both sell to [customer] and buy from [vendor])?

Unfortunately, based on the data available, these basic questions are surprisingly difficult to answer. Each system is updated independently with varying names, addresses, and attributes. Duplicate records and inactive records are stored in each system. The unfortunate truthful answer is "Don't Know" without a lot of research and reconciliation and until duplicates and inactive records have been removed. Potential answers could include the following.

1. How many vendors does company CO1 have?
If we consider the record counts in each system, then our potential answers can include 4,500 (SCM1 active), 6,000 (FI1 active), or 9,000 (BI1 application) based on the total records, or 1,000 (SCM1 transactions in the past two years), 950 (FI1 transactions), or 1,200 (BI1 transactions) based on the active records.

A number somewhere between 800 vendors and 10,000 vendors is unsatisfactory, and a reconciliation project to provide further details may be initiated. The record counts also exclude Corporate Linkage, which is an important factor in understanding your total spend.

2. How many customers does company CO1 have?
Again, if we consider the record counts in each system, our potential answers can include 3,000 (CRM1 active), 2,000 (SD1 active), 2,500 (FI1 active), or 6,500 (BI1 application) based on the total records, or 1,200 (CRM1 transactions in the past two years), 1,100 (SD1 transactions), 975 (FI1 transactions), or 1,300 (BI1 transactions) based on the active records.

This is a wide range of potential answers — a number of customers somewhere between 800 and 10,000 records is a best estimate. Also, as before, the number doesn't take into account the important Corporate Linkage, which will enable you to understand your total revenue from a company.

3. How many business partners does company CO1 contract with (i.e., a business partner we both sell to [customer] and buy from [vendor])?
This is a very difficult question based on the available data from Company CO1. Identifying and reconciling the master data across the five applications requires a lot of research and Corporate Linkage to provide total spend and revenue reporting.

Let's now move on to consider the financial and legal compliance implications of Company CO1's processes for master data management.

What Are the Implications for Financial and Legal Compliance?

Company CO1's current processes for maintaining vendor and customer records are weak and have evolved based on the use of its business applications over a number of years. There is a lack of data standards, and each organizational unit has developed its own individual processes.

However, during this period, the financial and legal compliance rules have changed. The Sarbanes-Oxley Act with its focus on internal controls and real-time disclosure now requires much tighter management processes. Company CO1 is now required to ensure that its business partner information is adequately protected, stored, used, shared, and transmitted. Its operational procedures should define which information is controlled, and you are expected to know what information is available and where it is, who can access it, and how to access it.

Designated people within your organization are required to have clear accountabilities with respect to all aspects of the management of the business partner master data. The data security must be considered, and you need to create, update, and delete data respecting the rights of others.

Compliance is challenged during the customer and vendor creation processes. You need to uncover the risk associated with an individual supplier and with its corporate family. A critical supplier, linked to a struggling corporate family could put your supply chain management at risk.

Sarbanes-Oxley Compliance

Sarbanes-Oxley has redefined the compliance rules for companies. Key features of the Act include a focus on internal controls, including the timely ability to access and analyze information with respect to a company's finances and operations.

You are expected to understand, verify, and authenticate your business partners, and, because of this, companies are now seeking to standardize their customer and vendor registration and management processes. Let's now move on to consider the implications and further complexity when Company CO1 merges with Company CO2 and inherits a further set of business applications and processes.

2.3   Case Study 2 — Impact of Mergers and Acquisitions

Companies often grow with mergers and acquisitions, which compounds the master data issues. Each of the merging companies will already have its own business processes, procedures, and business applications where customer and vendor records are maintained.

Let's now consider the example where Company CO1 (from Case Study 1) has recently merged with Company CO2. As already discussed, Company CO1 systems architecture has five applications. Now in addition, Company CO2 has one SAP ERP 6.0 application plus an SAP CRM and an SAP NetWeaver BI application.

Figure 2.2 shows the combined Company CO1 and Company CO2 system architectures.

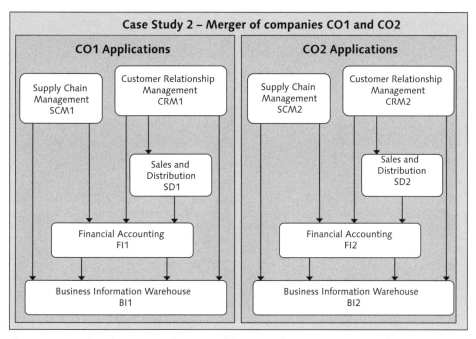

Figure 2.2 Combined Systems Architecture of the Merged Companies (Case Study 2)

Table 2.3 shows the applications and the organizational teams that initially maintain the customer and vendor data when the companies merge.

Although Company CO2 has an integrated SAP landscape, it hasn't understood the real business value of maintaining its customer and vendor records accurately. SAP ERP 6.0 provides good open ways to interface customer and vendor records into the LFA1 (vendor) and KNA1 (customer) tables, with the use of the CREMAS and DEBMAS interfaces. These require data standards and validation processes to be in place to avoid duplicate and incomplete records.

Unfortunately, these data standards are also not established for Company CO2. At the time of the Company CO2 data conversion process, all existing legacy records were transferred into the SAP ERP 6.0 application. This included duplicate, out-of-date, and inactive customer and vendor records.

Application	CO1 Application	CO1 Organization	CO2 Application	CO2 Organization
Supply Chain Management	Non-SAP	CO1 Supply chain management organization	SAP SCM	CO2 Supply chain management organization
Financial Accounting	SAP FI CO component (CO1 instance)	CO1 Financials team (AP) team	SAP FI CO component (CO2 instance)	CO2 Financials team (AP) team
Customer Relationship Management	Non-SAP	CO1 Marketing and sales representatives	SAP CRM	CO2 Marketing and sales representatives
Sales and Distribution	Non-SAP	CO1 Customer services division	SAP SD component	CO2 Customer services division
Financial Accounting application	SAP FI CO component (CO1 instance)	CO1 Financials team (AR) team	SAP FI CO component (CO2 instance)	CO2 Financials team (AR) team
Business Intelligence	Non-SAP	CO1 Marketing organization	SAP NetWeaver BI	CO2 Financials team

Table 2.3 Customer and Vendor Applications and Organizational Teams of the Merged CO1 and CO2 Company

---

SAP NetWeaver MDM and the Deployment of SAP ERP 6.0

It is invalid to assume that if a company has deployed an integrated SAP solution that it has also successfully tackled the master data issues. SAP ERP 6.0 deployments can be complex, and the quality of the master data can become a secondary issue for an implementation team when the pressures of an imminent go-live deadline approaches.

Your SAP NetWeaver MDM program should work closely with your major business deployment programs. Initially loading bad master data into a business application will severely impact the value of both the system and your SAP NetWeaver MDM program, and resolving the data issues after it has been created takes considerable effort.

The problems of managing the business partner master data processes and sharing the data across the systems are now compounded with the merger of Companies

CO1 and CO2. Let's now consider the customer and vendor record counts for the merged company as shown in Table 2.4.

Application Name	Vendor Active Records	Transactions in the Past Two Years	Customer Active Records	Transactions in the Past Two Years
CRM1			3000	1200
SCM1	4500	1000		
SD1			2000	1100
FI1	6000	950	2500	975
BI1	9000	1200	6500	1300
CRM2			12000	4000
SCM2	9000	3500		
SD2			9500	3750
FI2	8000	3300	7500	3500
BI2	15000	4600	16000	4300
	51500	14550	59000	20125

Table 2.4 Customer and Vendor Record Counts of the Merged Company

Your business leaders now have slightly different questions:

▶ Who are my most profitable customers in the combined company?

▶ How do I increase my revenue from my combined customers?

▶ Which customers are shared across the two companies?

▶ How do I improve my operational efficiency when dealing with a customer by reducing my business applications and integrating my organizational teams?

▶ What is my combined total credit risk with a customer following the merger?

▶ What is my total spending with a vendor in the combined company?

▶ Am I leveraging the scale of our company by understanding the global overview of my dealings with a vendor?

▶ Which vendors are shared across the two companies?

▶ What is my financial and trading risk information of a vendor following the merger?

▶ Am I trading with a "legitimate" vendor that has been authenticated in both organizations?

▶ Do I understand who I am dealing with and their financial health?

▶ What are the new combined company's potential strengths (and weaknesses) within the supply chain?

▶ How does the merger impact my procurement strategy?

▶ How do I implement purchasing controls across the two companies?

▶ Can I track issues such as health and safety status and diversity and inclusion?

Once again, it's back to the key master data questions. Before attempting to answer these important questions, you need to answer the following first:

▶ How many active vendors, customers, and business partners do the combined Company CO1 and Company CO2 have?

▶ How many active vendors, customers, and business partners are shared across Company CO1 and Company CO2?

Unfortunately, the questions are now even more difficult to answer. You can see from Table 2.4 that in total, there are 51,500 vendor records and 59,000 customer records set up in the various business applications across the two companies. However, there is no easy way to link the Company CO1 business partners to the Company CO2 business partners.

Adopting a new company data standard mandating that "All customers and vendors must be authenticated with a D&B D-U-N-S Number and be maintained with SAP NetWeaver MDM" would be a significant help for the newly merged Company CO1/CO2. The unique key, the D&B D-U-N-S Number, allows you to authenticate and to commonly identify vendors and customers across both sets of business applications. The D&B Corporate Linkage then enables you to aggregate your spend and revenue up to a Global Ultimate level. We'll return to these case studies in Chapter 4 when we describe how SAP NetWeaver MDM integrates the D&B services to your consuming systems.

Let's now consider how the master data silos issues further compound for large organizations.

2.4   Large Organizations – Multiplying the Data Silos Issues

The business partner master data issue is further multiplied for large organizations, which may have several hundred business applications, each creating customer and vendor master data records.

The issues highlighted in Case Study 1 and Case Study 2 are extrapolated across the organization. In this case, the master data is inconsistently managed across potentially hundreds of business applications. Duplicate vendors and customers may exist both within an application and across several applications. They are set up in each system with a different identifier such as a customer number or a vendor number, but there is no standard means of identification. Inactive records and records that have not been updated to reflect recent customer and vendor name and address changes add to the overall confusion. Searching for customer and vendor details is restricted to each master data silo.

The following factors compound the issue for large organizations.

2.4.1   Multiple Countries

Global companies can operate in more than 100 countries, and local business systems may be required for legislative reasons or because of your company's decentralized policies. In some organizations, each local business unit is run at arm's length and is fully accountable for its profits and losses. These units develop their own individual IT strategies and select their preferred business applications.

In large organizations, the key stakeholders are located across the globe, and cultural differences may present barriers to sharing master data.

2.4.2   Mergers and Acquisitions

We considered a simple example in Case Study 2. However, in the case of a large merger, each company will introduce several business applications and teams maintaining customer and vendor records, and it will take some time to integrate the people and processes.

Several mergers as part of a growth by acquisition strategy also result in multiple systems that each maintains master data records.

2.4.3 Multiple Business Units

You may have several business units each targeting the same customer but trying to sell different products. If each business unit has its own set of business applications, this will be another source of master data.

2.4.4 Multiple Financial Accounting Applications

If your company has multiple financial accounting applications, then this is an obstacle to measuring corporate business performance. Organizational business units often run independently, and so financial reporting is also handled independently.

2.4.5 IT Strategies

Even if your company has adopted an integrated SAP ERP 6.0 solution, you may have several production instances of data. Different production instances may be required because of geography, functional requirements, or organizational design. Each instance will have its own customer and vendor master data tables that may be linked through Application Link Enabling (ALE).

SAP NetWeaver MDM and the Large Organizations "As-Is" Review

A useful exercise is to produce a *business applications list* that registers all of the systems in which customer and vendor records can currently be created. When you consider your mergers, your geographies, your organizational units, and each of the various business applications (CRM, SCM, SD, FI, and BI in the case studies), you may find that the list is a surprisingly long one.

As a next step, it's also helpful to collect each of the various *master data request forms* for creating customer and vendor records. You may find that there are several different forms for one business application, especially if several organizational units share its use.

By gathering these application lists and creation forms, you are in a good position to understand the change management procedures you will need to introduce to effectively deploy SAP NetWeaver MDM.

2.5 Summary

In Chapter 2, we considered the issues faced by organizations with multiple business applications and master data silos, which currently manage their master data without SAP NetWeaver MDM. We then discussed two detailed case studies and considered the implications of mergers and acquisitions and how the issues are compounded for large organizations.

Let's now move on to show how by understanding the issues of the master data silos, this helps us develop a compelling SAP NetWeaver MDM business case for the management of customer and vendor records.

What is the business case for SAP NetWeaver MDM? In this chapter, we explore the business benefits and also a method to assess your SAP NetWeaver MDM program's progress.

3   The MDM Business Case and the MDM Program Assessment

This chapter examines the MDM business case and highlights the core MDM benefits of uniform, consistent master data. We explore how customer and vendor reconciliation and reporting are improved with MDM and also consider the financial and legal compliance implications, including the Sarbanes-Oxley Act.

We then drill down into the primary and secondary business benefits when MDM business partner master data is integrated with your SCM, CRM, Financial Accounting, and corporate and BI warehouse applications.

We consider why that if the business case is so compelling, MDM solutions have not been implemented more widely and describe the obstacles to MDM adoption. Finally, we discuss how to set up an SAP NetWeaver MDM Governance structure and introduce the SAP NetWeaver MDM assessment scorecard as a useful tool to measure the progress of your MDM program.

> **The Compelling SAP NetWeaver MDM Business Case**
>
> Effectively managing business partner relationships is a fundamental activity for most companies, and a successful MDM program will significantly improve the data quality of your customer and vendor information. Adding up the various MDM benefits throughout your organization soon builds up a compelling business case even for relatively small companies with few business systems.

3.1   The SAP NetWeaver MDM Business Case

Let's now try to understand where to find the business benefits in implementing SAP NetWeaver MDM in your company's systems.

A good starter question is, "As a benchmark, what are your current business costs for maintaining master data?" Understanding your current costs will help you to measure the returned business value over time. However, estimating the current business costs is not easy; as discussed in Chapter 2, they are hidden away in several places in the organization. The maintenance processes and reconciliation exercises of existing master data silos make this a complex exercise.

For example, do you know the total costs to your company of ad-hoc manual reconciliation exercises that are currently carried out to identify customers and vendors that will be avoided when the SAP NetWeaver MDM program is implemented? Not only do these reconciliation exercises tie up valuable people across your company, but they also add little business value. The MDM business case highlights and quantifies the current master data operational and process deficiencies. These should be continually re-examined throughout the SAP NetWeaver MDM program to understand the business value delivered.

It is a good practice for the SAP NetWeaver MDM program to record all quantifiable successes, such as the increased revenue or reduced spend when a better contract is agreed on a customer or vendor, due to the improved global information made available. Depending on the size of the contracts, a relatively small number of these improved deals can justify your program.

In the first part of this chapter, we consider the different types of SAP NetWeaver MDM services and benefits. Figure 3.1 shows how the core services and the primary and secondary benefits are linked together.

The *SAP NetWeaver MDM core services* are the intrinsic capabilities, systems, and processes that enable you to integrate accurate customer and vendor master data across your organization. The core services include providing a unique key to identify each master data record and to search and analyze your business partner legal entity structures. Your company requires uniform, consistent customer and vendor master data maintenance processes, including Lifecycle Management processes to keep the information up to date. Other core services include the capability to report and to reconcile customer and vendor master data and to meet all financial and legal compliance requirements. The core SAP NetWeaver MDM services are discussed shortly in Section 3.1 of this chapter.

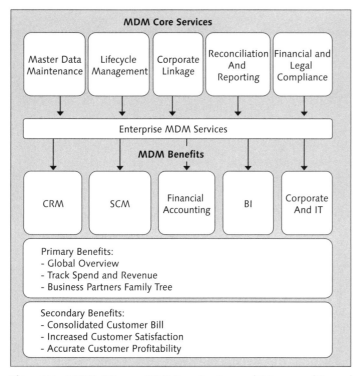

Figure 3.1 SAP NetWeaver MDM Core Services and Primary and Secondary Benefits

The *primary SAP NetWeaver MDM benefits* are "directly attributable" to an MDM program when MDM core services are integrated into a consuming system. The *secondary SAP NetWeaver MDM benefits* are "indirectly attributable" to an MDM program when MDM core services are integrated into a consuming system. The primary and secondary SAP NetWeaver MDM benefits are discussed in Section 3.2. Table 3.1 illustrates some examples of primary and secondary SAP NetWeaver MDM benefits.

Primary MDM Benefits	Secondary MDM Benefits
Reporting customer profitability by subsidiary and legal entity structure	Accurate determination of customer profitability
Providing customer credit risk information with a customer by subsidiary and legal entity structure	Savings due to single consolidated invoices and statements for customers (no duplicates)
Providing financial and trading risk information of a vendor by subsidiary and legal entity structure	Increased customer satisfaction due to complete accurate data

Table 3.1 Primary and Secondary MDM Benefits

93

> **MDM Is for Life – Not Just for Christmas!**
>
> Don't forget that MDM provides ongoing business value — these are not one-off benefits. By maintaining customer and vendor master data accurately, each benefit can be obtained year-on-year. There will be new global contract deals, new opportunities based on mergers and acquisitions, improved profitability analysis, better tracking of global spend, reduced compliance risk, reduced bad debt write offs, continued avoidance of manual reconciliations, and so on.
>
> MDM also requires a long-term business commitment with ongoing costs — the principles, standards, stewardship, and data quality must be maintained, and these objectives form part of a long-term program rather than a short-term project.

3.2   MDM Core Services

Let's now consider the five core services of MDM:

1. "Right first time" uniform, consistent master data processes

2. Lifecycle Management processes

3. Understanding company legal entity structures

4. Reporting and reconciliation

5. Financial and legal compliance

> **MDM Core Services Analogy — MDM as the "Home Heating System"**
>
> You can think of managing MDM customer and vendor master data as being the "heating system" of a house and the consuming systems being the rooms in the house: the kitchen, the living room, the bedrooms, and so on.
>
> Each of the rooms requires heat (MDM core services). By establishing a good heating system with uniform processes and providing consistent heat to all rooms, the rooms can be designed appropriately — without the need to even think to try to keep warm!
>
> MDM supplies consistent business partner core services (heat) to each part of the business organization (each room) throughout an entire company (house). The primary and secondary benefits will be experienced throughout.

Next, let's consider each of the core MDM services.

3.2.1   Uniform, Consistent Master Data Processes

Maintaining MDM master data is extremely important. You need to consider the following issues.

Unique Key

- ▶ Do your customer and vendor master data contain contradicting or duplicate information?

- ▶ Do you have a unique key to identify a master data record, is it a mandatory key, and are there any duplicate records?

Assuming the D&B D-U-N-S Number and MDM are implemented, you do have a unique key, which is extremely important.

Data Quality

- ▶ Do your data adhere to defined formats and standards?

- ▶ Do your data contain incorrect information?

- ▶ Do your data contain all of the necessary information?

The success of the MDM program is based on your data standards and the quality of the business partner name and address details. If this is not in place, then matching with D&B is impossible, thereby impacting the unique key.

Processes

This includes source identification, data collection, and data transformation (i.e., assembling the record of reference, data storage of the master data, and data governance).

- ▶ Have you established all of these processes?

- ▶ Do you consistently apply stewardship and workflow to provide the appropriate level of control?

MDM must have the best customer and vendor data in your company; it must be accurate, complete, and up to date. Your MDM data stewards and business processes must be rigorous and thought through.

Collection and Distribution

A key objective is to collect Worldbase data from D&B and to supply to multiple consuming systems with unique instances of each entity.

▶ Have you established the necessary integration steps?

You need a good technical solution with a robust architecture. Establishing interfaces to multiple consuming systems requires business process change management and careful design.

Documentation

▶ Have you documented the way customer and vendor master data is maintained and the reasons for the decisions you made?

Establishing and documenting MDM data standards will take time. Documentation is especially important when dealing with a wide variety of stakeholders and business users who will be impacted.

Measuring the Business Benefits

One measure of the MDM core benefits is to count the current active business partner records across each of the customer and vendor master data silos. After enrichment and cleansing the data with MDM, you can then recount the records:

▶ How many duplicate customer and vendor records are there in each data silo?

▶ What is the unit cost of creating a customer and a vendor record in each data silo?

The benefits of "right first time" customer and vendor master data with a unique key are the foundations of MDM.

3.2.2 Lifecycle Management Processes

Because business partner information supports critical business processes and drives business decisions, it's also important to manage and maintain the customer and vendor master data with rigor.

You need to establish processes to capture lifecycle changes of the business partner, such as changes in legal entity names and addresses, and customer and vendor mergers and acquisitions. You define and implement governance and processes so that over its useful life, business partner information is used, shared, stored, refreshed, and upgraded.

▸ You must keep the data up to date and ensure that customer and vendor master data is deleted and archived appropriately.

SAP NetWeaver MDM Data Quality and Processes

SAP NetWeaver MDM needs to become recognized by business users throughout a company as the "single source of truth," that is, the most accurate source of customer and vendor legal entity data, which is unique, complete, and up to date.

SAP NetWeaver MDM services are dependent on the uniqueness of the master data record, the data quality, the lifecycle maintenance processes, and the collection and distribution services.

Inaccurate or "bad" data in MDM severely damages the MDM program reputation — MDM must be viewed as having the best available business partner data in your company.

3.2.3 Corporate Linkage and Legal Entity Hierarchies

Accurate and accessible corporate linkage is needed to support corporate management processes, including setting customer and vendor master data goals and service levels. SAP NetWeaver MDM is the best place to maintain these corporate hierarchies. Legal entity hierarchies or D&B Corporate Linkage is true master data in every sense and should be included in your company's logical and physical corporate master data models.

D&B Corporate Linkage Hierarchies

The D&B Corporate Linkages are key business hierarchies for your company. They enable you to understand when your company is trading with the same customer and supplier or branches of the same customer and supplier. Where is your business partner legal entity hierarchies stored today? Do you trust the D&B services to provide you with corporate structures for all of your business partners?

The D&B Corporate Linkage is new information for you that was not previously available; this is a significant step forward. The D&B services provide you with a whole new set of useful master data to enable you to analyze your business partners by both parent and subsidiaries.

Also, it is important that you believe D&B will provide you with the complete and accurate list of legal entity master data, that is, the leap of faith we previously described as essential — that MDM must be viewed by all business users as the source of truth and the trusted source of business partner data that is complete, accurate, and up to date. Figure 3.2 illustrates the D&B Corporate Linkage model.

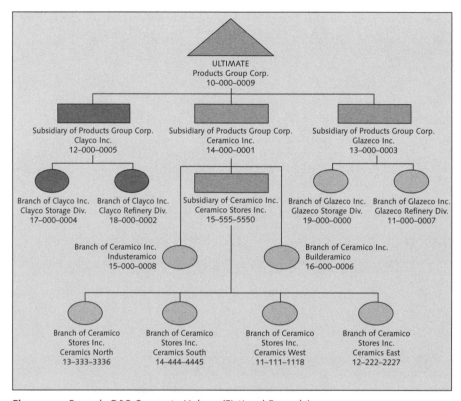

Figure 3.2 Example D&B Corporate Linkage (Fictional Example)

Business Value of Maintaining D&B Corporate Linkage in MDM

There is significant business value in understanding this D&B Corporate Linkage data. This information can be directly linked to the following benefits:

▶ Providing a global overview of business partner data

▶ Providing the information required to leverage the scale of the company

▶ Providing understanding of your business partner's family tree

Another core benefit of MDM is the ability to report and reconcile customer and vendor master data across your company's master data silos, which we'll discuss next.

3.2.4   Reconciling and Reporting Across the Master Data Silos

In Chapter 2, we discussed the issues of master data silos and uncoordinated organizational processes that result in duplicate master data records with out-of date, inaccurate, and incomplete information. No unique key is used, and D&B Corporate Linkage isn't available.

Chapter 2's Case Study 1 discussed the issues faced by Company CO1. Each system has a different version of the truth; there are differing numbers of active vendors and customers and no common unique identifier. You can't easily determine whether you are dealing with the same customer or supplier or branches of the same supplier.

Table 3.2 illustrates the customer and vendor record counts in Company CO1's systems.

CO1 Applications	Vendor Active Records	Transactions in the Past Two Years	Customer Active Records	Transactions in the Past Two Years
CRM1 – Customer Relationship Management			3000	1200
SCM1 – Supply Chain Management	4500	1000		
SD1 – Sales and Distribution			2000	1100
FI1 – Financial Accounting	6000	950	2500	975
BI1 – Business Intelligence	9000	1200	6500	1300
Totals	19500	3150	14000	4575

Table 3.2   Case Study 1 – Company CO1 Customer and Vendor Record Counts (Fictional Example)

Your business leaders — the CEO, CIO, CFO, head of marketing, and head of procurement — want to understand the company's relationships with its business partners. They are not aware of the implications of the master data silos and ask the following questions, expecting immediate responses:

- Who are my most profitable customers?

- How do I increase my revenue from my existing customers?

- How do I improve my operational efficiency when dealing with a customer?

- What is my credit risk with a customer?

- What is my total spending with a vendor?

- What is my financial and trading risk information of a vendor?

- Am I trading with a "legitimate" vendor that I have authenticated?

To answer each of these questions, you need accurate and accessible customer and vendor management information. However, in the case of Company CO1, this data is difficult to obtain. You initially need to answer some more basic questions:

- How do I uniquely identify my customers and vendors?

- Is the customer and vendor data accurate, complete, and up to date?

- How many vendors and customers does my company have?

- What is the legal entity structure of the customers and vendors I am working with?

> **Ad-hoc Master Data Reconciliation and Reporting**
>
> Manual master data reconciliation and reporting exercises tie up valuable business resources across an entire company, including marketing, customer services, procurement, accounting, management information, and IT resources.
>
> These ad-hoc exercises add little business value because they merely try to gather and interpret old information. These are the "hidden" business costs spread throughout a company's organization, which a successful SAP NetWeaver MDM program will remove.

3.2.5 Reconciliation and Reporting Issues

To answer the questions, you now need to identify a business partner in each of the master data silos. This is a time-consuming exercise that involves significant manual effort.

This identification exercise is so difficult for several reasons. Each master data silo has its own business partner create, maintain, and delete processes, and each master data silo contains inaccurate data (incomplete records, duplicate records, out-of-date records). It is difficult to differentiate when you are trading with the same business partner or branches of the same business partner.

Each master data silo is maintained using a different IT system with varying data models and processes. In each system silo, there are different definitions of customers and suppliers. The format, content, and data quality of the master data varies in each system.

Organizations may have tens if not hundreds of master data silos in different systems. This manual reconciliation exercise is likely to be repeated periodically. The management information questions will remain relevant, but the master data silos will continue to be isolated, and the transaction details will change day by day.

3.2.6   The Record of Reference in the Absence of MDM

Given these different silos, your company has to decide which record is the record of reference. The Financial Accounting system is often chosen because it is used for corporate reporting, Accounts Receivable (AR), and Accounts Payable (AP) purposes.

However, this proves frustrating for members of other parts of the organization (marketing, SCM, procurement, etc.) who invest significant effort in trying to understand their customers and suppliers based on specialized reporting from their individual systems. But a profitability report or a spend analysis report that doesn't reconcile with the Financial Accounting does not provide a satisfactory outcome.

Large management information projects can be set up to try to reconcile these differences. This is time consuming and more often than not fails to reconcile or aggregate due to the fundamental differences in the systems' data models and the data maintenance processes. Each of your company's organizational heads may create their own individual reconciliation projects, and the true business costs are "hidden" in several smaller silos of activity.

Also, in the cases of mergers and acquisitions, there are two Financial Accounting systems (in Chapter 2, Case Study 2 FI1 and FI2) both with their own versions of the customer and vendor truth. For any vendors and customers that are shared across FI1 and FI2, we are back to the familiar issue of contradictory business partner records numbers, duplicate records, data stored in different formats, and searching and matching errors!

3.2.7 The Business Value of MDM for Reconciliation and Reporting

MDM provides significant benefits in providing the ability to report and reconcile customers and vendors across multiple systems. By being the single version of truth, much like a central registry or "yellow pages" where everyone can look, MDM removes the need for many of the reconciliation process.

The benefits include providing the ability to measures the number of MDM records, the number of unique keys (D&B D-U-N-S Numbers), and the number of MDM customer and vendor updates (with refresh processes). You can also measure the number of consuming systems linked by the MDM data and produce KPIs in the form of a periodic status report (e.g., weekly reports). Accountancy, procurement, customer services, corporate and IT reconciliation and reporting requirements, and maintenance effort associated to translation tables are all reduced, which are significant benefits.

Let's now move on to see how MDM provides benefits in meeting financial and legal compliance requirements.

3.2.8 Financial and Legal Compliance

MDM and SOX Real-Time Disclosure (Section 409)

Legal compliance with Sarbanes-Oxley for organizations with tens or hundreds of silos of master data in different systems is problematic and is a key driver to implement an SAP NetWeaver MDM solution. If a large business partner is suddenly made bankrupt, a successful MDM program will *immediately* provide accurate information as to where that business partner is traded with throughout the enterprise.

Now consider your company's requirements to meet specific financial and legal compliance legislation, including Sarbanes-Oxley. These requirements also include managing financial and trading risk information on suppliers.

Compliance is a requirement throughout the supplier registration and evaluation process. Companies may use a manual qualification process to authenticate that a supplier is legitimate, which is difficult, time consuming and costly. In the absence of MDM, it isn't possible to leverage the legal entity and D&B Corporate Linkage information to validate your supply-based decisions. Third-party validation also helps to comply with the key components of SOX.

Your company may not have the ability to uncover the risk associated with an individual supplier and with a supplier's corporate family. A critical supplier, linked to a struggling corporate family, may mean that your inventory and revenues are put at risk. The Sarbanes-Oxley Act introduces a legal and regulatory focus on internal controls, including the timely ability to access and analyze information with respect to your company's finances and operations.

3.2.9 SOX Section 302 – Corporate Responsibility for Financial Reports

This requires that your company can produce accurate reports on internal controls and financial statements that CEOs and CFOs can sign off on with confidence.

The financial statements and related information must fairly present the financial condition and the results in all material respects. The signing officers are responsible for internal controls and have evaluated these internal controls within the previous 90 days and have reported on their findings.

MDM provides support for this because it delivers common definitions, a common key (the D&B D-U-N-S Number), and customer and vendor data quality metrics that can be used for audit purposes.

3.2.10 SOX Section 404 – Management Assessment of Internal Controls

Internal processes must be documented appropriately and this includes making sure that the customer and vendor information is properly protected, stored, used, shared, and transmitted. You need to define which information should be controlled — knowing what information is available, where it is, who can access it, and how to access it.

Designated people should have clear responsibilities and accountabilities with respect to all aspects of the management of the customer and vendor master data. It is a requirement to protect the customer and vendor data security (security rules and classifications) and availability of your information. You need to create, collect, and keep the data, respecting the rights of others.

Part of the Sarbanes-Oxley Act is the requirement for you to understand and authenticate your business partners. If your organization lacks proper traceability of customer and vendor data updates, it may end up with Sarbanes-Oxley issues. You may leverage the D&B Legal Entity and Corporate Linkage information to validate your supply-based decisions.

In the absence of MDM, companies can't uncover the risk associated either with an individual supplier or with a supplier's corporate family. A critical supplier who is linked to a struggling corporate family may put both your inventory and revenues at risk.

3.2.11 SOX Section 409 – Real-Time Issuer Disclosure

Sarbanes-Oxley requires real-time disclosure of any information concerning any material changes to a company's financial condition or operations that could affect a company's financial performance.

Compliance with Sarbanes-Oxley 409 for organizations with tens or even hundreds of silos of master data in different systems is problematic and is a key driver for implementing an MDM solution. For example, if a large company is suddenly made bankrupt, a successful MDM program will immediately provide information as to exactly where that company is traded throughout the enterprise.

Let's now move on to consider the benefits of integrating MDM with your major organizational units and business areas.

3.3   Integrating MDM with the Major Business Areas

This section considers the benefits of integrating MDM processes with your various organizational units, including Financial Accounting, SCM, CRM, BI, corporate administration, and IT departments.

We'll describe the primary and secondary benefits of MDM integration assuming that you have already linked your consuming systems to SAP NetWeaver MDM and the D&B external services. This integration process is described in Chapter 4; for now, let's assume that all of your customer and vendor records have been successfully linked to the appropriate D&B D-U-N-S Number and that the D&B Corporate Linkage is available in SAP NetWeaver MDM.

There are several potential benefits for you to consider when building up your MDM business case. In each section, we'll choose three or four sample benefits and provide example values for them over the next five years. To build your MDM business case, assess how these benefits will apply to your company; pick some obvious advantages and quantify the benefits.

3.3.1 Financial Accounting Integration

MDM will help you to improve your financial analysis capabilities, including global spend, corporate entity spend, and credit management reporting. You'll also see a reduction in ad-hoc accountancy reconciliation and reporting requirements.

D&B Corporate Linkage enables accurate and accessible assessment of company structures. It is needed to support management processes, including setting customer and vendor plans and service levels and reporting the results to a variety of stakeholders.

The number of bad debt write-offs will be reduced, and reliable financial information will be easily available to the people who need it.

Secondary benefits include a reduced number of accounts receivable open items and a reduction in invoice disputes. MDM provides shared services and reduces the maintenance effort associated with translation tables.

Table 3.3 lists four of the top Financial Accounting integration benefits.

Financial Administration and Management	Quantified Benefits	Year 1	Year 2	Year 3	Year 4	Year 5
Reduction in invoice disputes and AR open items	1% reduction in AR open items	$30,000	$35,000	$35,000	$35,000	$40,000

Table 3.3 Example Benefits of MDM and Financial Accounting Integration (Fictional Example)

Financial Administration and Management	Quantified Benefits	Year 1	Year 2	Year 3	Year 4	Year 5
Reduction in bad debt write-offs	2% reduction in bad debt write-offs and credit losses	$15,000	$20,000	$25,000	$30,000	$30,000
Reduction in financial services costs due to more accurate master data	2% reduction in financial services costs	$7,500	$10,500	$15,000	$18,000	$18,000
Less financial accounting ad-hoc reconciliation and improved short-term planning	10% reduction in ad-hoc financial reconciliation	$10,000	$12,000	$12,000	$12,000	$15,000
Total		$62,500	$77,500	$87,000	$95,000	$103,000

Table 3.3 Example Benefits of MDM and Financial Accounting Integration (Fictional Example) (Cont.)

3.3.2 Supply Chain Management Integration

MDM enables you to uniquely identify a vendor across all systems with the D&B D-U-N-S Number, so that you can understand which companies you are dealing with and their financial health. The D&B D-U-N-S Number is an accurate link to the other vendor maintenance systems (e.g., Financial Accounting system and BI warehouse), which provides consistent reporting without the need for your procurement and accounting teams to reconcile data.

D&B Corporate Linkage provides you with a global overview of supplier data. You can understand your vendor's family tree and know when you are trading with the same supplier or branches of the same supplier. All spend data can be classified and tracked so that you know which suppliers are being used and the levels of spend. You will be in a better position to leverage the scale of your company with groupwide deals and to identify potential strengths (and weaknesses) within the supply chain. You have a better understanding of joint ventures and can track health and safety status and diversity and inclusion metrics.

Secondary benefits include a reduction in errors in purchase orders and the ability to implement purchasing controls. MDM provides you with increased capability to reach out to suppliers for supplier enablement purposes with contact information data.

Table 3.4 illustrates three SCM integration benefits and the projected business value over a five-year period.

Supply Chain Management	Quantified Benefits	Year 1	Year 2	Year 3	Year 4	Year 5
Leverage global spend with improved global deals through MDM D&B Corporate Linkage analysis	1% reduction in global spend through MDM opportunities	$50,000	$100,000	$130,000	$190,000	$190,000
Reduced impact of supplier bankruptcy introducing supply chain disruption	5% reduction in supplier bankruptcy impacts	$15,000	$30,000	$39,000	$45,000	$57,000
Less vendor ad-hoc reconciliation and improved short-term planning	10% reduction in ad-hoc procurement reconciliation	$10,000	$12,000	$12,000	$12,000	$15,000
Total		$75,000	$142,000	$181,000	$247,000	$262,000

Table 3.4 Example Benefits of MDM and SCM Integration (Fictional Example)

3.3.3 Customer Relationship Management Integration

Also, by uniquely identifying a customer across your systems with the D&B D-U-N-S Number, you can now provide a global overview of customer data and classify and track all sales data. This enables you to track sales and again to leverage the scale of your company (this time using cross-selling and up-selling opportunities). You know which customers are being sold to and the level of sales. You can also assess your current pricing strategy across a corporation based on the D&B Corporate Linkage, which enables you to find and assess any inconsistencies in your current pricing models and again to leverage your scale to increase your revenue.

The D&B D-U-N-S Number provides you with an accurate link to your other customer maintenance systems (the Financial Accounting and Sales and Distribution systems), therefore providing consistent reporting without the need to reconcile. You know which customers you are dealing with and their financial health. You understand when you are selling to the same customer or branches of the same customer through the D&B Corporate Linkage.

You can implement credit-checking policies more systematically within the D&B Corporate Linkage structures and can reach out to customers with more accurate contact information data. Health and safety status can be tracked, and you can identify potential strengths (and weaknesses) within your overall customer relationships.

Secondary benefits can include an improvement in customer service and customer satisfaction due to complete and up-to-date data. There are potential savings due to the reuse of existing customer information and the use of consolidated invoices for customers. Identifying potential fraud in claims processes and reduced time spent on complaints and disputes also reduces losses.

Table 3.5 illustrates four CRM integration benefits and the business value over a five-year period.

Customer Relationship Management	Quantified Benefits	Year 1	Year 2	Year 3	Year 4	Year 5
Increased revenue due to cross-sell and up-sell deals based on D&B Corporate Linkage	0.5 % increase in revenue through MDM opportunities	$25,000	$35,000	$45,000	$48,000	$47,000
Increased revenue by implementing a consistent pricing strategy across a company based on D&B Corporate Linkage	0.5% increase in revenue through MDM opportunities	$25,000	$35,000	$45,000	$48,000	$47,000
Savings due to less reconciliation of CRM data with Financial Accounting and Sales and Distribution systems	10% reduction in ad-hoc marketing and customer services reconciliation	$30,000	$35,000	$40,000	$45,000	$47,000
Improved credit management based on entire company structures	5% reduction in credit losses	$10,000	$15,000	$15,000	$15,000	$18,000
Total		$90,000	$120,000	$145,000	$156,000	$159,000

Table 3.5 Example Benefits of MDM and CRM Integration (Fictional Example)

3.3.4 Business Intelligence Integration

SAP NetWeaver MDM and BI
Business information management systems (data warehouses, etc.) have so far focused on data access and movement — back to our house analogy, these systems are like the pipes and the plumbing.
MDM becomes a key component within day-to-day performance business information management because it allows unrelated applications to share a set of common master data.
The MDM view affects the master data that is scattered across a wide range of critical operational applications. Increasingly, organizations are looking to link their MDM and BI programs to deliver business value.

The additional D&B Corporate Linkage details provide multiple benefits, including the reporting of vendor spending, customer profitability, and trading and credit risk by subsidiary and legal entity structure. It will now be possible to track customer and vendor KPIs as well.

Your BI system will make reliable financial information easily available to the people who need it, when they need it. This will facilitate speedier, informed decision making because you can find information you need to quickly and with certainty.

Table 3.6 illustrates three BI integration benefits and the business value over a five-year period.

Business Intelligence	Quantified Benefits	Year 1	Year 2	Year 3	Year 4	Year 5
Improved profitability analysis reporting by corporate structures	3% increased usage in BI reports and analysis	$12,000	$15,000	$14,000	$15,000	$17,000

Table 3.6 Example Benefits of MDM and BI Integration (Fictional Example)

Business Intelligence	Quantified Benefits	Year 1	Year 2	Year 3	Year 4	Year 5
Reduced BI ad-hoc reporting and gathering inconsistent data from sources	10% reduction in ad-hoc BI reconciliation exercises	$20,000	$25,000	$25,000	$25,000	$25,000
Global spend tracking capability	5% more complete spend analysis reports and aggregation by corporate structure	$10,000	$15,000	$15,000	$15,000	$18,000
Total		$42,000	$55,000	$54,000	$55,000	$60,000

Table 3.6 Example Benefits of MDM and BI Integration (Fictional Example) (Cont.)

3.3.5 Corporate Integration

MDM helps you and your company with financial and legal compliance legislation, including Sarbanes-Oxley. Financial and trading risk information is now available on suppliers, and there is a reduced risk of trading with companies that are not legitimate.

There will be reduced merger and acquisition time and costs. Consistency in business rules and accurate and consistent MDM reports will facilitate this and accelerate any company integration.

You can now measure the number of business partners by the number of MDM records and unique D&B D-U-N-S Numbers. Also you can measure the number of MDM business partner updates (with refresh processes) as part of the Lifecycle Management and the number of consuming systems linked by the MDM data.

Secondary benefits include the achievement of strategic business objectives such as increasing corporate revenue and customer share. Table 3.7 illustrates four corporate integration benefits and the projected business value over a five-year period.

Corporate Administration	Quantified Benefits	Year 1	Year 2	Year 3	Year 4	Year 5
Improved corporate risk management	1% reduction in bad debt write-offs	$50,000	$50,000	$50,000	$50,000	$50,000
Reduced regulatory noncompliance issues and fines	2% reduction in Sarbanes-Oxley reporting issues and fines	$7,000	$4,250	$4,650	$4,900	$4,900
Reduced merger and acquisition time and costs	3% reduction in merger and acquisitions integration effort	$45,000	$48,000	$54,000	$54,000	$55,200
Accurate and consistent reports in structure and data	10% reduction in ad-hoc reconciliation reporting	$10,000	$25,000	$15,000	$15,000	$20,000
Total		$112,000	$127,250	$123,650	$123,900	$130,100

Table 3.7 Example Benefits of MDM and Corporate Administration (Fictional Example)

3.3.6 IT and Data Management

MDM plays a key role in the implementation of service-oriented architecture (SOA) initiatives. It provides an ownership structure, a governance mechanism, and a single version of the truth for the customer and vendor master data.

Your IT accounting team will spend less time in reconciling data. There are improved analysis capabilities, including global spend, corporate spend, and credit management. There is a reduction in ad-hoc reporting requirements and an opportunity for the use of shared services.

Development requests, reconciliation reporting requirements, maintenance effort associated with translation tables to map customer and vendor numbers across systems are all also reduced.

Table 3.8 illustrates three IT and data management integration benefits and the projected business value over a five-year period.

IT and Data Management	Quantified Benefits	Year 1	Year 2	Year 3	Year 4	Year 5
Reduced time spent in reconciling data	10% reduction in ad-hoc IT department effort in reconciling data	$16,000	$17,000	$17,000	$18,000	$18,000
Less ad-hoc development effort	10% reduction in ad-hoc IT development for reconciliation exercises	$20,000	$22,000	$22,000	$25,000	$23,000
SOA enablement	2% acceleration of the SOA program	$10,000	$12,000	$12,000	$12,000	$15,000
Total		$46,000	$51,000	$51,000	$55,000	$56,000

Table 3.8 Example Benefits of MDM and IT and Data Management Integration (Fictional Example)

3.3.7 Summarizing the MDM Business Case by Organizational Element

Finally, after analyzing each of your organizational elements and considering the business benefits of MDM, we can now compile the various organizational benefits to create a summarized MDM business case. Figure 3.3 illustrates this by aggregating the organizational benefits over a five year period.

	Year 1 Benefit	Year 2 Benefit	Year 3 Benefit	Year 4 Benefit	Year 5 Benefit
Corporate Administration					
Improved corporate risk management	$50,000	$50,000	$50,000	$50,000	$50,000
Reduced regulatory non-compliance issues and fines	$7,000	$4,250	$4,650	$4,900	$4,900
Reduced merger and acquisition time and costs	$45,000	$48,000	$54,000	$54,000	$55,200
Accurate and consistent reports in structure and data	$10,000	$25,000	$15,000	$15,000	$20,000
Financial Administration and Management					
Reduction in invoice disputes and AR open items	$30,000	$35,000	$35,000	$35,000	$40,000
Reduction in bad debt write-offs	$15,000	$20,000	$25,000	$30,000	$30,000
Reduction in financial services costs	$7,500	$10,500	$15,000	$18,000	$18,000
Less financial accounting ad-hoc reconciliation	$10,000	$12,000	$12,000	$12,000	$15,000
Supply Chain Management					
Leverage global spend with improved global deals	$50,000	$100,000	$130,000	$190,000	$190,000
Implement purchase controls for supplier segments	$15,000	$30,000	$39,000	$45,000	$57,000
Less vendor ad-hoc reconciliation	$10,000	$12,000	$12,000	$12,000	$15,000
Customer Relationship Management					
Increased revenue due to cross-sell and up-sell deals	$25,000	$35,000	$45,000	$48,000	$47,000
Savings due to consolidated bill of customers	$30,000	$35,000	$40,000	$45,000	$47,000
Improved credit management for entire company structures	$10,000	$15,000	$15,000	$15,000	$18,000
Business Intelligence					
Improved profitability analysis reporting by corporate structures	$12,000	$15,000	$14,000	$15,000	$17,000
Reduced MI ad-hoc reporting and gathering inconsistent data	$20,000	$25,000	$25,000	$25,000	$25,000
Global spend tracking capability	$10,000	$15,000	$15,000	$15,000	$18,000
IT & Data Management					
Reduced time spent in reconciling data	$16,000	$17,000	$17,000	$18,000	$18,000
Less ad-hoc development effort	$20,000	$22,000	$22,000	$25,000	$23,000
SOA enablement	$10,000	$12,000	$12,000	$12,000	$15,000
Total	**$402,500**	**$537,750**	**$596,650**	**$683,900**	**$723,100**

Figure 3.3 Summarized MDM Benefits by Organizational Element

You can see that the MDM business case is built on combining the business benefits of many parts of your organization. Don't be too ambitious with your business benefit claims; even with conservative quantified benefits; it is still possible to build a compelling case.

However, let's now move on to consider that even with a seemingly compelling business case, there are still some obstacles to overcome before MDM will be adopted.

3.4   Obstacles to MDM Adoption — One More Master Data System to Maintain

Why are MDM programs slow to develop? If the business case is so compelling, then why has MDM not been adopted more widely? We describe the key reasons for the business and IT inertia to implementing an MDM program in this section.

If a large company already has several business partner systems where customer and vendor master data is maintained, then introducing one more system (MDM) is not initially a popular move. All of these MDM activities are needed to create yet one more IT system and another set of business partner master data.

Is "Do Nothing" with MDM a Realistic Option?
It is worth considering the implications if you say "no" to MDM and do nothing with an MDM program at this stage.
In five years, will you be at a competitive disadvantage compared to others that do invest in MDM? Do you believe that they will make progress with their MDM programs and will be in a position to make more informed business decisions?

3.4.1   The Obstacles to MDM

The reasons for resisting change are significant in slowing down the adoption of MDM in companies. To drive through the business change, you need to overcome the various obstacles. Following are some of the key reasons for the slow adoption of MDM in companies:

- MDM program cost
- Business and IT inertia
- Time and business commitment required for cleansing master data
- MDM program not ready to scale
- MDM program focus on other master data objects and other technologies
- Lack of trust in external services
- Unwilling to use MDM services and to agree to service levels
- Leadership team commitment

Let's discuss each of these obstacles in turn.

1. MDM Program Cost

Mobilizing an MDM program requires a significant investment. You need data governance and data stewards, an MDM program team, SAP and D&B licenses, SAP NetWeaver infrastructure, and integration with consuming systems. MDM requires senior sponsorship and a clearly articulated business case with measurable business benefits.

2. Business and IT Inertia

Due to a lack of awareness of your existing master data management processes and the subsequent issues that arise, your business leaders and users do not understand the true costs of managing the customer and vendor data with the current processes, nor do they understand the benefits of an MDM program and linking to the D&B services of the D&B D-U-N-S Number and D&B Corporate Linkage.

The current business costs are hidden in many places; the master data management and reconciliation processes tie up resources across the organization, but there is no overall view of the total costs. "Live" customer and vendor master data already exists and is maintained in existing systems with established operational procedures.

An MDM program impacts your organizational units' existing programs and project timelines. MDM is not necessarily a planned business unit activity, and your organizational units are already busy with other business activities that are perceived to have a higher priority than MDM.

Your organizational units may also be opposed to the use of external services such as D&B. The MDM – D&B Worldbase lookup is seen to be yet one more step in the customer and supplier registration process. Also, this step is not controlled by the local organizational unit and increases their reliance on others.

3. Time and Business Commitment Required for Cleansing Master Data

Cleansing master data requires dedicated business effort and has associated costs. It results in business change, including the deletion and end dating of records in existing systems. Sometimes, only scarce business specialists such as expert customer services team members can make the transactional changes because there are several data dependencies. For example, Financial Accounting open items must be settled before a duplicate customer or vendor record can be blocked or end dated.

4. MDM Program Not Ready to Scale

The MDM program can try to move too quickly to establish MDM. If there is a lack of MDM program governance, data standards, or data stewardship skills available, this will impact the MDM program delivery. Similar negative impacts will occur if the technical solution and the D&B integration are not operationally tested.

5. MDM Program Focus Placed on Other Master Data Objects and Technologies

The MDM program may focus on other master data objects, and the attention to business partners is diluted. It's easy to get distracted with MDM! There's often a tendency to seek out other problems to solve with master data because you have this technical solution in place, so why not use it elsewhere? You should carefully consider the MDM business case for other master data objects — a compelling case for customer and vendor master data maybe just a nice idea for another object with no real tangible business benefits.

The MDM program can also spend a lot of time analyzing alternative technologies rather than delivering a solution with the SAP NetWeaver MDM and D&B solution. Many potential MDM solutions are available in an emerging market, and your technical architects can have great fun investigating them, without delivering any real business value.

6. Lack of Trust in the D&B External Services

There is likely to be internal challenges as to why you need to pay for the external D&B services of the D&B D-U-N-S Number and the D&B Corporate Linkage. Questions will be raised when D&B, on rare occasions, does not provide the expected answer; for example, there are no D&B Worldbase details available, an incorrect D&B Entity Match or Corporate Linkage, or a lack of coverage in a region. Some may believe that the required company data can be found on the internet by internal people.

Also, lifecycle process changes can take time; on occasion, changes in D&B company names and addresses or mergers and acquisitions have a delay before they are "officially" updated on the D&B Worldbase record. However, these changes are known in advance by your company's internal people through their business contacts.

7. Unwilling to Use MDM Services and to Agree to Service Levels

Some will challenge why you have to look up data from outside an application and a master data silo because this will impact your organizational unit's business processes. It's important to set up MDM Service Level Agreements because you need to publish agreed timescales for providing your D&B lookup and for creating the record in the consuming system. These service levels should be carefully monitored, and weekly reports should be produced by the MDM data stewards for your organizational units to review.

8. Leadership Commitment

This is one of the most serious obstacles. Somehow, the MDM program needs to grab your leadership's attention because often they will have other more urgent priorities to consider as compared to the existence of duplicate customer and vendor master records across systems.

Longer term, it will be a huge advantage if you can convince them of the need to introduce corporate standards mandating the use of MDM services. This will include the business reasons why the setup of a customer and vendor will always include an MDM D&B Entity Match lookup.

3.4.2 Overcoming the Obstacles

Chapter 5 describes how to mobilize an MDM program team to deliver the business values. We also describe the importance of managing the key stakeholders throughout the organization, and we introduce the concept of an MDM Stakeholder map. At this early stage, when your company is still considering the MDM business case and whether or not to implement MDM, the following initial steps will help you.

Obtain Leadership Commitment

You need to obtain strong commitment from senior business leaders (CEOs and CIOs), which means spending time with them to talk through the MDM program and to explain the business benefits. Somehow you need to transform them into MDM champions so they will support you on each step of your implementation journey.

Set Up a Good MDM Program Team

You need a strong enterprise services team spanning the organization. The MDM program team requires good consultancy skills and an ability to present the case for MDM throughout the organization. You also need skilled SAP NetWeaver MDM technical resources.

Articulate the MDM Business Cases

You've seen how to develop the MDM business case in this chapter; it should be carefully articulated and supported, and include measurable business benefits. This is essential to justify the MDM program costs and to obtain senior level sponsorship.

Produce Aggressive MDM Roadmaps

Your MDM program needs to set aggressive timescales. Even for large companies, there is no insurmountable business or technical barriers to implementing a customer and vendor MDM program within two years. Try to set ambitious quarterly targets — much can be achieved in an MDM program in a three-month period.

3.4.3 Setting Up MDM Governance — The Role of the MDM Steering Board

An MDM Steering Board is an excellent forum to establish MDM Governance for business partner data. The role of an MDM Steering Board is to bring together cross-functional teams to agree to rules and to resolve issues.

The MDM Steering Board will include a combination of local business unit leaders; corporate, financial, and compliance leaders; and MDM program leaders. It will provide the MDM governance and will be the mechanism by which MDM program decisions are made. It will agree on the MDM program vision, scope, and funding levels, and also ensure that a clear MDM roadmap is produced.

The MDM Steering Board will monitor the delivered business value from the MDM program against defined KPIs. It will also establish MDM data stewardship accountabilities and agree on the MDM service levels. It will communicate and champion the MDM program to key stakeholders throughout your organization. It will also react to and resolve any issues arising from noncompliance with the agreed-on MDM decisions and rules.

Establishing MDM Governance and the role of the MDM Steering Board are discussed further in Chapter 5. Let's now move on to discuss the two major phases of an MDM program and introduce you to the MDM business partner assessment scorecard.

3.5   The MDM Business Partner Scorecard

The MDM program can be broken down into two phases:

▶ MDM Phase 1
Establishing the MDM program and creating the first live MDM services.

▶ MDM Phase 2
Rolling out the MDM services throughout your organization so that all customers and vendors records are maintained through the established MDM processes.

Let's now discuss each of the phases in detail and also introduce you to the MDM business partner assessment scorecard.

3.5.1   MDM Phase 1

In Phase 1, you establish the MDM program and create the basic MDM business processes, including the first live services referred to in Figure 3.4, which shows the program activities needed to develop an initial operational service.

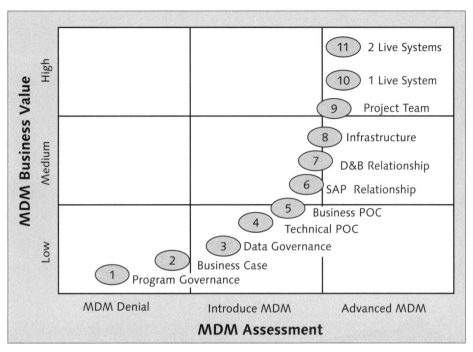

Figure 3.4 MDM Phase 1 Business Value Map

Each of the steps 1 to 11 is important in creating a live operational MDM system. We will discuss these steps in much more detail in Chapter 5 when we consider how to mobilize an MDM program. For now, we will produce an MDM Phase 1 program assessment scorecard.

3.5.2 MDM Phase 1 Program Assessment Scorecard

This is a method of assessing how far an MDM program is along the Phase 1 journey. Table 3.9 illustrates this by completing an MDM program assessment scorecard for a recently started MDM program.

MDM Program Scorecard – Initial Stage of an MDM Program	Score	Ranking
1. MDM Business Case: Has the business case been signed off on? Is there senior sponsorship? Are there quantified measurable benefits? Have the "As-is" business costs been estimated as a benchmark?	4	0 – No business case 2 – Proof of concept agreed 4 – Six-month program agreed 6 – One live system and operational support agreed 10 – 2-3 year funding for global rollout
2. MDM Program Governance: Is there an established governance process? Is there an MDM Steering Board? Does the MDM Steering Board agree with the MDM program objectives on a frequent (2-3 month) basis?	4	0 – No steering board 2 – Small team approves proof of concept 4 – Steering Board approves 12-month roadmap 6 – Operational Steering Board with "live" system accountabilities 10 – MDM mandated as a corporate standard
3 MDM Data Governance and Stewardship: Is a team of MDM data stewards in place to manage Lifecycle Management processes? Are agreed data standards established?	10	Yes (10) or No (0)
4 MDM Business Proof of Concept: Has a trial been carried out with a subset of a company's business systems? Has an exercise to match company data using the D&B Entity Matching process been carried out? Has the D&B Corporate Linkage been assessed for complex company structures? Has a recommendation report been produced?	0	Yes (10) or No (0)
5 MDM Technical Proof of Concept: Has a trial been carried out on a company's infrastructure? Have prototype processes been analyzed and a recommendation report produced?	0	Yes (10) or No (0)

Table 3.9   MDM Business Partner Assessment Scorecard

MDM Program Scorecard – Initial Stage of an MDM Program	Score	Ranking
6 Relationship with the SAP team: Have licenses been agreed on? Does your team include a member of the SAP MDM Customer Council?	4	0 – No relationship 4 – Licenses purchased 10 – SAP MDM Global Council
7 Relationship with D&B: Are relationships with D&B established? Are there regular status updates?	4	0 – No relationship 2 – Licenses purchased 4 – Trial of D&B Legal Entity matching processes 6 – D&B service levels agreed on 10 – Close relationship with agreed-on shared roadmaps
8. NetWeaver Infrastructure: Is the infrastructure established? Are development, test, and production environments available and supported for SAP NetWeaver Portal, SAP NetWeaver MDM, and SAP NetWeaver Process Integration (PI)	0	Yes (10) or No (0)
9. Mobilizing the Project Team: Is the required team with the required skills in place? Are the program managers, technical design authority, NetWeaver solution architects, working on the project?	0	Yes (10) or No (0)
10. MDM Roadmap: How many consuming systems will be linked into MDM this year?	0	0 – Zero Live systems 2 – One Live system 4 – Two Live systems 6 – 10 live systems 10 – 80% live systems
Total Score	26	

Table 3.9 MDM Business Partner Assessment Scorecard (Cont.)

We will now assess the score to see how your company's MDM program is rated. Table 3.10 matches your score to the appropriate rating and assessment.

Score	Rating	Assessment
0-10	MDM denial	MDM program is yet to start, and there is little interest.
11-30	MDM beginner	The first signs of enthusiasm in an MDM program are shown.
31-60	MDM designed	The principles are established, and the MDM program team is mobilized and ready to build a solution.
61-95	MDM intermediate	Significant MDM progress has been made, and the MDM program is close to a live operational system.
95-110	MDM advanced	A live MDM solution has all of the core functions in place and is ready to scale across the enterprise in Phase 2.

Table 3.10 MDM Assessment Score Evaluation

So we've now considered the building blocks to create a live MDM infrastructure with links to a couple of consuming systems. Let's now discuss what is needed to scale the solution and to implement MDM throughout your organization in MDM Phase 2.

3.6   MDM Phase 2

In MDM Phase 2, you integrate MDM with multiple consuming systems and also achieve financial and legal compliance. Phase 2 varies according to the size of your organization, your existing systems architecture, and your MDM roadmap. It may take two or more years to implement depending on your company's size, complexity, and enthusiasm for MDM.

During MDM Phase 2, a company will develop from an intermediate level (having establishing the MDM program and the basic MDM processes and services) into a world-class MDM organization with a competitive advantage in its application of master data. The tangible business benefits are delivered in this phase. Figure 3.5 illustrates the MDM Phase 2 milestones.

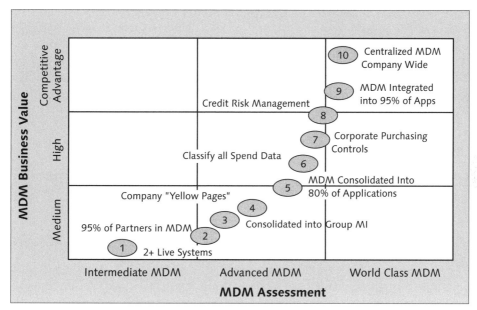

Figure 3.5 MDM Phase 2 Business Value Map

Let's now discuss in detail the Phase 2 milestones.

3.6.1 Two or More Live Systems Linked to MDM

Achieving an MDM go-live is a key milestone in an MDM program. The components now established provide a good foundation from which MDM business benefits can be derived. The following components are now in place both from a business and technical viewpoint.

Business Achievements

Data governance is in place, including MDM data standards and MDM data stewardship. You have experienced a real example of data migration and data cleansing with D&B Entity Matching; you have end-dated and blocked duplicate and inactive records in a consuming system.

Technical Achievements

You have a live MDM system with development, test, and production environments in place. Your MDM functionality is designed, built, and in operational use.

Security, disaster recovery, and business continuity procedures are established, as well as release and change management procedures. Web Services are in place along with operational interfaces to D&B and to consuming systems.

If possible, starting off with relatively small vendor and customer consuming systems is a sensible, low-risk approach that allows the MDM Data Stewards time to understand and refine the MDM workflow processes without significant maintenance overheads.

3.6.2 MDM Contains 95% of All Business Partners Within a Company

As you saw in Chapter 2, business partner master data is often maintained in multiple silos using several systems. An important aim of the MDM program is to establish MDM as the best and most complete source of business partner master data in your company.

Achieving 95% of all business partners within a company in MDM can be more straightforward than it may initially seem. By establishing links with D&B, you have a D&B D-U-N-S Number, which is a unique key, and D&B Corporate Linkage. Lifecycle Management processes are in place so that the MDM vendor and customer data can be refreshed periodically. You have established processes to quickly match large files of vendors and customers by batch Entity Matching requests with D&B.

Even if an MDM record is not yet consumed in a system, if it's recognized that a system record is linked to a D&B D-U-N-S Number, then it can be set up in the SAP NetWeaver MDM business partner repository so that it is available to be searched and distributed as required to other consuming systems.

Scaling MDM to maintain a full set of company business partner data is an important step for your SAP NetWeaver MDM program: It gives confidence that MDM is the definitive source of data. A typical take-on process for a new business partner record is to distribute an existing MDM record to a new consuming system. In large organizations, a business unit somewhere in the organization is probably already dealing with the business partner either as a customer or a vendor. In these cases, the existing MDM record can be referenced in the request without the need for the requestor to re-key the name and address.

A key requirement is to avoid duplicate records in both MDM and your consuming systems. By using the D&B D-U-N-S Number as a unique key, you can avoid duplicates in MDM. By making it easy to search MDM, you also help to avoid creating duplicates in consuming systems.

3.6.3 MDM Is Consolidated into a Large Business Intelligence Warehouse Solution

Linking MDM to a large business intelligence warehouse is a big step forward in achieving the MDM business benefits. This will enable business users to drill down and analyze both sales and spend data to understand the aggregated views across a business partner. It will also enable users to drill down through the D&B Corporate Linkage hierarchy from the Global Ultimate to the Domestic Ultimate and then to the Parent and Subsidiary records.

Depending on the scale of your Business Intelligence warehouse, by consolidating MDM you can now provide a global overview of your business partner data. You understand who your business partners are and their contribution to both sales and spend. You can track sales and leverage the scale of the company and also classify and track spend data. You understand who you are dealing with and their financial health and also understand when you are trading with the same business partner or branches of the same business partner through the D&B Corporate Linkage.

Again, this is a relatively straightforward MDM step that can quickly deliver significant business value.

3.6.4 Business Users Are Searching the MDM "Yellow Pages" to Understand the Business Partner's Corporate Structure

As a next step, it's important that business users can quickly and accurately search the MDM data to make better informed decisions. It's useful to produce some metrics on how the MDM company search is being used. If many users across the company are using the functionality, then this is a positive sign, and you will be stopping at the source the creation of duplicate business partner records in a simple and effective way.

Mandating the MDM company search as a standard step of all customer and vendor creation processes is a final step on the journey. This can be introduced when the MDM services are fully tested and MDM has a complete and accurate set of business partner data.

3.6.5 MDM Is Consolidated into 80% of Applications

Given the appropriate key stakeholder support, this again can be achieved relatively quickly. By linking all of your existing business partner records to a D&B D-U-N-S Number and recording the link in the SAP NetWeaver MDM consolidation repository, you can make significant and speedy progress.

You will now target the big consuming systems, that is, your largest systems where the most customers and vendors are maintained. By integrating these systems to MDM, you can now start to scale the solution and deliver increasing business benefits.

3.6.6 All Spend Data Is Tracked and Classified

By achieving this milestone, your company starts to become a world-class MDM operator delivering high business value and competitive advantage. Your procurement specialists now have the tools to drill down into your suppliers' Corporate Linkage details to classify and track all of your spend data accurately across it.

The negotiation process with vendors will change with this important information; for example, volume discounts can now be more easily analyzed, and leveraging your company's scale becomes a common process.

The D&B Worldbase data also provides you with Standard Industry Classifications for vendors, which enables your company to segment group spend into different buckets that can also be useful in the negotiation process.

3.6.7 Corporate Purchasing Controls Are Implemented

By now, with a rich data set in MDM and all business partners established, the supplier registration process can be improved. For example, if your company is already dealing with 20 IT providers, should another IT provider be established without due consideration? How many IT suppliers optimally should your company deal with?

Your company can now look to enforce purchasing controls by refining the vendor-creation processes to meet with your procurement strategies and standards.

3.6.8 Credit Risk Management Programs Use the MDM and D&B Corporate Legal Entity Structures

Better credit risk management is now possible with the MDM D&B Corporate Linkage. D&B is a leading credit-reporting provider; by structuring the data in the same way and using the same D&B D-U-N-S Number, applying such credit services reporting becomes straightforward.

The previous complexities (reconciling and reporting across master data silos) by now have disappeared. Companies are in a position to use the MDM data and D&B Corporate Linkage to understand credit risk from the Global Ultimate, Domestic Ultimate, Parent, and Subsidiary levels. Again, this is important new business information sourced by good MDM data.

3.6.9 MDM Is Integrated into 95% of Systems

The final steps up the MDM program mountain! Your company may well have many small applications that are not considered worthy of MDM integration — hence the 95% target. If a system is strategic and will exist in the mid-term, then MDM ideally should be integrated with it.

If MDM links to a key SAP system in a centralized way (1:1 relationship, and MDM is the single source of business partner data), and if a system such as SAP CRM is a satellite of the SAP ERP 6.0 system, then both SAP ERP 6.0 and SAP CRM follow the MDM integrity rules. MDM is considered integrated with both systems in these circumstances.

3.6.10 Centralized MDM Processes Are Implemented Groupwide

And finally the top of the MDM mountain! All systems are not only linked to MDM, but there is a 1:1 match of MDM legal entity records to the consuming systems. Creating a new business partner record mandates the use of the MDM "search and create" process. Utopia!

MDM is now integral to your company's operations — all of the primary business benefits and many of the secondary benefits are now being delivered. A truly world class implementation!

3.7   Summary

In this chapter, we examined the MDM business case and highlighted the core MDM benefits of uniform, consistent master data and Lifecycle Management processes. We explored the MDM reconciliation and reporting benefits and also discussed financial and legal compliance implications, including Sarbanes-Oxley.

We defined the primary and secondary benefits of integrating MDM with your SCM, CRM, Financial Accounting, management information, corporate administration, and IT systems. We also aggregated the business benefits across an organization.

We discussed the obstacles to MDM adoption and suggested ways to overcome these. We considered the role of the MDM Steering Board. Finally, we described the two main phases of an MDM implementation and also developed an MDM business partner master scorecard assessment to help you to monitor your progress. These techniques will help you to develop a suitable two or three year MDM roadmap for your organization. Let's now move on to look at the Dun & Bradstreet services in much more detail.

Why is the D&B global database "the best global company database in the world?" In this chapter, we'll consider the Dun & Bradstreet services and further explore the D&B D-U-N-S Number, Corporate Linkage, and Entity Matching.

4   The Dun & Bradstreet Services

In this chapter, you'll see how the Dun & Bradstreet services can help you maintain your customer and vendor master data. We define the D&B D-U-N-S Number and further describe the core D&B concepts of the Worldbase database, Corporate Linkage and Entity Matching. We also analyze the SAP NetWeaver MDM D&B enrichment adapter.

You'll learn how you can integrate D&B services and SAP NetWeaver MDM into your company. We revisit the earlier case studies to illustrate how the D&B solution can be applied to link multiple applications. Finally we re-examine the key management questions after the D&B services and the D&B D-U-N-S Number has been successfully implemented.

4.1   Dun & Bradstreet Services

Let's begin our analysis of the D&B services by considering the D&B Worldbase database and how D&B maintains company master data.

D&B claims that its Worldbase database is "the most comprehensive global company database in the world." This section explains why D&B makes this claim and answers some fundamental questions about D&B's management of master data.

4.1.1   How D&B Maintains Company Data

The D&B business model requires the company to be very good at these processes because it sells services that rely on the completeness and accuracy of its company master data records. As an example, the D&B company credit risk and credit ratings reports are of little value if the Corporate Linkage is inaccurate or doesn't reflect the latest business mergers and acquisitions. Also, D&B provides information services of global companies who may have thousands of legal entities around the world. The data therefore has to be not only up to date, accurate, and complete but also available from every country in the world. In meeting these requirements, D&B has developed specialist skills and techniques, which are considered best practices, that underpin its service offerings.

Next, let's consider the D&B D-U-N-S Number, which is the D&B unique key used to identify a business globally.

4.1.2   The D&B D-U-N-S Number Defined

The *D&B D-U-N-S Number* is a unique, nine-digit, nonindicative identification number assigned to every business entity in D&B's database. It is a unique key used to identify a business globally. No other numbering system is as established, recognized, and globally accepted.

The following questions and answers provide more details regarding the D&B D-U-N-S Number:

▶ **How many D&B D-U-N-S Numbers are there?**
The D&B D-U-N-S Number uniquely identifies more than 132 million business company records.

▶ **Is the D&B D-U-N-S Number a unique identifier?**
D&B operational processes make sure that no two businesses will ever receive the same D&B D-U-N-S Number.

▶ **Is a D&B D-U-N-S Number ever reused?**
No, D&B D-U-N-S Numbers are never recycled.

▶ **How long is a D&B D-U-N-S Number retained for?**
The D&B D-U-N-S Number is retained for the life of a business.

▶ **How is a D&B D-U-N-S Number assigned?**
There are global policies for D&B D-U-N-S Number assignment that provide for consistent company identification. A D&B D-U-N-S Number is never reassigned and follows a business through every phase of its life, including bankruptcy.

▸ **What is the D-U-N-S verification process?**
A D&B D-U-N-S Number is not assigned until multiple data sources have confirmed a business's existence.

▸ **How does a D&B D-U-N-S Number enable business authentication and help you with Sarbanes-Oxley compliance?**
The D&B D-U-N-S Number enables you to authenticate your customers and vendors. D&B authenticate that a company is who it say it is by using multiple sources. By then accurately linking your company record to the correct D&B D-U-N-S Number, you can authenticate who you are dealing with. Sarbanes-Oxley requirements include supplier verification and also reporting any material information about companies that impact your company's financial condition or operations.

▸ **Is the D&B D-U-N-S Number a standard, and who recommends it?**
A D&B D-U-N-S Number acts as an industry standard for business identification. It is recommended by the United Nations, the European Commission, and more than 50 industry groups.

▸ **Which other data attributes are stored in the Worldbase database, along with the D&B D-U-N-S Number?**
Other attributes include the business name and address, demographics, Corporate Linkage, financial information, and diversity and inclusion details.

▸ **What happens if a company moves within a country?**
A D&B D-U-N-S Number is retained when a company moves anywhere within the same country.

Now that you know the specifics about the D&B D-U-N-S Number, let's consider the D&B Worldbase database.

4.1.3 D&B Worldbase Database

D&B claims that the Worldbase database is "the most comprehensive global company database in the world" because D&B provides a global service covering 132 million business records and 225 countries. Country information is aggregated from more than 20 regional databases.

Figure 4.1 shows how D&B gathers company data from a variety of local country sources, validates the data, carries out global linkage build and finally stores it in the global Worldbase database.

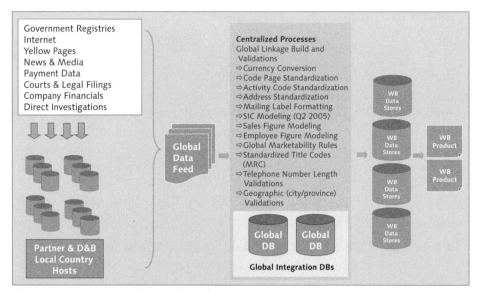

Figure 4.1 The D&B Worldbase Architecture

D&B uses multiple sources to collect and to verify the company information, including business owners, government sources, public records, customer files, and third-party data, as shown in Figure 4.2.

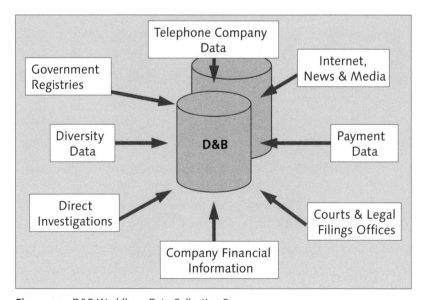

Figure 4.2 D&B Worldbase Data Collection Sources

Table 4.1 lists some of the D&B data collection sources from across the world.

Record Source	North America	Europe	Asia	Middle East
Government Registries	X			
Newspapers and Publications	X	X	X	X
Payment Experiences	X			
Telephone Interviews	X	X	X	X
Business Internet Sites	X	X	X	
Yellow Pages	X			
Postal Address Changes	X			
Banking Information	X			
D&B Customer Experiences	X	X	X	X
Public Company Financial Filings	X			
Courts and Legal Filings Offices	X	X		
Business Registries		X		
Company Financials (public and private)				
Financial statements/Annual returns		X		
Insolvency records		X		
China conformity assessment			X	
Chinainfobank.com			X	
Shanghai and Shenzen Stock Exchange			X	
Administration of Industry and Commerce			X	
People's Court Newspaper			X	
National Part-Time Network for Court			X	
Registry of Companies or Ministry of Commerce				X
Correspondents on Location				X

Table 4.1 Examples of D&B Global Collection Sources

D&B also uses the services of strategic partners to create a global service. Approximately 60% of the D&B Worldbase records are created "internally" by the D&B organization, and 40% of records come by external partners.

You can see from Table 4.1 that creating and maintaining 132 million global D&B D-U-N-S Numbers involves significant research and administrative effort. Verifying the data from the data sources requires manual checking and then processes to update the Worldbase records. The multiple source approach to collecting company data enables D&B to confirm the accuracy of the data collected and also to identify new companies. This provides a complete picture of each company and access to nearly all companies around the world.

Next let's explore D&B Corporate Linkage.

4.1.4 D&B Corporate Linkage

D&B provides a sophisticated view of company structures that enables you to see where your customers and suppliers fit within their larger corporate hierarchies. D&B Corporate Linkage can reveal relationships between your suppliers and customers that you would otherwise never have known existed.

Corporate Linkage is the relationship between different companies within a corporate family. Linkage occurs in the D&B database when one business entity "controls" another business entity because it has financial or legal responsibility for it, thereby creating a Headquarters to Branch or a Parent to Subsidiary relationship.

Corporate Linkages are updated monthly and reflect mergers and acquisitions and company openings and closures through a period.

Table 4.2 lists some of the key D&B Corporate Linkage terminology.

D&B provides linkages from Branch to Headquarter, from Subsidiary to Parent, to Domestic Ultimate and to Global Ultimate. Figure 4.3 shows an example D&B Corporate Linkage structure. In this fictional example, we can see how 15 legal entities are linked to one Global Ultimate *"Products Group Corp."* There are four levels of hierarchy and we can see that the Branch *"Ceramics East"* is part of the *"Subsidiary of Ceramico Inc"* which is in turn part of the *"Subsidiary of Products Group Corp"* under *"Products Group Corp"*. The ability to link these legally related companies is extremely important when you consider the total spend, revenue, and credit risk faced by your organization.

Term	Definition
Global Ultimate	The Global Ultimate is the top most responsible entity within the corporate family tree.
Domestic Ultimate	The Domestic Ultimate is a subsidiary within the global family tree that is the highest-ranking member within a specific country.
Headquarters	A Headquarters is a family member that has branches or divisions reporting to it and is financially responsible for those branches or divisions. If a Headquarters is more than 50% owned by another corporation, it is also a Subsidiary. If it owns more than 50% of another corporation, then it is also a Parent.
Branch	A Branch is a secondary location of its Headquarters. It has no legal responsibility for its debts, even though bills may be paid from the Branch location.
Parent	A Parent is a corporation that owns more than 50% of another corporation. A Parent can also be a Headquarters if it owns Branches.
Subsidiary	A Subsidiary is a corporation that is more than 50% owned by another corporation and has a different legal business name from its Parent. There are also single location Subsidiaries where the Subsidiary does not have anything reporting to it.
Affiliate	Affiliated companies are related to a business through common ownership by the direct Parent company. All of them share the same Parent company. A direct Parent company is a corporation that owns more than 50% of another corporation's capital stock.

Table 4.2   D&B Corporate Linkage Terms

Corporate Linkage allows you to identify how much you are spending with your suppliers, your total revenue from customers, and your total risk exposure. The potential business benefits from Corporate Linkage are significant. You can gain an understanding of the total risk exposure within a corporate family and also recognize the relationship between bankruptcy or financial stress in one company and the rest of its corporate family.

▶ Sales can be increased through up-sell and cross-sell within the corporate family and by finding new prospects to penetrate existing customers. D&B Corporate Linkage maximizes the revenue opportunity from the entire corporate family. It provides an understanding of where purchase decisions are made and increases your leverage with vendors. Possible conflicts of interest can be identified and your company research time is reduced, which saves business effort and cost.

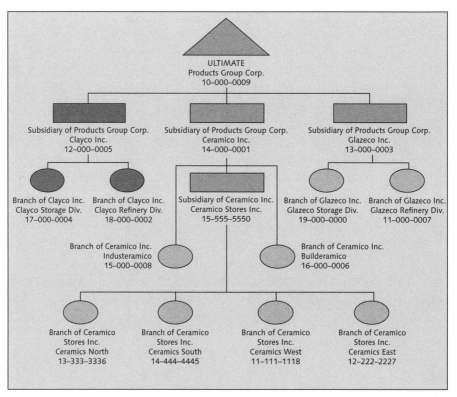

Figure 4.3 The D&B Corporate Linkage Model (Fictional Example)

Now that we've discussed D&B Corporate Linkage, let's consider how D&B keeps the Worldbase data up to date.

4.1.5 D&B Lifecycle Management Processes

Lifecycle Management is a key requirement for managing customer and vendor master data. In today's dynamic business environment, your company is required to keep track of changes to company structures and to understand how they impact you. It's easy to see why compliance, in particular internal controls and real-time disclosure obligations, is so challenging given the following D&B Worldbase change statistics.

Table 4.3 provides some examples of the number of Worldbase records typically updated in a given period.

In the next year...*	21% of CEOs will change.	17% of business names and 20% of all addresses will change.	18% of telephone numbers will change.
In the next month...*	There will be 14-20 million unique monthly updates to the D&B Worldbase database.		
In the next day...*	There will be 1.5 million unique monthly updates to the D&B Worldbase database.		
In the next 60 minutes, globally ...*	251 businesses will have a suit, lien, or judgment filed against them; this is material information required for SOX real-time disclosure. 289 companies will change their phone numbers. 60 new businesses will open. 30 businesses will close.	7 businesses will file for bankruptcy. With the new regulations, companies are asking themselves, are any of these bankrupt suppliers material to my business, in which case, you are obliged to report it with your total exposure. 257 corporate suits, liens, or judgments will be filed. 60 credit ratings will change. 30 companies will change their names.	353 companies will move. 125 corporate phone numbers will be disconnected. 1 company will change ownership. 5 firms will file a bankruptcy petition.

Averages based on changes in the D&B Worldbase as at January 2008

Table 4.3 D&B Worldbase Change Metrics

D&B provides tools to search through the Worldbase database to find the appropriate D&B D-U-N-S Number and Worldbase record, as we'll discuss next.

4.1.6 D&B Entity Matching

D&B has developed intelligent Entity Matching processes to link your company's business partner details to the appropriate D&B D-U-N-S Number for any given enquiry. Enquiries can be submitted either using a batch process or by using online real-time searches such as the D&B DTI toolkit or the SAP NetWeaver MDM enrichment adapter.

Batch processes are typically used to match and cleanse your existing customer and vendor records before they are migrated into MDM. These processes involve your MDM data stewards and a D&B data analyst working together to prepare the data. The MDM data steward arranges the extraction of your customer and vendor name and addresses details from the consuming systems and sends these details to D&B in a flat file or spreadsheet for analysis. The D&B data analyst then returns the file or spreadsheet with the appropriate D&B D-U-N-S Number and Worldbase details added to each record.

Online processes are typically used in the daily MDM operational processes to match new customer and vendor records; these provide the D&B D-U-N-S Number and Worldbase details in real time directly into your SAP NetWeaver MDM repository.

Both the batch and the online processes use the same three Entity Matching processes: cleansing and parsing, candidate retrieval, and decision-making. Figure 4.4 shows the D&B Entity Matching processes, starting with cleansing and parsing, moving to candidate retrieval, and finishing with decisioning.

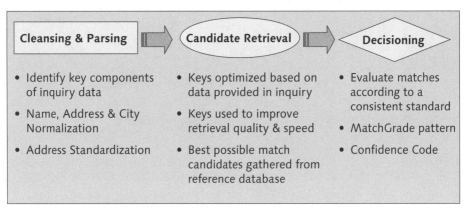

Figure 4.4 D&B Entity Matching Processes

The D&B Entity Matching processes enable you to find the best candidate D&B D-U-N-S Number against the submitted name and address parameters. The more accurate and complete the name and address data you provide, the higher the matching success rate. The following D&B matching techniques are among the best in class and have been continuously improved following several years of experience:

▶ Using the D&B patented MatchGrade technology

▶ Using multiple search algorithms to efficiently retrieve the best candidate records

▶ Standardizing addresses, including name, address, and city normalization

▶ Using in-memory keys and new keys such as latitude/longitude, acronyms, modified soundex, shingles, and various name, address, and telephone combinations

▶ Efficiently passing records through the match process using a Customer File Process (CFP) workflow tool

The Entity Matching elements are described in more detail in Figure 4.5. A rating letter (A, B, Z, or F) is assigned to each of the 7 name and address components (11 components for U.S. companies) to create a *MatchGrade pattern*.

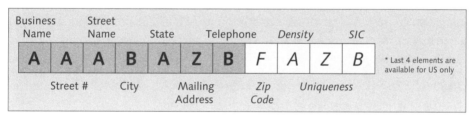

Figure 4.5   D&B Entity Matching Elements

Table 4.4 illustrates how a business name parameter "ABC Widget MFG" will be rated when matched to the various D&B Worldbase records:

Rating	Name	Range	Example Name Component Match	Score
A	Same	80-100	ABC WIDGET MFG versus ABC Widgeting MFG	94
B	Similar	35-79	ABC Widget MFG versus ABC MFG	73
F	Different	0 – 34	ABC Widget MFG versus XYZ MFG	34
Z	Null	Null	One or both are null (blank)	1

Table 4.4   D&B Component Matching Example

Each of the 7 components (11 for U.S. companies) is compared in this way and is scored either as an A, B, F, or Z rating.

MatchGrade has the following features:

- Overall MatchGrade ratings are developed for the various combinations of match patterns that can occur (such as name has exact match, phone has similar match, city has exact match, country has exact match, etc.).
- MatchGrades are mapped to confidence codes (1-10) and to a probability percentage.
- The best candidate D&B D-U-N-S Number records are selected by using components of the name and address to produce an overall MatchGrade score.

If, as a result of Entity Matching, a record is found with an overall confidence code of 8, 9, or 10, then it's a good match to the D&B record. You can be confident that your business record matches to this D&B D-U-N-S Number.

For those records with a confidence code of 7 and below, more research is required. The best candidate records will be returned for the MDM data steward to review and then to decide if any accurate matches exist. It could be that the company name and address you provided is another type of business partner function (e.g., a delivery or invoice name and address) and is not a valid legal entity with a D&B D-U-N-S Number.

D&B also provides benefits through external services, particularly in regard to financial and legal compliance, which we'll discuss next.

4.1.7 D&B and Financial and Legal Compliance

Understanding your customers' and vendors' Corporate Linkage helps you aggregate your total risk exposure across a corporate family. This is important especially given the continual change in ownership from mergers and acquisitions. Companies that have undergone mergers over the past few years are likely to have integrated systems and processes quickly. This rapid change and speed of integration has implications for data integrity and ultimately for real-time reporting to meet the Sarbanes-Oxley requirements.

Understanding your total risk exposure will enable you to make different decisions in cases such as the former Enron Corporation. This is a good example of "areas of risk" and "liability to your financial condition" that the Sarbanes-Oxley Act is intended for.

Figure 4.6 illustrates how D&B can help you aggregate your risk exposure using D&B Corporate Linkage.

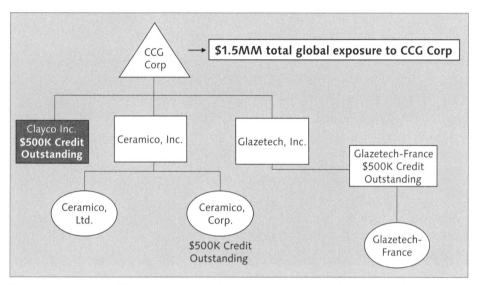

Figure 4.6 Example of Total Risk Exposure Analyzed by Corporate Linkage (Fictional Example)

In this example, you can see there is a total exposure of $1.5 million with the global ultimate company CCG corp consisting of the following:

- ▸ $500K exposure with Clayco Inc.
- ▸ $500K exposure with Glazetech-France
- ▸ $500K exposure with Ceramico Corp.

The D&B Corporate Linkage makes this analysis possible — without it there's no way of knowing that the companies are interrelated based on the company names and addresses stored in local systems.

Understanding the D&B Corporate Linkage structures enables you to better understand your global spend and revenues and to reduce your risk exposure and bad debt write-offs.

4.1.8   D&B Maintenance of Joint Venture Corporate Linkage Structures

However, a limitation of the D&B Corporate Linkage model is found in the case of joint ventures. You've seen that D&B defines a Parent to be "a corporation that owns more than 50% of another corporation." Similarly, a subsidiary is defined as "a corporation that is more than 50% owned by another corporation and will have a different legal business name from its parent company."

In the case of a joint venture, the Parent company or Subsidiary company may be split on say a 51% to 49% basis. D&B defines the Parent or Subsidiary as the 51% stakeholder. However, this can then distort the reporting figures when aggregated up to the Domestic Ultimate and Global Ultimate levels. Credit risks and spend analytics reports can be skewed.

For example, if total spend with company C is $10m and company C is a subsidiary of a Joint Venture between Company A (51%) and Company B (49%), then the D&B Corporate Linkage would indicate a spend of $10m with Company A ($4.9m overstated) and $0 with Company B ($4.9m understated). If the level of spend is high, as in this case then overall spend analytic reports produced by Global Ultimate will be misleading.

In these joint venture cases, you should consider setting up "alternate" hierarchies in SAP NetWeaver MDM. The functional design and the maintenance processes need to be carefully thought through; for example, how will you maintain the alternate hierarchies for future mergers and acquisitions? Discussions with your D&B team can help you develop an appropriate solution for the situation.

Let's now consider the SAP NetWeaver MDM Enrichment Architecture, which is an impressive technical feature.

4.1.9   The Dun & Bradstreet – SAP NetWeaver MDM Enrichment Architecture

By integrating D&B Entity Matching services with the SAP NetWeaver MDM enrichment adapter, you enable real-time customer and vendor matching processes to retrieve the best D&B D-U-N-S Number. D&B Worldbase data can be automatically integrated into the SAP NetWeaver MDM repository.

> **D&B SAP NetWeaver MDM Enrichment Adapter**
>
> With the D&B SAP NetWeaver MDM enrichment adapter, you can search 132 million Worldbase records in seconds using Web Services to find the best candidate records and then automatically import the appropriate D&B D-U-N-S Number and Worldbase package into the MDM business partner repository. This is impressive!

The D&B SAP NetWeaver MDM enrichment adapter components allow you to search for your new business partners against the D&B Worldbase database so that they can be identified with a D&B D-U-N-S Number and then enriched. This is a two-step process as now described.

Step 1: Identify the Candidate DUNS Records

The candidate D&B records are presented to the MDM data steward so that the "best candidate" record can be selected based on the company name and address details you provided. This selection process uses the D&B Entity Matching MatchGrade algorithms as described earlier in this chapter (Section 4.1.5). When the candidate records are returned to SAP NetWeaver MDM, it's also a good idea to design your solution to automatically check your business partner repository to see if you already have the D&B D-U-N-S Number. This is a quick and efficient way to avoid creating duplicate records in SAP NetWeaver MDM.

Step 2: Enrich the MDM Record with the D&B Worldbase Details of the Chosen DUNS Record

For the selected D&B D-U-N-S Number, D&B then returns you the Worldbase details with the Corporate Linkage to enable you to automatically store in the Sap NetWeaver MDM repository.

The D&B Worldbase plus linkage package enrichment details include mailing addresses, industry classifications, legal and "doing business as" names, Corporate Linkage, branch indicators, marketing demographics, business status, annual sales, and employee counts. Figure 4.7 shows the workflow steps.

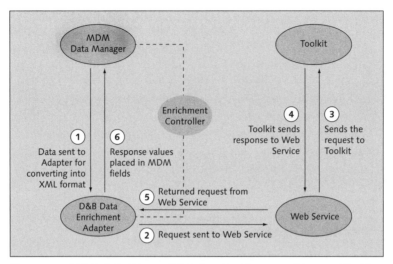

Figure 4.7 D&B SAP NetWeaver MDM Data Enrichment Architecture Workflow

The SAP NetWeaver MDM enrichment adapter integrates D&B Worldbase data real-time directly into the repository. The following series of workflow steps are executed:

1. **STEP 1** – A workflow step triggers the syndication of the request from the SAP NetWeaver MDM Data Manager, and the Enrichment Controller routes the query to the D&B data enrichment adapter.

2. The adapter passes the request to the D&B Web Service.

3. The D&B Web Service sends the request to the D&B toolkit.

4. D&B returns information on the candidate companies that best match the query — the best candidate matches against the 132 million DUNS records on Worldbase — to the Web Service.

5. The D&B Web Service returns the request to the D&B Enrichment Adapter.

6. The SAP NetWeaver MDM Enrichment Controller sends these response values to the Data Manager using an automated import process.

7. The MDM data steward selects the best candidate (or changes the parameters and requests another set of candidate records) and submits the chosen D&B D-U-N-S Number for the Worldbase package request.

8. **STEP 2** – Workflow steps 1 through 6 are then repeated this time to return a single Worldbase record with the D&B Worldbase details for the chosen D&B D-U-N-S Number.

You'll learn much more about the technical features of SAP NetWeaver MDM and D&B integration in Part 2 of this book. We introduced the SAP NetWeaver MDM D&B enrichment processes at this stage given its direct relevance to D&B and SAP NetWeaver MDM integration.

Let's now discuss the potential integration methods and the implications of introducing D&B services and SAP NetWeaver MDM into your company.

4.2   Dun & Bradstreet – Implications for an Organization

Returning to our example Company CO1 as introduced in Case Study 1 in Chapter 2, we'll illustrate how the D&B D-U-N-S Number and Worldbase data and SAP NetWeaver MDM can be integrated with your existing systems.

As a reminder, in our case study, Company CO1 has five business applications: a Supply Chain Management application (SCM1), a Customer Relationship Management application (CRM1), a Sales and Distribution application (SD1) a Financial Accounting application (FI1), and a Business Intelligence system (B11). Business partner details are maintained in each of these applications.

Figure 4.8 shows the new CO1 systems architecture when the external D&B services and SAP NetWeaver MDM have been introduced.

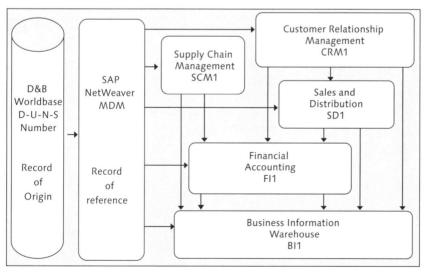

Figure 4.8 Company CO1 Systems Architecture, Including D&B External Services and SAP NetWeaver MDM

Now let's discuss the architecture design and the key principles in linking your existing systems to D&B external services and SAP NetWeaver MDM.

4.2.1 Architecture Principles in Using D&B External Services

D&B, SAP NetWeaver MDM, and Consuming Systems Integration
D&B services with the D&B D-U-N-S Number and Corporate Linkage provides valuable business information. The SAP NetWeaver MDM program's role is to design and appropriately link the D&B record of origin to the customer and vendor records in the consuming systems. All third-party business partner records should be linked to a D&B D-U-N-S Number; if you can't accurately identify and authenticate a company, then you face risk and compliance issues. All business partner records should be linked to the correct D&B D-U-N-S Number so that they can be verified correctly.

Table 4.5 describes the key principles in integrating D&B services and SAP NetWeaver MDM with your consuming systems.

The Business Information Warehouse (BI1) integration with the D&B Worldbase data and SAP NetWeaver MDM follows a slightly different model. In this case, you also integrate the SAP NetWeaver MDM D&B Corporate Linkage structure into the warehouse. An interface from MDM to BI1 enables customer and vendor reporting not just at the company level but also at group, country and parent level (D&B Global Ultimate, Domestic Ultimate and Parent / Headquarter levels).

Principle	D&B Worldbase	SAP NetWeaver MDM	Consuming Systems
Record definition	Record of origin: The system where the legal entity record is created and maintained.	Record of reference: The system where the legal entity is referred to. The single point of reference within your company.	The records of the business-facing applications where relationships with business partners are managed. The records are linked to the SAP NetWeaver MDM record of reference.

Table 4.5 D&B, SAP NetWeaver MDM, and Consuming Systems Integration Principles

Principle	D&B Worldbase	SAP NetWeaver MDM	Consuming Systems
Role	The system where the D&B D-U-N-S Number is created (originate). The single source of truth of D&B Corporate Linkage, which is accurate and up-to-date.	The "bridge" between the record of origin and the consuming systems. SAP NetWeaver MDM is the single definitive place where the D&B D-U-N-S Number and Worldbase details are stored in your systems. Consuming application details are maintained in SAP Netweaver MDM so that you can audit each system where the D&B D-U-N-S Number is consumed.	The consumers of the MDM records and services. The MDM data stored in the consuming system varies depending on the integration model chosen, for example, consolidated, harmonized, or centralized models.
Number of records	132 million	The number of unique customers and vendors of your company.	The number of records per consuming system as described in Case Study 1; this will be reduced if a centralized model is chosen and duplicate records are blocked.
Unique key	D&B D-U-N-S Number	MDM ID and D&B D-U-N-S Number	All relevant business partner records should be linked to an appropriate D&B D-U-N-S Number. If you apply a consolidated model, there can be several occurrences of a D&B D-U-N-S Number.

Table 4.5 D&B, SAP NetWeaver MDM, and Consuming Systems Integration Principles (Cont.)

Principle	D&B Worldbase	SAP NetWeaver MDM	Consuming Systems
Data model	D&B Worldbase data, including Corporate Linkage.	D&B Worldbase data, including Corporate Linkage *plus* links to all consuming systems.	Mixture of legal entities and partner functions. Data attributes include the relevant business partner name and address details and other local attributes as required by the business system.
Maintained by	D&B – multiple sources	Refresh processes from D&B plus MDM data stewards who manage the refresh processes and distribution of MDM records to consuming systems.	Local business users with feeds of global attributes from MDM, including key identifiers (MDM IDs and D&B D-U-N-S Numbers).
Search processes	Search using D&B entity mapping – sophisticated patented search engine.	Initially search the internal SAP NetWeaver MDM business partner repository to see if the business partner is already used in the company. Then search the D&B Worldbase using the SAP NetWeaver MDM enrichment adapter.	Initially search the local business application (FI1, SD1, etc.) to see if the record exists. If the record is not found, then search the SAP NetWeaver MDM repository to see if the record exists. If found, request distribution. If not found, request a new company record from the MDM Data Stewards who will look-up with D&B using the SAP NetWeaver MDM enrichment adapter.

Table 4.5 D&B, SAP NetWeaver MDM, and Consuming Systems Integration Principles (Cont.)

Now let's consider how to link each of your customer and vendor master records to the D&B D-U-N-S Number and the D&B Worldbase data.

4.2.2 The D&B D-U-N-S Number as a Unique Key

The first objective is to uniquely identify each of your records. The D&B Entity Matching functionality will be used to match each of your consuming systems master data records and to find the appropriate D&B D-U-N-S Number for each vendor and customer.

Dun & Bradstreet Matching – Phase 1

D&B Entity Matching is usually initially set up as a batch process — your MDM data steward arranges for the extracts of the company name and addresses from each of the consuming systems and sends these to D&B for analysis. The MDM data steward soon builds up specialist knowledge of how company structures are set up and also how D&B Entity Matching processes are best organized. Table 4.6 provides some fictional results from the first iteration of a D&B Entity Matching process.

4.2.3 Persuading Local Business and System User Groups

A useful technique to help you persuade your local business and system user groups is to compare the D&B approach to customer and vendor master data management with your company's existing processes. As an example, let's assume that your company is the recently merged company (CO1 plus CO2) as introduced in Chapter 2, Case Study 2.

Table 4.7 compares the D&B processes with those of the Case Study 2 Companies.

How Does Your Company Compare?
Try this comparison exercise for your company: ▶ How do you authenticate new customers and vendors? ▶ Do you understand their current corporate structure? ▶ Can you uniquely identify each company that you deal with? ▶ How rigorous are your company search processes, and are duplicate master data records ever created? ▶ How do you update your customer and vendor records when they move or merge?

CO1 Systems		Vendor Active Records	Used in Past Two Years	Vendor Linked to DUNS	Vendor Unique DUNS Records	Customer Active Records	Used in the Past Two Years	Customer Linked to DUNS	Customer Unique DUNS Records
Customer Relationship Management	CRM1					3,000	1,200	840	790
Supply Chain Management	SCM1	4,500	1,000	740	680				
Sales and Distribution	SD1					2,000	1,100	685	600
Financial Accounting	FI1	6,000	950	845	810	2,500	975	920	900
Business Intelligence	BI1	9,000	1,200	990	940	6,500	1,300	975	905
Totals		19,500	3,150	2,575	975	14,000	4,575	3,420	965

Table 4.6   First Iteration of D&B Entity Matching for Company CO1 (Fictional Example)

Master Data Feature	Dun & Bradstreet	Company CO1/CO2 from Case Study 2
Unique key	The D&B D-U-N-S Number — 132 million records globally.	No unique key. There are duplicate records in each of the master data silos. Users cannot easily differentiate between a legal entity and other business partner function relationships.
Single MDM database repository	The D&B Worldbase database.	No central repository.
Create business partner process	Rigorous process, including global verification and validation by several sources. A D&B D-U-N-S Number can only be created when a business has been authenticated.	Minimal local database checking with limited data entry standards and occasional verification.
Data model and Corporate Linkage	Detailed company data model, including Corporate Linkage.	Vendors and customers are created using varying data models with few data standards. Corporate Linkage is not available; you cannot view the corporate structure.
Update business partner process: Lifecycle Management	Continuous improvement; D&B team continuously research their data sources. Mergers and acquisitions updates are included.	Data is infrequently updated with varying local system processes. Inactive records are not maintained or end dated.
Search business partner processes	Sophisticated D&B Entity Matching processes with patented algorithms and built-in controls and confidence codes.	Simple searches by users checking an individual data silo based on name and address matching. Often, the searches are ineffective, and duplicate records are created.

Table 4.7 Comparison of D&B Master Data Processes and an Example Company

Returning to our example now, you may be surprised that D&B doesn't match 100% of records the first time with a D&B D-U-N-S Number, especially because

D&B has 132 million company records and a sophisticated matching engine. Do they really have the global coverage they claim?

Why Does D&B Entity Matching Not Initially Match 100% Linkage of Your Business Partner Data?

Typically, on the first round of D&B Entity Matching, you can expect somewhere between a 60% to 80% Entity Matching success rate. In these cases, a D&B D-U-N-S Number will be identified with a match score of between 8 and 10 so that you can confidently link it to your customer or vendor record. In our example of the Financial Accounting system FI1, D&B managed to match 845 out of 950 vendor records with a D&B D-U-N-S Number. Table 4.8 shows a fictional example D&B Entity Matching report.

	Score	Number	Percentage	Cumulative Percentage
Confidence Code	10	680	71.6%	71.6%
Confidence Code	9	95	10.0%	81.6%
Confidence Code	8	70	7.4%	88.9%
Confidence Code	7	35	3.7%	92.6%
Confidence Code	6	24	2.5%	95.2%
Confidence Code	5	13	1.4%	96.5%
Confidence Code	4	10	1.1%	97.6%
Confidence Code	3	1	0.1%	97.7%
Confidence Code	2	0	0.0%	97.7%
Confidence Code	1	0	0.0%	97.7%
Confidence Code	0	22	2.3%	100.0%
Total Confidence Codes		950	100	100

Table 4.8 Iteration 1 – D&B Confidence Code Report Produced for Financial Accounting System FI1 (Fictional Example)

The MDM Data Steward will investigate all matches where the confidence code is 7 or below. Table 4.9 lists the key reasons for these "no matches" and also the actions your business will take to ensure a higher success rate in future iterations.

Reason	Description	Actions
1. The business partner name and address you provided is not a legal entity name and address but is of some other business partner relationship.	The business partner name and address is for a different type of partner account. For a vendor, this may be a purchase ordering address or an address to which payments are sent. In the case of a customer record, it may be a ship-to (or delivery) address, a bill-to (or invoicing address), or a payer (or payment address).	Analyze nonmatched records and review the company structures. Consider if the name and address is really a valid legal entity. Consider your consuming system design to see how it reflects these different kinds of relationships.
2. The business partner name and address is incomplete in your consuming system.	Business users often key minimal information into a system as a shortcut to save time, especially if the full details are not readily available. If a country, a ZIP code, a street, or a city are not mandatory fields and are not provided on a request form, then these will be omitted from the data entry process. The business names that are set up may also be partially completed; for example, a system may limit a name field to say 30-50 characters when a legal name can be more than 100 characters in length.	Review incomplete addresses. Work with the business application users to complete the country, city, name, street, ZIP codes, and so on. Establishing and mandating the data entry standards for complete and accurate business name and address data is a key building block for a successful MDM program.
3. The business partner name and address has not been kept up-to-date in your consuming systems.	Over time, a company may merge, change its name, or move. A business partner record in your business application may be several years old, and may not reflect such changes.	Look up the latest company details with D&B, and amend your business name and address details accordingly.

Table 4.9 Reasons for a "No Match" with D&B Entity Matching

Reason	Description	Actions
4. The business partner is not a company but is a natural person.	Relationships with individuals (natural persons) may be set up in the same system tables as the company's legal entities. These types of records will not be known by D&B.	Remove these records from the analysis. Natural persons should not be sent to D&B and should be set up using different account groups and processes.
5. D&B does not have the legal entity set up in the Worldbase database.	This is rare but is often used by "internal opponents" of the D&B service as a reason not to use it. It is highly likely (>99%) that for most countries if a legal entity exists, then it will be in the D&B Worldbase database. The four reasons already discussed are more likely to explain why a record cannot be matched to a D&B D-U-N-S Number. In a few developing countries, the D&B match rate may not be as high. Also, in a few cases, the company may be a brand-new startup company that has yet to be investigated by D&B.	For these exceptional cases, you will need to agree on policies and procedures with D&B who will investigate if the company is a valid one, create a new D&B D-U-N-S Number in the Worldbase database, and then distribute to your SAP NetWeaver MDM system.

Table 4.9   Reasons for a "No Match" with D&B Entity Matching (Cont.)

Persuading Local Business and System User Groups

To be persuasive, you need some early D&B and MDM successes, such as 100% of your customer and vendor records in one important system being successfully matched to a D&B D-U-N-S Number. A critical success factor for the D&B and SAP NetWeaver MDM solution is data quality; your business users must believe that both D&B and your SAP NetWeaver MDM repositories have the very best, most complete, and most accurate company data available. Employ good MDM Data Stewards, and work closely with the business users to cleanse and to successfully link a key system to MDM.

It will be a major help if your businesses can obtain some early MDM value or quick wins, for example, negotiating an improved global deal through a better understanding of the D&B Corporate Linkage structures.

4.2.4 Measuring D&B Entity Matching Progress

For you to successfully match 100% of your business partner records to a D&B D-U-N-S Number, you'll need a few iterations. Exception reports will be produced for your business users to act upon and these will highlight the nonmatched records, the reasons, and the likely actions to take. An initial focus is likely to be on improving the completeness of your business name and address details, which will quickly increase the match rates. Understanding complex company structures may take a little longer and a few more cycles.

Duplicate D&B D-U-N-S Numbers in Your Systems

During the data analysis phase, you are also likely to discover that multiple records within one system are linked to the same D&B D-U-N-S Number, as illustrated by Figure 4.9.

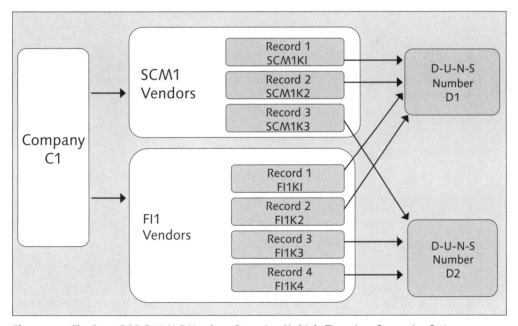

Figure 4.9 The Same D&B D-U-N-S Numbers Occurring Multiple Times in a Consuming System

The D&B Entity Matching highlights to you that there are multiple records within your SCM1 and FI1 applications that are linked to the same D&B D-U-N-S Number. As an example, in the SCM system SCM1, there are two records (Key records: SCM1KI and SCM1K2) matching to the same D&B D-U-N-S Number D1. In addition, there are two records in the Financial Accounting system FI1 (Key records: FI1K1 and FI1K2) also linked to the same D&B D-U-N-S Number D1. Table 4.10 lists the reasons why duplicate records are found.

Cause of Duplicate Records	Reasons
Master data maintenance processes in SCM1 and FI1 are not "rigorous"	Incomplete data entry, for example, is missing address details.
	Business users maintaining the data do not search the existing SCM1 and FI1 databases before creating a new record.
	Name and address data was for a partner function to the legal entity, for example, ordering address or payment address.
	Data has been automatically added via batch processes to the SCM1 and FI1 due to mergers or acquisitions. These were not fully validated due to time constraints before loading.
Limitations of the SCM1 and FI1 applications	In some applications and with some implementation designs, it's necessary to set up multiple business partner records because of other features in the customer and vendor setup design.
	For example, if different sales organizations within your corporation have different contracts with a supplier, they may require multiple vendor records to be set up (e.g., to store different payment terms or different bank details).

Table 4.10 Reasons for Duplicate D&B D-U-N-S Numbers in Systems

Dun & Bradstreet Matching – Phase 2

After a few iterations, the D&B matching processes provides better results. This results from many activities to cleanse and improve the quality of the names and addresses in the CO1 applications. Table 4.11 provides the revised D&B D-U-N-S Numbers counts.

CO1 Systems		Vendor Active Records	Used in Past Two Years	Vendor Linked to DUNS	Vendor Unique DUNS Records	Customer Active Records	Used in the Past 2 Years	Customer Linked to DUNS	Customer Unique DUNS Records
Customer Relationship Management	CRM1					3,000	1,200	925	875
Supply Chain Management	SCM1	4,500	1,000	775	695				
Sales and Distribution	SD1					2,000	1,100	785	680
Financial Accounting	FI1	6,000	950	905	850	2,500	975	930	905
Business Information Warehouse	BI1	9,000	1,200	1,050	975	6,500	1,300	1,100	940
Totals		19,500	3,150	2,730	1,020	14,000	4,575	3,740	1,060

Table 4.11 D&B Entity Matching for Company CO1 – Final Iteration (Fictional Example)

Some Observations and Conclusions – Speed and Repeatability

Three key parties are involved in the D&B Entity Matching process. The local business users cleanse, delete, and complete the name and address details so that the nonmatched records will match next time. The D&B data analyst provides you with the Entity Matching files and reports to link your records to a D&B D-U-N-S Number. The MDM data steward coordinates the data match and cleansing activity.

After you've established the D&B, SAP NetWeaver MDM, and business partner maintenance processes, taking on new systems becomes a routine process. D&B Entity Matching becomes a tried and tested method with a quick turnaround. In three months, you can link D&B D-U-N-S Number to many of your customer and vendor records.

Let's now consider how to analyze D&B Corporate Linkages and business partner functions in your systems and what options you have to link them with SAP NetWeaver MDM.

4.2.5 D&B Corporate Linkages and Business Partner Functions in SAP NetWeaver MDM

Figure 4.10 illustrates how D&B Corporate Linkage structures and business partner functions link together.

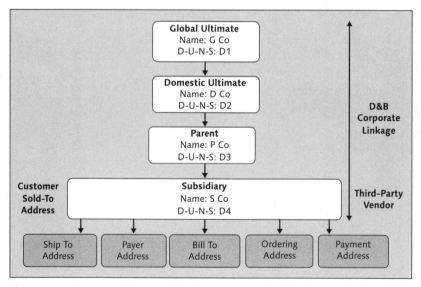

Figure 4.10 Corporate Linkage and Partner Functions Combined

D&B provides the legal entity and Corporate Linkage details, which are the top four layers of the hierarchy as shown in Figure 4.10. This information is important for setting up customer and vendor contracts because these are the legal companies you transact with and whose corporate structures you need to understand for credit risk exposure and compliance reasons. It's sensible to store all of the D&B Worldbase details in MDM; the D&B Worldbase package attributes underpin your SAP NetWeaver MDM business partner repository design.

However, in your various business systems, you'll also hold other useful pieces of information about your business partners. For customers, you hold ship-to addresses (or delivery addresses), bill-to addresses (or invoice addresses), and payer addresses (or payment addresses). Similarly, for vendors, you hold the ordering address (or addresses from which you purchase goods and services) and the payment address (or address from which payment is made).

Even for your customers and vendors with a very simple structure, that is, a single address that serves as the ship-to, the sold-to, the payer, and the bill-to address, there are often extra details of useful business information. For example, the ship-to address may also store the contact person details and some special delivery instructions, and the payer address may be located in a different room or part of a building with different contact and department details.

The various business partner relationships become a factor in the creation of duplicate records in the master data silos. When the name and address details vary slightly, "duplicate" record entries are created. In the absence of the D&B Entity Matching process and the unique D&B D-U-N-S Number, these duplicate entries are difficult to identify.

An important design decision for the SAP NetWeaver MDM program is how much of the business partner function details you'll store and maintain in SAP NetWeaver MDM and also how much you'll link through to the consuming systems.

Design options to consider include the following:

▶ **Partner functions details are not stored in MDM.**
The consuming system masters and maintains the business partner details (ship-to, bill-to, payer name, addresses, etc.). MDM is linked to the sold-to record only and the D&B D-U-N-S Number is stored in the sold-to records as a key mapping in the consuming system. (This is a simple consolidated model.)

▶ **Partner functions key mappings are maintained in MDM.**
This is similar to the previous option, but in this case, the D&B D-U-N-S Number is also tagged to each relevant business partner record in the consuming system — sold-to, ship-to, bill-to, payer, and so on. (This option is a variant of the consolidation model.)

▶ **Partner functions attribute details are mastered in MDM.**
With this option, MDM is the master of all business partner name and address details, including the partner functions. In this case, the consuming system's local data validation rules and processes need to be replicated in MDM, which is likely to require software development. The non-D&B sourced data in MDM must be maintained through the business partner lifecycle. (This option is a variant of the centralized model.)

Consolidated, harmonized, and centralized models are discussed more fully later in this chapter in Section 4.2.7. First, let's consider the MDM Lifecycle Management and D&B refresh processes.

4.2.6   Lifecycle Management

By establishing the D&B look-up as part of the create vendor and create customer business processes, you can guarantee that each new record gets a D&B D-U-N-S Number. By refreshing the data from D&B, you also ensure that the name, address, and Corporate Linkage data is kept up to date throughout a company's lifecycle.

Lifecycle Management changes are made available to you by periodically refreshing your D&B Worldbase data (e.g., on a monthly or quarterly basis) and then importing these details to the SAP NetWeaver MDM business partner repository. You can then review all of the changes that have occurred and decide on the relevant actions. As an example, if a legal name or address has changed, you can then inform the appropriate consuming systems support team and update your SAP NetWeaver MDM repository.

A carefully designed refresh strategy is an important deliverable from an MDM program. You may initially store the latest D&B Worldbase file in a separate "staging" SAP NetWeaver MDM repository and then produce comparison reports to highlight any changes compared to your "live" repository. Some changes such as a change of CEO or SIC code are likely to only impact the individual SAP NetWeaver MDM repository. However, other changes such as bankruptcy or credit rating changes are more significant, and all interested consuming systems business teams should be notified. D&B Corporate Linkage changes need to be reflected and interfaced to your Business Intelligence warehouse.

After careful consideration, the latest D&B Worldbase file details will be incorporated into your SAP NetWeaver MDM business partner repository to keep it up to date. Changes made in this way to the repository should be easily auditable.

Now let's consider how to scale the solution so that MDM can link to many consuming systems and how the consolidated, harmonized, and centralized MDM models affect this.

4.2.7 Scaling the Solution

The MDM program can apply different integration models to scale the solution and to integrate D&B data and SAP NetWeaver MDM to business partner data with *all* consuming systems. Full and accurate business partner data linked to the D&B D-U-N-S Number is the most important factor — this should be mandatory!

However, the decision whether to consolidate, harmonize, or centralize a consuming system's data with SAP NetWeaver MDM is an integration choice. Let's first consider the "weakest" form of integration, which is the consolidated model.

Consolidated Model

In the consolidated model, MDM is used to collect master data from several systems and to store the details in the central MDM business partner repository. Consolidation allows you to detect and to clean up duplicate and identical records and to update the consuming systems key fields for cross-system key mapping linkage. The key identifier of the D&B D-U-N-S Number (or possibly the unique SAP NetWeaver MDM record identifier the MDM ID) will be tagged onto each of the consuming system's records; this is the only MDM attribute stored in the consuming system.

The business partner maintenance processes are still driven in the local consuming systems. Records continue to be created in the consuming systems (which remain the "master" systems). MDM is the "slave" and receives the records sometimes later through periodic interfaces or extracts.

MDM is at the back end of the process rather than being an integral part of the create customer and vendor processes. A 1:1 relationship does not necessarily exist among an MDM record, a D&B D-U-N-S Number, and a consuming system record.

Finally, with the consolidated model design, there will still be duplicate records in the consuming systems, so many of the MDM benefits will not be realized. However, this is relatively quick to implement and does enable you to develop a global view of your business partners and the associated leverage of scale advantages. The business users can access the SAP NetWeaver MDM information to perform company-wide analysis and consolidated reporting.

Harmonized Model

In the harmonized model scenario, MDM enhances the consolidation model by also forwarding global master data attributes to consuming systems. This enables you to synchronize globally relevant attributes across your company's landscape.

The number of global attributes to be harmonized needs to be carefully considered, and there are questions you need to address before deciding. Do you mandate the legal name as provided by D&B in the consuming systems? Do you mandate the legal address? Does this have implications for your existing consuming systems design and interfaces? Are the consuming systems' data model and data attributes consistent with the SAP NetWeaver MDM repository design?

With the harmonized model, there is a stronger relationship between MDM and the consuming systems. However, it isn't as strong as in the case of the centralized model; it may still be possible to create new records in a consuming system without the rigor of the SAP NetWeaver MDM – D&B external services look-up process.

The harmonized model is quicker to implement than the centralized model and allows the legacy systems to continue to store duplicate records. This may apply, for example, in cases where two vendor records are needed in a consuming system because of multiple bank details or multiple payment terms across sales organizations.

The D&B D-U-N-S Number is still an important key (although not necessarily a unique key) within a consuming system, thereby enabling the enterprise spend and revenue reporting requirements to be met.

Centralized Model

The tightest form of MDM integration is the centralized model. With this model, SAP NetWeaver MDM is the "master" system and the consuming systems are the "slaves."

Whereas the emphasis in the consolidation scenario is on local data maintenance, the centralized scenario focuses on creating and maintaining the global data in the central SAP NetWeaver MDM repository. Global data attributes are then syndicated to the consuming systems, where the local attributes can be added.

It isn't possible to create a vendor or a customer record directly in a consuming system because the record must first be created in MDM and then distributed. This is the cleanest, purest approach and achieves all of the MDM primary business benefits.

There are 1:1 relationships between an MDM record, a D&B Worldbase record, and a consuming system legal entity third-party record. Existing business partner data must be initially cleansed in the consuming systems, and new records cannot be created without an MDM – D&B external look-up process, therefore avoiding future duplication.

Global attributes can be updated automatically with periodic refreshes from D&B into the SAP NetWeaver MDM repository and then passed on to the consuming systems.

This integration model requires the most business effort with data clean up activities and also includes completing transactions and open items financials settlement for the business partners that we want to end date, in order that duplicates can be removed. This approach also results in the most MDM business benefits.

External numbering is a potential option for you to consider with the central master data model. In this case, MDM controls and creates the vendor and customer number in the consuming systems. MDM can ensure that the vendor and customer numbers are unique and consistent so that the backend BI or the SCM systems automatically pick them up. This helps to simplify reporting consolidation.

A situation where central master data management can be achieved is when your company is implementing a new SAP ERP 6.0 system. Usually, considerable time is invested in preparing the data for the new application. Data conversions are practiced, data cleansing teams are set up, and business partner data will be restructured. For example, only active business partners (e.g., business partners where financial transaction have taken place in the past three years) may be migrated, and dedicated effort is spent in cleaning the business partner master data.

The centralized model is the ideal MDM model; however, the SAP NetWeaver MDM program may be restricted by the pace of the data cleanup process or by the deployment, which can take several months. This can slow down the pace of your program and delay the benefits of setting up accurate and aggregated enterprise master data.

Deciding on Your MDM Scaling Strategy

By designing your SAP NetWeaver MDM repositories appropriately, you can enable all three integration models at the same time; the MDM repository designs are determined by the local rules of the consuming systems.

The decision to consolidate, harmonize, or centralize will take into consideration you existing systems and their expected life spans. If you plan to integrate MDM to a new system currently being implemented or to a strategic long-term system, a centralized model may be appropriate. For older legacy systems that are about to be decommissioned, a harmonized or consolidated model is more practical.

The design decision is also dependent on the progress of your MDM program. You need to have established a live operational SAP NetWeaver MDM system with D&B links, MDM data stewards, and data standards before you can move to a centralized model.

A practical MDM implementation strategy to get things moving includes the following:

▶ Tag each customer and vendor record in the consuming system with a D&B D-U-N-S Number.

▶ Add the D&B Worldbase details, including Corporate Linkage, to your BI reporting system.

▶ Clear up the duplicate records in your consuming system over time (using the D&B D-U-N-S Number as a KPI).

▶ Implement policies and procedures so that all future records are created and validated through the SAP NetWeaver MDM – D&B external services look-up process before creation in the consuming system.

So let's now imagine that you've established D&B services through SAP NetWeaver MDM and linked the D&B D-U-N-S Number to all of your consuming systems. You can now revisit the earlier case studies questions.

4.3   Applying the D&B Solution – The Case Studies Revisited

You are now in the position where all new customer and vendor records are created using the MDM and D&B external services look-up process. Each of your consuming systems has had all of its records tagged with the appropriate D&B D-U-N-S Number, and you have started end dating and blocking duplicate records. Let's revisit the questions from Chapter 2 to see if we have some better answers. Refer to Table 4.12 for each of the latest answers.

Question 1: How many *vendors* does Company CO1 have?

Is it 4,500 (SCM active records), 6,000 (FI active), or 9,000 (BI system), or 1,000 (SCM transactions in the past two years), 950 (FI transactions in the past two years), or 1,200 (BI transactions in the past two years)?

In Chapter 2, we answered:

"A number somewhere between 800 vendors and 10,000 vendors is unlikely to be satisfactory; a project to reconcile the data across the systems may be initiated."

Now with D&B external services established, we can see:

We can now answer the question with certainty.

Company CO1 has in total 1,020 unique vendor records. It has 695 unique DUNS vendor records in SCM1, 905 unique vendor records in FI1, and 975 vendor records in BI1.

In Chapter 1, we introduced the concept of the Vendor System Index (VSI) defined as the following:

Vendor System Index (VSI) = (Number of Available Vendor Records / Number of Unique Active Vendor Records) − 1) × 100%

We now know that the VSI for SCM1 is 547%, for FI1 is 562%, and for BI1 is 823%. Each of the systems is "obese" according to our VSI metric!

CO1 Systems		Vendor Active Records	Used in Past Two Years	Vendor Linked to DUNS	Vendor Unique DUNS Records	Customer Active Records	Used in the Past Two Years	Customer Linked to DUNS	Customer Unique DUNS Records
Customer Relationship Management	CRM1					3,000	1,200	925	875
Supply Chain Management	SCM1	4,500	1,000	775	695				
Sales and Distribution	SD1					2,000	1,100	785	680
Financial Accounting	FI1	6,000	950	905	850	2,500	975	930	905
Business Intelligence	BI1	9,000	1,200	1,050	975	6,500	1,300	1,100	940
Totals		19,500	3,150	2,730	1,020	14,000	4,575	3,740	1,060

Table 4.12 D&B Entity Matching for Company CO1 – Final Iteration (Fictional Example)

The DUNS key provides you with key mappings in each consuming system so you can identify the shared vendors across SCM1, FI1, and BI1, and also the number of vendors in SCM1 only (and not FI1), and so on.

Corporate Linkage enables you to integrate these details with the business intelligence warehouse and to aggregate your vendor reporting at the group (global ultimate and domestic ultimate levels) and parent levels.

Question 2: How many *customers* does company CO1 have?

Is it 3,000 (CRM active records), 2,000 (SD active records), or 2,500 (FI active records), or 6,500 (BI records), 1,200 (CRM transactions in the past two years), 1,100 (SD transactions in the past two years), 975 (FI transactions in the past two years), or 1,300 (BI transactions in the past two years)?

In Chapter 2, we answered:

"Again there is a wide range of potential answers; a number somewhere between 800 and 10,000 records again is a best estimate."

Now with D&B external services established, we can see:

Again you can answer the question much more accurately. Company CO1 has in total 1,060 unique customer records. There are 875 unique DUNS records in CRM1, 680 unique records in SD1, 905 unique records in FI1, and 940 BI1 records for customers.

In Chapter 1, we also introduced the concept of the Customer System Index (CSI) defined as the following:

Customer System Index (VSI) = (Number of Available Customer Records / Number of Unique Active Customer Records) – 1) × 100%

We now know that the CSI for CRM1 is 242%, for SD1 is 194%, for FI1 is 176%, and for BI1 is 591%. Each of the systems is again "obese" according to our CSI metric!

We know the exact number of customers shared across CRM1, SD1, FI1, and BI1, and the number of customers in CRM1 only (and not FI1). We also can analyze the D&B Corporate Linkage reporting.

Question 3: How many counterparties does company CO1 have (i.e., business partners we both sell to [customer] and buy from [vendor])?

Chapter 2 answer:

We said, "What a difficult question!"

Now with D&B external services established, we can see:

By matching the D&B D-U-N-S Number key across CRM1, SCM1, SD1, FI1, and BI1 systems, you understand and can make decisions both on your sales and procurement positions. By matching the Global Ultimate DUNS and the Domestic ultimate DUNS details, you can understand your relationships across counterparty organizations.

Question 4: For the combined Company CO1 and Company CO2, how many vendors, customers, and business partners are there? How many vendors, customers, and business partners are shared across the two companies?

In Chapter 2 we answered: "Unfortunately, the answers are even more difficult to estimate. In total, there are 51,500 vendor records and 59,000 customer records set up on the various systems. There is no easy way to link Company CO1 business partners to Company CO2 business partners."

Now with D&B external services established, we can see:

By using the D&B D-U-N-S Number key, we can identify the number of combined and shared customers across CRM1 and CRM2, SD1 and SD2, FI1 and FI2, and BI1 and BI2.We know the number of combined and shared customers across SRM1 and SRM2, FI1 and FI2, and BI1 and BI2. We also can identify the number of combined and shared business partners across each of the CO1 and CO2 systems.

Revisiting the Management Questions of Chapter 3

Finally, we can revisit the questions your business leaders raised in Chapter 3 in trying to better understand your company's relationships with your business partners. Previously, they were not aware of the implications of the master data silos and asked the following questions:

▸ Who are my most profitable customers?

▸ How do I increase my revenue from my existing customers?

▸ How do I improve my operational efficiency when dealing with a customer?

▸ What is my credit risk with a customer?

▶ What is my total spending with a vendor?

▶ What is the financial and trading risk information of a vendor?

▶ Am I trading with a "denied" vendor?

As a result of the D&B services and linking all of your company records to the D&B D-U-N-S Number, you can again provide accurate answers to all of these questions, which can be quickly repeated. This is a huge step forward!

4.4 Summary

In Chapter 4, we considered the D&B services. We defined the D&B D-U-N-S Number and also further explained the Worldbase database, Corporate Linkage, Entity Matching, and Lifecycle Management processes. We considered the company master data maintenance processes, including global verification and Lifecycle Management. We analyzed the features of the SAP NetWeaver MDM D&B Data Enrichment Adapter.

We revisited our earlier case studies to illustrate how the D&B external services can be applied to link customer and vendor details in multiple systems using the D&B D-U-N-S Number as a common key. We discussed the potential ways of integrating D&B services and SAP NetWeaver MDM into your company, including the consolidation, harmonized, and centralized models. Finally, we returned to the key management business intelligence questions from Chapters 2 and 3 to answer with much greater accuracy and certainty.

Let's now move on to consider how to mobilize an MDM program.

This chapter covers the people and key stakeholders you engage with to mobilize your MDM program. You'll learn how to establish MDM program governance and what skills are needed in your MDM program team. We'll also discuss how to develop a realistic MDM roadmap for your organization.

5 Mobilizing for MDM: People and Planning

To mobilize your MDM program, you'll need specific people and skills. We'll describe how to establish MDM program governance, including the role of the MDM Steering Board, and we'll also introduce the MDM Stakeholder map. This chapter then moves on to the roles and skills you will need in your MDM program team. You'll learn how to build relationships with SAP and Dun & Bradstreet, and then how to carry out both a business and a technical SAP NetWeaver MDM proof of concept. Finally, we'll discuss the varying SAP NetWeaver MDM program skills you'll need during Phases 1 and 2 of your MDM journey.

5.1 Establishing MDM Program and Data Governance

To start your MDM program, you need senior business support and funding. You need to clearly articulate the MDM business case and the business benefits as discussed in Chapter 3. The core MDM business benefits include uniform, consistent master data and Lifecycle Management processes. There will also be reconciliation and reporting benefits and financial and legal compliance improvements.

Your business case will include the primary and secondary benefits of integrating MDM with your SCM, CRM, FI, management information, corporate administration, and IT systems. Ongoing measurement of the business benefits delivered by the MDM program is also important.

Let's now consider how to set up the governance of your MDM program and the role of your MDM Steering Board.

5.1.1 MDM Program Governance and the Role of an MDM Steering Board

The MDM Steering Board is an important forum for MDM Governance. Its primary role is to agree on the MDM decisions and to resolve issues. The MDM Steering Board is the forum through which the MDM program can highlight its integration challenges, identify the key stakeholders, and clarify accountabilities. The MDM Steering Board agrees on the MDM program objectives and meets on a frequent basis, either each month or every two months. It is likely to include a combination of local business unit leaders; your corporate, financial, and compliance leaders; and the MDM program leaders. The board agrees on the MDM program vision and the two-year roadmap, signs off on the MDM program scope, and secures the funding.

The MDM Steering Board monitors the delivered business value from the MDM program against defined KPIs. The board agrees on the MDM service levels and the MDM data stewardship accountabilities, and communicates and champions the MDM program throughout your organization.

The board also produces a documented set of decisions and accountabilities for your organizational units that define the business procedures to be executed according to the established MDM consolidated, harmonized, or centralized models.

Finally, the MDM Steering Board also reacts to and resolves any issues arising from noncompliance with the established MDM decisions and rules. This governance is particularly important when an MDM program finds that it can't make the required progress and need decisions.

Let's now consider the organizational impacts of MDM and who drives the MDM agenda in your organization.

5.1.2 Organizational Impacts

An important question to ask is "Who drives your MDM agenda?" The answer will vary from company to company. It can be a business led initiative, for example, driven by your procurement organization whose objective is to deliver global purchasing benefits by leveraging your company's scale.

Your Financial Accounting organization can drive the MDM program agenda through the perceived risks of non-compliance. This is influenced by concerns about regulatory initiatives, such as Sarbanes-Oxley and the associated requirements to authenticate your customers and suppliers.

A Business Intelligence (BI) program can drive the MDM program agenda where the intent is to provide better analysis, reconciliation, and reporting throughout your organization. As an example, this may be driven by a corporate procurement management initiative to better understand your supplier metrics.

Finally, your IT department may drive the MDM program agenda as part of a technical infrastructure program. For example, this may be driven by a desire to move to a service-oriented architecture (SOA) and the master data barriers of inconsistent data sources and data models.

Who drives the MDM agenda is often determined by who the MDM champions and key stakeholders are. You can assess this using the MDM Stakeholder map, which is a tool discussed later in this section.

In Figure 5.1, the head of procurement is your initial MDM champion, and your MDM program is initially a business-led initiative. However, as the MDM program gains momentum, other key stakeholders such as your CEO, CFO, CIO, Head of Marketing, and Head of Business Information Reporting can also become your MDM champions.

By successfully mastering your customer and vendor records in MDM, you'll provide benefits for each of these key stakeholders. However each stakeholder will have different objectives and priorities for the MDM program. This is why the constituents of your MDM Steering Board should be carefully considered, and cross-functional representation is so important.

Let's now move on to consider how you'll mandate MDM as a company standard.

Establishing MDM as a Company Standard

During MDM Phase 1, you'll assess the internal politics and recognize that your key stakeholders start from different positions of MDM awareness and enthusiasm. It's important that the MDM program quickly builds momentum and achieves some early wins.

By MDM Phase 2, you'll need to gain sufficient stakeholder support to ensure that MDM becomes a corporate way of doing things. Eventually, this leads to the creation of a company data standard with which all organizational units must comply.

There are three approaches to establishing MDM as a company standard: the top-down approach, the strategic approach, and the bottom-up approach. Let's now consider each in turn.

The *top-down approach* is a formal and recognized form of governance and an approach where your senior business leaders mandate MDM.

For example, your company could mandate that: The D&B D-U-N-S® Number is a mandatory attribute for every customer and vendor legal entity record. A legal entity is a customer sold-to record, and any third-party vendor against whom a purchase order can be raised. All systems must comply within two years by the date dd-mmm-yyyy.

The *strategic approach* is a softer approach where MDM is seen as a strategic goal and is "generally encouraged" for the long term. This is an informal, unrecognized form of governance. For example, your company could set a target of the D&B D-U-N-S Number will be an attribute linked to customer and vendor records in 70% of systems within two years.

The *bottom-up approach* is an approach where the MDM program initially works with a small number of enthusiastic organizational units to establish an enterprise data service and design the solution to scale later. The advantages of this approach include that it is agile, able to proceed at a pace, and can deliver an initial solution. The disadvantage is the risk that MDM will become just one more business partner silo with no firm commitment to implement across your entire corporation.

A Bottom-Up Approach Followed by a Top-Down Approach

A successful bottom-up approach in Phase 1 of your MDM program is a good lever for a top-down approach in MDM Phase 2.

In MDM Phase 1, you'll discover which MDM models are the most suitable for your organization and which attributes you want to make global attributes. This knowledge will help you define practical and achievable company standards.

The desired outcome is that the MDM D&B D-U-N-S Number lookup process will become a mandated company standard for the management of your customer and vendor records.

We'll now consider the importance of communicating with your key stakeholders and introduce you to the MDM Stakeholder map.

Communicating with Stakeholders

The MDM Stakeholder map is a tool that allows you to categorize each of your key stakeholders. On the *x*-axis, you'll assess the stakeholder's current enthusiasm for MDM — whether he supports or opposes the MDM program. On the *y*-axis, you'll assess his current awareness of the MDM program and score it as high, medium, or low. Figure 5.1 shows an example MDM Stakeholder map.

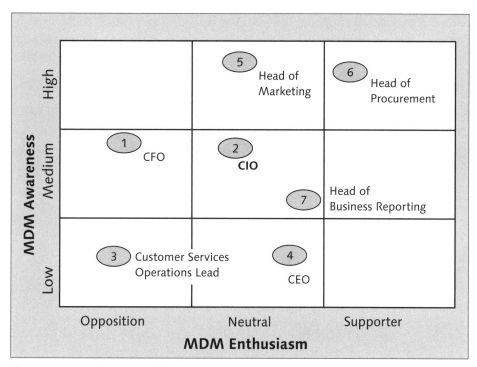

Figure 5.1   Example MDM Stakeholder Map

Initially, your key stakeholders will have differing views of the MDM program. In Figure 5.1, we see that the Head of Procurement is an initial MDM champion. He can visualize the benefits that MDM will bring to the procurement organization, particularly the abilities to authenticate each supplier and to aggregate their overall expenditure using the D&B Corporate Linkage. He is currently frustrated by the data in the BI warehouse because the information he receives is incomplete and can't be aggregated to make informed procurement decisions.

However, the Customer Services Operations Lead initially opposes the MDM program. He has formed the customer services team, which is directly under his control. He is wary of introducing another customer maintenance system into the current processes, particularly because he doesn't personally manage MDM. He has heard some rumors of cases where MDM gave incomplete results and does not trust MDM to meet his service levels. He believes it will be slow to implement and that it will distract attention from his current projects. The Customer Services Operations Lead can initially be found in the bottom-left box on the MDM Stakeholder map.

The aim of the MDM Stakeholder map is to try to move as many stakeholders as possible into the top-right box. In this box, you'll find your MDM champions who will support the integration of MDM throughout your organization.

> **Using the MDM Stakeholder Map**
>
> Review your MDM Stakeholder map periodically. How many of the key stakeholders currently support the MDM program? Have you managed to recently move any business leaders toward the box on the top right? Are regular meetings and updates taking place with your key stakeholders? Is there increasing enthusiasm for the MDM program, and have more MDM champions been identified?

Identifying your initial senior-level MDM champions is important. These are your business sponsors, and they will help you mobilize your MDM program. Be prepared to engage with new stakeholders because they will continually change throughout the two MDM roll-out phases. Assess and revise your priorities to meet the new stakeholder's requirements, and engage with new projects as they emerge.

Continually communicate with your stakeholders, repeating the MDM messages and highlighting all successes. Demonstrate to them the current functionality and show how you can now identify your customers and vendors using the D&B D-U-N-S Number and the D&B Corporate Linkage. Build their trust, and keep delivering your MDM program promises. Set short, sharp targets with definite MDM advancement every three months, and always meet them.

> **Success Breeds Success, and Good MDM Projects Get Better Every Day**
>
> If your MDM program is seen to consistently deliver both on time and on budget, the program will gain the respect and confidence of your organization. The MDM program will gain momentum, and your MDM champions will communicate this to the other stakeholders.
>
> Your MDM Stakeholder map will then have several of your key stakeholders in the top-right box, and you'll have many MDM champions. This will be a huge step forward!

Let's now consider the implications of the consolidated, harmonized, and centralized models on your data governance and stewardship.

5.1.3 Data Governance and Stewardship

The consolidated, harmonized, and centralized MDM models were already discussed in Chapter 4. The MDM model that you choose to implement impacts your MDM data governance and data stewardship.

Consolidated Model

By implementing a consolidated model, MDM is used to collect the master data details from several systems and then to store them in your central SAP NetWeaver MDM business partner repository. You can detect and clean up duplicate records and update the consuming systems key fields for cross-system key mapping linkage. The only SAP NetWeaver MDM attribute stored in the consuming system is the key identifier of the D&B D-U-N-S Number, which is tagged onto each of the customer and vendor records.

In Chapter 4, we also described two variations of the consolidated model as follows.

Option 1 – Only Legal Entity Details Are Stored in MDM (Partner Functions Details are Not Stored)

In this scenario, if we consider customer master data, the consuming system masters and maintains the customer details (the sold-to, ship-to, bill-to, payer name and addresses, etc.). Simply put, SAP NetWeaver MDM is linked only to the customer sold-to record, using the D&B D-U-N-S Number as a key mapping tag in the consuming system. Your consuming system links the partner functions to the sold to record.

Option 2 – Partner Functions Key Mappings Are Also Mapped in MDM

This is similar to Option 1, but in this case, the relevant D&B D-U-N-S Number is also tagged to each partner function record in the consuming system — the sold-to, ship-to, bill-to, payer, and so on. All company records are tagged in each consuming system.

The consolidated MDM model requires the least MDM data governance and data stewardship. Your master data standard will state that the D&B D-U-N-S Number is a mandatory attribute for every customer and vendor record in your consuming systems and that it must be authenticated and mapped to the SAP NetWeaver MDM business partner repository. Your business users will continue to maintain your customer and vendor master data using the current procedures and the same local systems.

Harmonized Model

By implementing a harmonized MDM model, you extend the consolidated model and also forward selected global master data attributes from SAP NetWeaver MDM to your consuming systems. This enables you to synchronize globally relevant attributes across your company's landscape.

You must carefully consider which global attributes to harmonize. The following questions will help you:

- Do you mandate that the consuming system legal name is provided by MDM based on the D&B legal name?
- Do you also mandate that the consuming system legal address is provided by MDM and is based on the D&B legal address?
- Are attributes such as bank details and payment terms global attributes to be distributed?
- What are the implications for your existing consuming systems interfaces?
- Are the consuming systems data model and data field attributes consistent with the MDM data model and data attributes?

The harmonized model introduces further data stewardship requirements and wider reaching MDM data governance. For example, your company may introduce a new master data standard stipulating that the D&B D-U-N-S Number and the MDM legal name and address are mandatory attributes for all customer and vendor legal entity records in your systems.

Your data stewards will periodically cross-check SAP NetWeaver MDM and the consuming systems to ensure that the legal names and addresses are being maintained consistently. Any exceptions will then be highlighted and may be raised to your MDM Steering Board.

Centralized Model

The tightest form of MDM integration is the centralized model where SAP NetWeaver MDM is the "master" system, and the consuming systems are the "slaves." Whereas the emphasis in the consolidation scenario is on local data maintenance, the centralized scenario focuses on creating and maintaining the global data attributes in the central MDM data repository, which are then distributed to the consuming systems where the local attributes are added.

With the centralized model, it isn't possible to create a vendor or a customer record directly into a consuming system. The master record must first be created in MDM and then distributed.

You'll need to consider which attributes are global and mastered in MDM. The legal name and addresses are obvious candidates, and you'll also decide whether to define attributes such as bank details and payment terms as global attributes.

You may also decide to master in MDM all of the business partner functions details, including the business partner name and address details and the partner functions. The consuming systems' data validation processes must be replicated in MDM, which requires software development. You'll effectively develop the equivalent of the SAP R/3 create and change customer and vendor transactions in MDM.

With this scenario, the non-D&B sourced data in MDM, such as the vendor ordering addresses and payment addresses, must be maintained through the business partner lifecycle. You'll need business procedures for the MDM data stewards to maintain the partner functions when changes occur. The centralized model requires the most MDM data governance and data stewardship activity. Your consuming systems now rely on the MDM master data services to provide the customer and vendor general data and global attributes. You'll establish Service Level Agreements that will define the allowed timeline for a new customer or vendor request in SAP NetWeaver MDM to then be created as a record in a consuming system.

The SAP NetWeaver MDM data stewardship activity also includes managing the D&B services, both for the D&B Entity Matching and for the investigations processes.

In this case, your MDM master data standard defines the global master data attributes and the defined rules for synchronization to consuming systems.

Lifecycle Management

Because your MDM business partner master data supports critical business processes and drives business decisions, it's important to manage and maintain it with rigor. You'll develop processes to maintain your customer and vendor D&B Worldbase details and Corporate Linkage through company lifecycle changes. These include changes to legal entity names and addresses when companies move or are involved in mergers and acquisitions.

You'll implement governance and processes so that over its useful life, the business partner information can be appropriately shared, stored, refreshed, and upgraded. You'll keep the data up to date and ensure that it is deleted and archived appropriately.

Lifecycle process changes can take time to implement. On occasion, changes to the D&B Worldbase names and addresses or D&B Corporate Linkage for mergers and acquisitions will take time before they are "officially" updated on the D&B Worldbase record. However, these changes may be known in advance by your company's internal organization through its business contacts. You'll develop a process to handle these situations.

How you refresh the latest D&B details into your SAP NetWeaver MDM repository and your consuming systems needs careful consideration. This will require processes to compare the latest D&B data with the data in your live repository. A SAP NetWeaver MDM staging repository and developing appropriate match and merge rules will help. Your consuming systems will also be refreshed, and you'll design rules for updating each of your global attributes.

Figure 5.2 illustrates the various ways that SAP NetWeaver MDM receives Lifecycle Management changes.

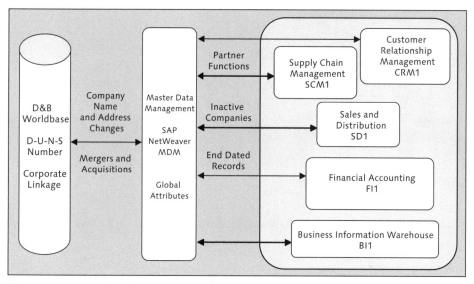

Figure 5.2 MDM Lifecycle Management Changes

Figure 5.2 also highlights that, over time, your company's relationships with customers and vendors will change. Some of your customers and vendors will become inactive and will be blocked or end dated in your consuming systems. Your SAP NetWeaver MDM repository details will be impacted by this and will need to be updated to reflect this. You'll also need an overall archiving strategy for the SAP NetWeaver MDM business partner repository when an MDM record is no longer consumed by any system.

Maintaining the SAP NetWeaver MDM repository details so that it's consistent with the latest D&B Worldbase data and Corporate Linkage and with where it is currently consumed in your systems is a critical success factor for your MDM program. You'll lose the trust and confidence in your solution if it isn't maintained consistently.

Let's now explore the advantages of building relationships with SAP and D&B.

5.2   Building the Key MDM Program Components

The people skills and the relationships you'll need to develop with both SAP and D&B are crucial for a successful MDM program.

5.2.1   Relationships with the SAP Team

Working closely with SAP can help you extend your SAP NetWeaver MDM network, discover MDM best practices, and work with the SAP NetWeaver MDM roadmap. The SAP MDM Customer Council provides you with some useful insights.

SAP MDM Customer Councils

The SAP MDM Customer Council is a useful forum for your MDM program to engage with. By building good relationships with SAP, your MDM program gains three major benefits described as follows.

1. Extended MDM Network

Establishing a set of external MDM contacts is beneficial. Within your company, your MDM program can become a "niche" with a small number of specialists developing a detailed understanding of the benefits and challenges of establishing MDM within your organization.

It's helpful to meet with SAP NetWeaver MDM specialists from other companies who also understand master data issues. Setting up audio calls and further workshop sessions with companies whose SAP NetWeaver MDM solutions overlap with yours can accelerate your learning process.

2. Company Benchmarking and Best Practices

The SAP NetWeaver MDM Customer Council also provides you with an opportunity to benchmark your SAP NetWeaver MDM solution. How good is your company's solution compared to others? How does your MDM scorecard assessment compare to others?

You'll discover best practices and a variety of new SAP NetWeaver MDM ideas and ways of thinking. Meeting with others helps to develop your confidence that your MDM program is heading in the right direction as well as helping to build trust with your internal key stakeholders.

3. SAP NetWeaver Technical Roadmap

The SAP NetWeaver MDM Customer Council enables you to meet with the SAP NetWeaver MDM development team and to obtain insights into the strategic direction of the SAP NetWeaver MDM platform roadmap. You are given the opportunity to influence and prioritize the future SAP NetWeaver MDM technical developments to meet your company's key requirements.

5.2.2 Relationships with the D&B Team

There are various ways in which you can build relationships with the D&B team. Let's now discuss your D&B Service Level Agreement and the Project Engagement process.

D&B Service Level Agreements

Your D&B Service Level Agreement defines how the D&B data refresh processes will be implemented operationally. As companies change (e.g., legal name and address changes, D&B Corporate Linkage, etc.), you will refresh your SAP NetWeaver MDM business partner repository periodically with the latest available data from D&B. These refresh procedures need to be defined and established.

You'll define how to trigger an investigation process to request a new D&B D-U-N-S Number in cases when a valid company that you need is not on the D&B Worldbase database. Such an example could be a brand new startup company that has yet to be validated by D&B.

You'll also document in your MDM business procedures how to create a customer or vendor record when it's temporarily without a D&B D-U-N-S Number and is awaiting a D&B investigation.

D&B Project Engagement

The process of cleansing, de-duplicating, setting up your customer and vendor records in MDM, and linking them to the D&B D-U-N-S Numbers is an iterative one. With each attempt, your data will be improved, and you'll increase your successful D&B Entity Match rates. Your business users will ensure that the company name and address fields are completed more accurately and that old business partner records are end-dated.

D&B provides you with data analyst support for the D&B Entity Matching process. Matched data and exception reports are returned to you within short time scales to meet your MDM program objectives. Regular discussions with D&B to track the outstanding data migration items and to resolve any issues are beneficial.

Weekly status reports and meetings with D&B are helpful throughout your MDM program. You'll discuss the various project activities, including your current project engagements and the status of the D&B Entity Matching processes.

An awareness of the D&B technical architecture and D&B's strategic direction is also helpful. D&B recently acquired their own MDM solution so understanding how your SAP NetWeaver MDM architecture will integrate with D&B will evolve and should be considered by your SAP NetWeaver MDM solution architect.

Now let's discuss your SAP NetWeaver infrastructure requirements.

5.2.3   SAP NetWeaver Infrastructure

We will now consider the key software license and infrastructure building blocks you need. Software licenses are essential prerequisites that you need to purchase from SAP for the use of the various NetWeaver components (e.g., Portal, MDM, PI, and SAP Interactive Forms).

You will also agree on the necessary licenses and service levels with D&B to use their D&B Worldbase data and Corporate Linkage.

You'll work closely with your IT operations and infrastructure team to establish an appropriate SAP NetWeaver infrastructure. Your SAP NetWeaver "stack" will include several servers because you'll need development, test, and production environments for the SAP NetWeaver Portal, SAP NetWeaver MDM, and SAP NetWeaver Process Integration (SAP NetWeaver PI) components. You'll also establish policies, processes, and support arrangements for the transport of code across the environments and also with your operational support team.

The relevant firewalls and ports will be opened to enable external Web Services, such as the D&B Enrichment Adapter architecture. Disaster Recovery and Business Continuity processes will also be tested.

SAP provides you with a lot of advice on how to set up your SAP NetWeaver infrastructure. Follow this carefully, and also work closely with your security and operations infrastructure teams. Allow yourself plenty of time to set up your SAP NetWeaver infrastructure. The Change Management processes can be complex and require careful planning.

Service Packs

Applying SAP NetWeaver MDM service packs and upgrades is a necessary process that should be incorporated into your SAP NetWeaver MDM roadmap. Each SAP NetWeaver component (Portal, MDM, and PI) requires the regular application of service packs and requires coordination beyond your MDM program team.

MDM is a relatively new SAP product, and many new features are available to you in each new service pack release. Allow your MDM program team time to evaluate the new features, and typically aim to apply the new service pack within three months to your production environment.

Be aware that the service pack changes can cause changes to your current application. Changes such as the use of APIs, workflow processes, and attribute validation can differ. Create a regression-testing plan of your SAP NetWeaver MDM application for each new service pack.

Next we'll discuss the collective team skills and the individual skills you'll need in your MDM program team.

5.3 Mobilizing the MDM Program Team

The collective skills you'll need from your MDM program team include communication skills, team spirit, patience, and trust. The barriers to implementing a successful MDM solution are often related to do people skills rather than technical issues.

Excellent *stakeholder communication skills* reflect a key competency for each of your MDM program team members. MDM will impact the length and breadth of your organization – from your top leadership to the end business users who maintain the customer and vendor data in your systems. Each of these people is a key MDM stakeholder, and you'll need to engage and communicate repeatedly and effectively with them all.

Develop a good *MDM team spirit*. What you are trying to achieve is difficult, and you'll experience setbacks along the way. Be warned that not all parts of your organization will welcome you, and you may initially be treated with some suspicion. Allow time to develop your MDM service offering and to build the core capabilities to distribute master data to consuming systems.

Be *patient* with the SAP NetWeaver development activities, trust your technical team to deliver a working solution, and also recognize that this will be an iterative process. Don't expect to move directly from a position of no MDM to a fully integrated MDM solution without some mistakes and taking a few detours along the way.

Look for MDM team members you can *trust* and who will stick together; each will learn a considerable amount about SAP NetWeaver MDM, D&B, and the existing master data business processes throughout your organization. Encourage your MDM program team to innovate, and don't be afraid to try things out. There is no single right answer for MDM; you can find considerable MDM benefits from some simple ideas.

> ### Building Your MDM Program Team
>
> Look for team members with previous MDM experience, but be aware that this can be both an advantage and disadvantage. Examine your candidate's delivery track records, and look for people who have delivered a successful MDM program. Many MDM projects have been abandoned part way through due to a badly thought through design or poor execution.
>
> You need people with good business consultancy skills who have a good understanding of customer and supplier business processes and data. Team members with a solid experience of SAP ERP implementations are also an advantage; a thorough understanding of the customer and vendor SAP transactions is beneficial.

Let's now consider the various individual roles you need to fill to create a successful MDM program team.

5.3.1 Required Skills and Roles

Your MDM program team needs to have a combination of business and technical skills and roles. The number of people involved in an MDM program will vary through the two MDM phases. At a peak point in the MDM program, you may need 30 or more people, which require careful coordination.

Let's now discuss the roles of the MDM program manager, the MDM technical design authority, the SAP NetWeaver MDM solution architects, and the MDM data steward in more detail.

5.3.2 MDM Program Manager

The MDM program manager communicates and builds relationships with your MDM stakeholders. He needs to manage the stakeholder expectations for the MDM program and to resolve conflicts in priorities. Strong relationships are needed across business, financial and compliance, business intelligence, and IT domains.

He covers the end-to-end SAP NetWeaver MDM system integration, aligns the MDM program deliverables with the business needs, and ensures that subsequent benefits are on track for realization. He also ensures that the delivery of the MDM program is in line with the service levels and costs, and challenges these to ensure best value.

The MDM program manager ensures that the SAP NetWeaver MDM design captures clear requirement definitions and assists with technology design and architecture decisions. He also ensures adherence to your company standards and project methodologies.

He also leads the exploitation of the SAP NetWeaver MDM solution and identifies key opportunities to improve the business partner master data processes in terms of accuracy, ease of use, performance, compliance, and risk.

5.3.3 MDM Technical Design Authority

The MDM technical design authority also requires good communication skills with the various MDM stakeholders plus a solid SAP NetWeaver MDM technical awareness. He creates the architectural strategies and principles and facilitates a rapid SAP NetWeaver MDM technical deployment.

Key aspects of the communication with stakeholders include aligning the MDM steering group, the MDM data stewards, and the MDM program team with the architectural decisions. He champions the use of MDM to a wide range of internal and external communities, including architecture forums, business leaders, and project teams.

He engages with SAP NetWeaver MDM and D&B technical architects to agree and refine the SAP NetWeaver MDM architecture to enable continuous improvement. He consults with your major project teams and interprets how to apply the SAP NetWeaver MDM processes and systems solution.

The MDM technical design authority develops the strategy and architectural principles for how SAP NetWeaver MDM repository data will be obtained and consumed. He defines the MDM instance strategy, the workflow processes, the D&B enrichment processes, and the overall SAP NetWeaver architecture. He also extends the architecture to cope with multiple consuming systems with multiple models (centralized, harmonized, and consolidated) through the SAP NetWeaver MDM repository design. He also considers the various user interfaces, including MDM Data Manager, SAP NetWeaver Portal, SAP Interactive Forms, and Web Services, depending on your end user requirements.

He defines an appropriate SAP NetWeaver MDM technical architecture, including instance strategy, production and development environments, disaster recovery, Internet facing, versions and upgrades, patching, security, and backups. He is the focal point for the design of the technical SAP NetWeaver MDM solution and ensures that the infrastructure meets the requirements of the growing business needs.

The MDM technical design authority facilitates rapid technical deployment by prototyping the business partner master data processes and systems solution. He provides a complete, clearly scoped solution and accelerates the MDM program speed to market by reducing the project lifecycle.

The Need for SAP NetWeaver MDM Technical Skills

You need a variety of SAP NetWeaver technical skills on your MDM program team; a SAP NetWeaver Portal developer with Web Dynpro skills is a different individual than an SAP NetWeaver MDM data architect and an SAP NetWeaver PI interface developer.

SAP MDM is a NetWeaver technical component or toolkit, so you need to design and build the workflow processes and SAP NetWeaver Portal user interface with a number of Web Dynpros to meet your company's requirements.

5.3.4   SAP NetWeaver Solution Architects

You need three types of SAP NetWeaver solution architects who specialize in the various SAP NetWeaver MDM, SAP NetWeaver PI, and SAP NetWeaver Portal components. Let's now consider each of these roles in turns.

SAP NetWeaver MDM Solution Architect

The SAP NetWeaver MDM solution architect works closely with your data analysts to identify the business requirements for the SAP NetWeaver MDM solution. He identifies the core master data objects in your organization using data discovery and data context setting processes. He collects both business and technical requirements and tracks how these requirements will be met.

The SAP NetWeaver MDM solution architect then designs the enterprise data architecture. This includes the technical framework of the SAP NetWeaver MDM solution, which consists of the master data management processes, the integration architecture both to source and consuming systems, and the final data model, data definitions, and data standards.

He designs the solution landscape for the SAP NetWeaver MDM environments, including the development, test, and production stacks. He designs and builds the critical configuration and system parameters in the system.

The SAP NetWeaver MDM solution architect designs the key SAP NetWeaver MDM processes to be consistent with the overall data quality standards. He incorporates in the design the appropriate business rules and data governance processes using workflows and validations. He specifies the end user interface requirements, including the screen flow, the data validation, and the security requirements. He also assists the MDM data steward in preparing the standard operating procedures for data stewardship, exception handling, and system administration.

He designs the customer and vendor master data model and builds it in SAP NetWeaver MDM. He designs the data matching and merging rules based on cleansing and standardization requirements and also designs the data-enrichment processes in coordination with D&B.

The SAP NetWeaver MDM solution architect plays a key role throughout the MDM implementation. He designs the SAP NetWeaver MDM data staging repository and the data import and syndication processes. He also creates the MDM test plan and test scenarios and executes the initial master data load and the cutover processes.

Finally, he validates the SAP NetWeaver MDM design with performance metrics. He monitors the deployment of the solution and the post go-live performance and usage of the system. He identifies and configures the appropriate reports to enable effective data management.

SAP NetWeaver PI Solution Architect

The SAP NetWeaver PI solution architect designs and implements the SAP NetWeaver PI integration solution in your system landscape. He evaluates the integration requirements and design solutions to interface SAP NetWeaver MDM with both the D&B services and your consuming systems. He aligns the integration requirements with the standard integration content provided by SAP NetWeaver PI.

He designs and prepares the mapping specifications and message routing conditions for the master data objects, between source and target systems. He defines the integration business scenarios and then designs the inbound and outbound interfaces to meet the MDM scenarios. He designs and registers the technical systems, the business systems, and the software integration components in the System Landscape Directory (SLD), the Integration Builder (Integration Repository [IR], Integration Directory [ID]), and the Integration Server.

The SAP NetWeaver PI solution architect designs the message types and the interface mapping between the SAP NetWeaver MDM system and the source and consuming systems. He also designs the Business Process Management (BPM) scenarios and implements the various interfaces, including the File-to-IDoc, IDoc-to-IDoc, File-to-RFC, File-to-JDBC, and HTTP-to-JDBC interfaces. He also implements the necessary SAP NetWeaver PI adapters such as FTP, HTTP, SOAP, and JDBC for communicating with both SAP and non-SAP consuming systems.

Finally, the SAP NetWeaver PI solution architect builds the integration scenarios. He creates the SAP NetWeaver PI test plan and the test scenarios and validates the design and build based on high availability and performance scalability requirements.

SAP NetWeaver Portal Solution Architect

The SAP NetWeaver Portal solution architect designs and implements the SAP NetWeaver Portal user interface application to the MDM repository. He evaluates the user interface, the security, and MDM data flow requirements to define the solution. He also aligns your specific application requirements with the standard MDM business content provided in the SAP NetWeaver Portal.

The SAP NetWeaver Portal solution architect defines the technical framework layer for the portal development. He designs the site topology, the migration strategy, and the SAP NetWeaver Portal content and navigation structure. He also designs the user roles, the mapping to work sets and pages, and the application flow logic.

He implements the performance coding, testing, and fine-tuning in the J2EE architectures. He defines the processes for sign-on with integration to LDAP, MDM connections, and the use of MDM Java APIs to manage data in the portal applications.

The SAP NetWeaver Portal solution architect analyzes the requirements for custom applications and reports, and design solutions leveraging the SAP NetWeaver Portal functionality. He designs and builds the SAP NetWeaver Portal integration with the SAP NetWeaver MDM workflows.

Finally, the SAP NetWeaver Portal solution architect develops the methodology for the management of reusable solution software. He also prepares the SAP NetWeaver Portal test plan and the test scenarios.

Let's now consider the role of the MDM data steward.

5.3.5　MDM Data Steward

The MDM data steward manages the business partner master data maintenance processes, including the external interfaces with D&B, data conversion projects, and operational processes. He develops the operational processes for customer and vendor data maintenance working with your SCM, CRM, and FI business teams across your company.

The MDM data steward implements and manages the business aspects of the systems solution and also the subsequent enhancements in new releases. He leads the exploitation of the business partner master data service and identifies key improvement opportunities.

The MDM data steward coordinates the data migration projects, including data cleansing from consuming systems into MDM and data enrichment with D&B. He checks and imports your customer and vendor master records and also imports the matched D&B Worldbase and Corporate Linkage records.

He works closely with local business users to process valid requests via workflow. This includes requesting data enrichment from D&B and then checking returned records. He updates the master records in your MDM repositories and distributes new or changed master data to consuming systems.

The MDM data steward runs MDM performance reports, produces management summary reports, and deals with any identified issues such as duplicates or missing key data. He also provides MDM awareness presentations to your organization as part of the MDM program.

Let's now consider the role of a systems integrator in your MDM program.

5.3.6 The Role of Systems Integrators

As we've discussed, there is a requirement for a number of SAP NetWeaver specialist technical roles in your MDM program. Your company may want to develop these competencies internally or you may decide to contract with a systems integrator (SI) who has these skills readily available.

Each approach has its advantages and disadvantages; you need to consider your existing available skills and your IT strategy. A combination of an internal team providing the business process consultancy and the technical design authority with a SI providing the appropriate SAP NetWeaver MDM technical skills can be a good model.

If you engage with a SI, you go through your usual due diligence processes. Engage with your procurement team to produce a procurement strategy and send out a Request for Proposal (RFP) to your IT suppliers.

Meet with the SI team you will be working with during the RFP process. You will rely heavily on a few key individuals, so check out their resumes and ask detailed questions. Are they enthusiastic, and have they implemented a successful SAP NetWeaver MDM program before?

Consider the MDM implementation track record of your proposed team members. SAP NetWeaver MDM is a relatively new product and having hands-on experience through to a live environment is a significant advantage. An in-depth knowledge of the SAP ERP create vendor and create customer transactions is also helpful because there are many constraints with interfacing MDM to your consuming systems.

An ability to leverage experience from others within a SI organization is also an advantage. For example, configuring SAP NetWeaver MDM with D&B enrichment processes takes time to understand, and specific technical knowledge of the D&B Enrichment Adapter is useful.

When you've chosen the best SI, then set up a fair contract, so that both your company and the SI organization can benefit. You should clearly articulate what you expect of the SI and define the accountabilities of both your internal team members and the SI team.

Build ways of working together as an MDM program team; ideally the MDM program team members, including the MDM data stewards, are co-located. This speeds up the design and build. Some build activities can be managed by an off-shore development team to reduce the development costs, but we recommend a strong onshore presence for your MDM program.

5.4   The MDM Discovery Phase

A good way to start your MDM program is with both a business and a technical proof of concept. These enable you to learn a great deal both about D&B and how to implement SAP NetWeaver MDM. You gain hands-on experience and discover what is possible.

Encourage your MDM team to experiment and to be prepared to try things out to uncover the various strengths and weaknesses. Try some difficult and complex functionality, and be prepared to step outside your comfort zone because there will never be a better opportunity to learn.

Let's now discuss some ideas for your business proof of concept.

5.4.1   Business Proof of Concept with Dun & Bradstreet

You should carry out a business proof of concept with D&B to quickly establish ways of working with the company. You can assess the D&B services and how D&B can help you maintain your customer and vendor master data. While developing the proof of concept, you gain a better understanding of the D&B D-U-N-S Number and become familiar with the core D&B concepts of the Worldbase database, D&B Corporate Linkage, and Entity Matching. You can also try out the SAP NetWeaver MDM D&B Enrichment Adapter and discover how the two-step workflow processes work in practice.

You can test the D&B Entity Matching process by extracting the company name and address details from one of your key business applications and send these in a file to D&B. In return, you receive the matched D&B D-U-N-S Number, the Worldbase package details, and Corporate Linkage.

Review the D&B Entity Matching reports, which summarize the findings and highlight the possible reasons for unsuccessful matches. You can investigate a sample of the records that are not matched and find out why. Possibly, the business partner name and address you provided is not a legal entity name and address but is of some other business partner relationship or maybe the business partner name and address is incomplete or has not been maintained in your system.

You can also test D&B with a complex customer or vendor that your company has a lot of dealings with. Some large companies have several hundred or even a few thousand entities with a D&B Corporate Linkage linked to one Global Ultimate company. If you can extract an entire company that you deal with, you can then load the D&B Corporate Linkage into one of your BI systems and provide some total risk exposure reports. This type of new BI reporting will interest your leadership team and may help to convert some MDM stakeholders into supporters, or even "MDM champions."

Also, in the business proof of concept, test your company! You can arrange with D&B to extract your own company records linked up to your Global Ultimate company. Have D&B maintained your records accurately? Is the D&B Corporate Linkage accurate and up to date, taking into account any recent mergers and acquisitions in your company? Check with your company's legal team if this is the case, and analyze the details carefully. This helps build confidence in the D&B data.

If your company carries a lot of business in a country or region where you feel D&B may not have good coverage, then test this during the business proof of concept. As before, you can follow up on any unsuccessful matches to find out the underlying reasons.

Allow yourself some time to review the D&B Worldbase data. Legal names and addresses follow varying conventions in different parts of the world; for example, legal name abbreviations are handled differently in the United States where spaces are included in the name. Company XYZ plc may have a legal name of "X Y Z plc" to follow the convention. In some countries, such as France, the rules for registering a legal entity are more thorough, so you may find many more D&B Worldbase records in that country when compared to others.

Next, we'll discuss some ideas for a technical proof of concept using SAP NetWeaver MDM.

5.4.2 Technical Proof of Concept using SAP NetWeaver MDM

Why Conduct a SAP NetWeaver MDM Technical Proof of Concept

A technical proof of concept enables you to assess the SAP NetWeaver MDM functionality against your key master data maintenance requirements. You can test detailed scenarios to show how SAP NetWeaver MDM can be integrated with both your SAP and non-SAP systems. Example scenarios can include MDM hierarchy management with D&B Corporate Linkage. You can also configure the MDM workflow to create a business partner request process involving different roles using the SAP NetWeaver Portal and MDM.

SAP NetWeaver MDM Web Services and BI integration to report spend analysis against the D&B Corporate Linkage is also worth investigating.

As a first step, gather a detailed list of MDM requirements. The technical proof of concept assesses the SAP NetWeaver MDM product against these requirements. Carry out a series of workshops with key stakeholders to define the business scenarios and use cases.

Design a SAP NetWeaver MDM business partner repository, and document the details (field and structural mapping). Initial configuration and developments are carried out in the SAP NetWeaver Portal, SAP NetWeaver MDM, and SAP NetWeaver PI systems. The configured SAP NetWeaver MDM solution is then linked with the selected SAP and non-SAP test systems to support the integrated proof of concept scenarios.

Try out as many things as you can. Conduct the technical proof of concept on your company's infrastructure (to understand the environment setup implications) rather than relying on third-party infrastructure or seeing a "canned" demo. Use "real" customer and vendor data from your business systems, and make a technical assessment of the D&B Worldbase database and its application as a record of origin for business partners.

During the technical proof of concept, you assess the out-of-the-box support for business partner data models and how these can be extended. You review functionality such as key mapping and hierarchy management as well as the match, merge, and harmonize capability, including normalization and de-duplication. You also explore the data extraction and loading, mapping, and data enrichment functionality as well as reviewing the MDM search capability and workflow management.

Investigate the technical interface the SAP NetWeaver MDM Java APIs and Web Services (SOA) capability along with exception handling, notification, and standard reporting capability. Test the integration with D&B and the SAP NetWeaver Portal and also consider the future proofing and upgrades strategy.

> **Review Your SAP NetWeaver MDM Security Setup**
>
> During the technical proof of concept, conduct a detailed security assessment that includes your user profiles setup and audit trail, history, and version control. This helps you avoid problems later on and is important when you consider that your SAP NetWeaver MDM system may store sensitive data about customers, possibly including customer credit ratings. Unauthorized access to such information results in a loss of credibility and lacks internal control. The SAP NetWeaver MDM system is also relevant to your company's compliance to the Sarbanes-Oxley Act.

A key output from the SAP NetWeaver MDM technical proof of concept is the recommendation report. You document your assessment of the SAP NetWeaver MDM capability to meet your functional and technical requirements surrounding MDM.

Several benefits come from conducting an MDM technical proof of concept. It's a low risk, relatively small initial investment to test out MDM, and it should be possible to achieve a good quality proof of concept within three months. You mobilize the MDM program team, and initial MDM Governance processes are established to review your findings and to agree to sponsorship.

You mobilize the SAP NetWeaver MDM technical team so that if you choose to outsource, your SI is in place, and the MDM program team spirit starts to develop. The technical proof of concept enables practical learning, and your MDM team begins to understand the key requirements for your organization.

The documented deliverables are useful outputs for your first MDM implementation. Setting up a SAP NetWeaver MDM development environment ready for your MDM program is another big advantage. SAP NetWeaver MDM can be a complex landscape that requires several servers.

To summarize, carrying out business and technical proof of concepts are excellent ways to start your MDM program. Now let's consider how the skills and roles of your MDM program team will vary during the two phases of an MDM program.

5.5 MDM Planning and Roadmaps

The pace of an MDM program is driven by your organization. As discussed earlier in this chapter, this can be a top-down approach where your senior business leaders mandate the MDM approach. Alternatively, you may adopt a strategic approach where MDM is a strategic goal and is "generally encouraged" for the long term. Finally, you may adopt a bottom-up approach where the MDM program initially works with a small number of enthusiastic local business units to establish an enterprise data service and design with scaling in mind for later.

The chosen approach influences the size of your MDM team and the MDM program time scale. Let's now consider the MDM Phase 1 activities and required skills.

5.5.1 Phase 1 – Establishing the MDM Program and Services

Figure 5.3 illustrates the activities that take place in Phase 1 of the MDM program.

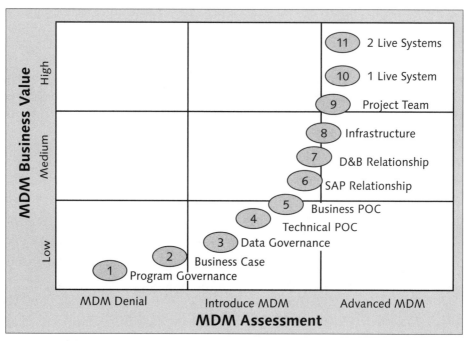

Figure 5.3 MDM Phase 1 Activities

The MDM Phase 1 setup activities were discussed in Chapter 3. Establishing the MDM program governance and agreeing to the business case require sponsorship and support from your key MDM business champions.

In MDM Phase 1, you need significant SAP NetWeaver MDM technical development. The technical proof of concept gets you started, and you need a combination of SAP NetWeaver Portal, SAP NetWeaver MDM, and SAP NetWeaver PI expertise. By the end of MDM Phase 1, you will be "live," and MDM will be integrated to one or two business applications. You will be impacting some of your business users but not the majority of your organization.

MDM Phase 1 is the time to prepare your business procedures to scale the solution across your organization. You'll learn from what has worked well (and not so well) and use this experience to guide you as to what can practically be achieved in MDM Phase 2 and implementing MDM across your organization.

5.5.2 Phase 2 – Integrating MDM Throughout a Company

Figure 5.4 illustrates the activities that are then carried out during Phase 2 of an MDM program.

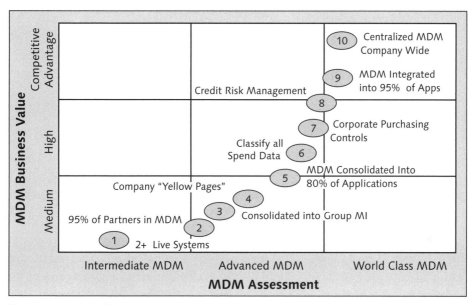

Figure 5.4 MDM Phase 2 Activities

MDM Phase 2 involves a much broader business engagement. You transition from just one or two business systems being linked to MDM to your entire organization being integrated. This requires excellent communication with the key stakeholders across your organization. You need to convert several more MDM stakeholders into MDM champions for this to be successful.

SAP NetWeaver MDM technical development also occurs during MDM Phase 2. Functional enhancements extend the initial solution, which was suitable for a go-live with one or two systems, to cope with the wider requirements. Scaling your MDM solution requires careful design discussions. You may need to design a combination of consolidated, harmonized, and centralized models of integration, which will impact your SAP NetWeaver MDM repositories. You will also need to develop additional interfaces to integrate SAP NetWeaver MDM with your various business applications.

As you move through MDM Phase 2, you will both support an existing operational SAP NetWeaver MDM system and also further develop your functionality and interfaces. This is an unusual support model; you need to set up continuous improvement processes to allow frequent updates of your SAP NetWeaver MDM software and controlled releases into your production environments.

The SAP NetWeaver MDM change management processes can take time to establish and need to be carefully considered, particularly if you are sharing components such as the SAP NetWeaver Portal with other parts of your organization.

5.6   Summary

In Chapter 5, we considered how to mobilize your MDM program. We discussed how to establish MDM data governance and standards, the role of the MDM Steering Board, and the importance of communicating with key stakeholders. We discussed MDM data stewardship and Lifecycle Management processes, and also how to develop relationships with both SAP and Dun & Bradstreet.

We then moved on to discuss how to mobilize an MDM program team and the team and individual skills you should look for. We described how to carry out a business and a technical proof of concept and the benefits these will provide. We ended the chapter with a review of how your MDM program activities and skill sets will differ during MDM Phases 1 and 2.

You are now aware of the variety of business and technical skills you'll need to resource your MDM program throughout the phases. Finding the right people both internal and external to your organization is a key activity that you should plan for. Also, allow plenty of time to communicate with your key stakeholders to convert them into "MDM Champions."

This completes Part 1 of our book where we have discussed the business justification and the necessary people skills for an MDM program. Let's now move on to Part 2 where you'll first learn how to develop an SAP NetWeaver MDM Technical Framework and a Solution Architecture for your organization.

PART II
SAP NetWeaver MDM Technical Framework and Solution Architecture

The enterprise MDM architecture provides the solution framework for your build and deployment teams. Practical approaches to your architecture design ensure that the MDM solution is simple and complete. The design encompasses solutions from all SAP NetWeaver components, providing seamless user and system interfaces.

6 Developing an SAP NetWeaver MDM Architecture for an Enterprise

Defining an SAP NetWeaver MDM architecture for an enterprise consists of two distinct phases. During the first phase, you design the *SAP NetWeaver MDM Technical Framework*, which includes defining the MDM scenarios, the data management processes, and the integration scenarios. This phase is driven by the MDM program scope and identified key business requirements to deliver the business benefits.

After the Technical Framework is established, you then move on to design the *SAP NetWeaver MDM Solution Architecture* for the master data objects. This involves designing the data model, context (taxonomy or hierarchy), validations, and workflows to comply with your data standards and security design. The SAP NetWeaver MDM Solution Architecting phase is also driven by your MDM business case and by the Technical Framework definition.

MDM programs can tend to make the solution design a multilayered and complex process. We advocate a practical approach that gives the necessary attention to defining the framework and architecture, while leaving the lower-level definition and micro-modeling to the consuming business applications. Don't try to bring too much complexity into MDM, and trust the functionality in your business applications for the local validations. You are not trying to re-create the SAP ERP logic and processes for managing local attributes in SAP NetWeaver MDM. A simple and standards-based architecture is crucial for the enterprisewide success of your MDM program.

Proof of Concepts

Some MDM programs find it difficult to envision the fit-gap analysis between the SAP NetWeaver MDM product features and your business requirements. In this case, a separate proof of concept is recommended for the fit-gap analysis.

A best practice is to decouple your MDM architecture definitions and the product features analysis. Don't confuse the "wish list" of what you want an MDM system to do in all circumstances, with a pragmatic MDM architecture to meet the business requirements and to deliver the business benefits.

6.1 Designing the SAP NetWeaver MDM Technical Framework

Your SAP NetWeaver MDM Technical Framework definition will answer the following key questions:

▶ What governance principles drive your MDM solution? What are your data standards and your organization's appetite to enforce those standards?

▶ Following the governance principles, what master data scenarios, such as consolidation and central data management, will the solution map to?

▶ Which MDM objects and processes will the solution define?

▶ What are the system of origin and the record of origin, and how will you design the Lifecycle Management processes?

▶ Which consuming business applications will the MDM solution integrate with?

To address these core questions, your MDM program mobilizes the architecture team, including the business leads, the Technical Design Authority, and the SAP NetWeaver solution architects. This team must understand the roles and responsibilities for executing the MDM architecture design activities. These activities are very different from designing a planning, transaction processing, or reporting application.

There can be two extremes when you design your SAP NetWeaver MDM Technical Framework. If your MDM program is a business information reporting initiative, you may find that your SAP NetWeaver MDM repository is updated periodically with the master data from your transactional systems. In this scenario, the only consuming system is BI. This is a very "light" technical framework, which, unfortunately, does not address the issues of the master data silos as described in Chapter 2.

At the other extreme, you may design your SAP NetWeaver MDM solution as the single point of data entry for customers and vendors. Interfaces are then built to link SAP NetWeaver MDM to each business application for both the legal entity and the partner function details. This "heavy" technical Framework is an expensive solution because, effectively, you'll need to replicate in SAP NetWeaver MDM the transactional logic from each of your ERPs, which will have different data models and functionality.

> **Don't Try to Build "All-Inclusive" Solutions**
>
> Be pragmatic when designing your SAP NetWeaver MDM Technical Framework. Don't be too "heavy" in your design. Only aim to master the global attributes, and don't try to reinvent business applications functionality.
>
> The MDM architecture team, while taking input from various applications, retains its focus only on MDM. The team leaves the solution design involved in aligning and modifying the end user applications (both the transactional and the reporting systems) to the respective IT and business teams.

6.1.1 Architecture Roles

A core team of the MDM business leads, the Technical Design Authority, and the SAP NetWeaver solution architects develop the SAP NetWeaver MDM Technical Architecture Framework.

Master data subject matter experts in the organization provide the business inputs. For business partner master data, this expertise comes from your procurement organization for vendors and from your customer services teams for customers. Existing SAP ERP design leads and data analysts from the data warehousing teams provide valuable inputs to the technical framework definition. Your IT services organization contributes with systems and integration architects.

Typically, the MDM Technical Design Authority is an enterprise architect from your company's internal organization. The SAP NetWeaver solution architects are provided by the MDM program team, which may include a systems integrator (SI).

Table 6.1 lists the roles of the Technical Design Authority and SAP NetWeaver solution architects using a RACI Matrix. For each activity, the respective role is assessed to be Responsible, Accountable, Consulted, or Informed.

Activity	Responsibility Matrix – Responsible, Accountable, Consulted, Informed	
	Technical Design Authority	SAP NetWeaver Solution Architects
Acquire system of origin and system of reference data layouts and sample data.	RA	I
Acquire consuming business applications data layouts and sample data.	RA	I
Specify and prioritize the key business requirements for the MDM processes.	RA	CI
Define the legal, compliance, and validation requirements.	RA	CI
Define the record of origin and the data enrichment services.	RA	CI
Define the MDM requirements for data standards and data quality metrics.	RA	CI
Define the MDM data security and data privacy/protection requirements.	RA	CI
Collate and arrange sign-off for the MDM requirements matrix.	AI	R
Design the logical and physical MDM data models.	I	RA
Design the MDM business scenarios.	CI	RA
Design the data interface architecture.	CI	RA
Design the Data Enrichment Architecture.	CI	RA
Finalize design and sign off.	A	R

Table 6.1 RACI Matrix for the Technical Design Authority and Solution Architects

The RACI Matrix is not an exhaustive list for all of the roles in the architecture definition phase, and the matrix also varies for individual projects. It highlights the criticality of the Technical Design Authority role, which is primarily a business-facing function that makes the decisions to help finalize the entire MDM architecture.

6.1.2 Consolidated and Centralized Master Data Architecture

After the MDM architecture design team is in place, the team moves on to the task of defining the SAP NetWeaver MDM Technical Framework components. They consider the various MDM scenarios and typically discuss these through a series of workshops with key stakeholders. Let's now consider the MDM consolidated scenario and the MDM centralized scenario.

MDM Consolidation Scenario

The MDM Consolidation scenario allows you to identify identical master data objects within a landscape and to merge identical objects centrally. You can assign unique identifiers to provide the relevant key mapping information for further use in business operations or analytics. The consuming business applications continue as before with each record tagged with the MDM key as an additional attribute. Figure 6.1 shows the SAP NetWeaver MDM application landscape in such a consolidation scenario.

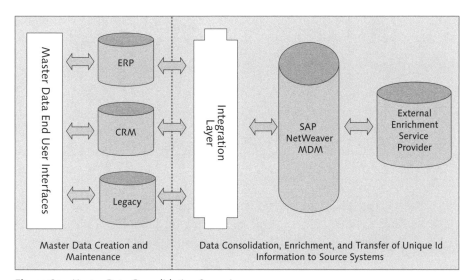

Figure 6.1 Master Data Consolidation Scenario

MDM Centralized Scenario

In this scenario, the master data record is centrally created in MDM and then automatically distributed to the consuming systems. MDM holds the "master" details, and the consuming systems are the "slaves." The obvious advantage of the central data model is that it enables the maintenance of a single source of truth.

The role of MDM in this scenario is to act as a "yellow pages" of companies used by an organization. MDM is a directory storing the global information about the business partners, with further extensions of the transaction-relevant master data occurring in the individual business applications.

This scenario supports the companywide quality standards by ensuring that the central processing of the master data begins as soon as the data is created.

Figure 6.2 shows the data flow of the central MDM scenario.

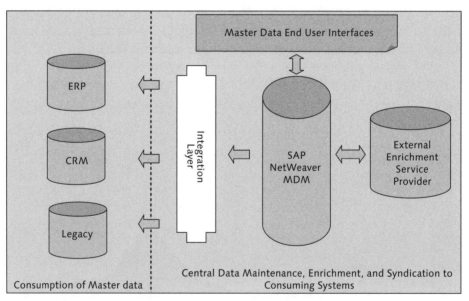

Figure 6.2   Central MDM Scenario

Your SAP NetWeaver MDM Technical Framework defines the master data scenario that is applicable for the object and the consuming business application in question. Key organization factors that drive the scenario definition are listed here:

▶ Does the MDM program have a mandate from the organization's senior business leaders to implement an SAP NetWeaver MDM solution with enterprise-wide data standards and common user interfaces?

▶ Is the MDM program going to run in parallel with a major business application implementation? Do the MDM program roll-out timelines align with the business application rollout?

▶ Does the organization have the aspiration to redefine the master data maintenance processes in the existing financial, procurement, and sales applications?

▶ Do the existing business applications have an open architecture to enable them to integrate in real time with the SAP NetWeaver MDM solution to access centrally authored data?

▶ Finally and critically, is there a big gap among the data definition, the data context, data, and the data standard and quality in the operational transaction systems and the MDM Governance process standards? Do the business applications and master data silos contain redundant, inactive, duplicate, and inaccurate master data, and is there an appetite to improve this?

The answers to these questions will help you decide whether to adopt a consolidation or a central MDM solution. Table 6.2 summarizes the evaluation parameters to be considered:

Evaluation Parameter	Fits the Consolidation Model	Fits the Central Model
The organization is embarking on a major implementation of SAP applications.		Yes
The mandate of the MDM program is to have enterprise-wide data standards, including common user and application interfaces based on enterprise SOA principles.		Yes
External data enrichment with the assignment of a unique D&B D-U-N-S Number is defined in the solution.		Yes
The organization requires a six-sigma level data quality in all transactional applications.		Yes

Table 6.2 Evaluation of Consolidation and Central Management Scenarios

Evaluation Parameter	Fits the Consolidation Model	Fits the Central Model
The capability to change the master data maintenance processes in consuming business applications does not exist.	Yes	
The primary business requirement is to tag a unique identifier to each master data record, to be referenced only by BI reporting and analytical systems.	Yes	
The master data quality in the business applications is not very high.	Yes	
The data definition and context in the business applications and reporting systems are very disparate and vary considerably from application to application.	Yes	
There is one major SAP ERP application, and the requirement is to enrich this data using SAP NetWeaver MDM and to feed data to the reporting and analysis systems.		Yes

Table 6.2 Evaluation of Consolidation and Central Management Scenarios (Cont.)

External enrichment addresses the issue of Lifecycle Management of business partner master data and fits both the consolidation and the centralized models.

Let's now consider the advantages of aligning your central MDM program along with a major SAP ERP 6.0 deployment program. The MDM program scope can be aligned to the scope of the SAP application deployment project with respect to the master data business processes, the business objects involved, and the geographies in scope.

It's easier to implement a central SAP NetWeaver MDM solution when it's "piggybacked" on an SAP ERP 6.0 implementation. If MDM is done separately, the master data must be consolidated first and then centralized. The business organization will be more enthusiastic to embark on the MDM journey because it's bundled with the value provided by the SAP ERP 6.0 implementation.

The regulatory and compliance issues, data privacy, and data protection can be handled together, without the ERP implementation waiting for a separate master data solution to handle the requirements. The time frames for implementing the new MDM processes can also be aligned with the ERP delivery time frames.

Both the MDM and the ERP programs can leverage resources, such as the data analysts, the integration architects, and the system administrators, more effectively. There is a single process for data cleansing and migration and an integrated cutover approach.

By following this approach, you avoid the need to modify the master data processes in the legacy business applications and to build new interfaces to them. The SOA-based architecture for the integration of the master data look-up and maintenance processes can be integrated with the ERP business scenarios. There is reduced effort in the ERP deployment because the MDM processes are mapped by the MDM team, who also drives the master data cleansing processes that are often ignored due to other urgent priorities.

Standard MDM processes take care of complex hierarchy management and attributes that are not managed in ERP. This, in turn, reduces the need for custom development efforts in ERP. The key business functionality, such as extended hierarchy management, high performance master data search, and integration with third-party data service providers, can be handled by SAP Netweaver MDM. However, there are also some limiting factors to consider when aligning the MDM program with a major SAP application rollout. The business subject matter experts must standardize the MDM processes, in addition to the SAP application transactional business scenarios, and there is increased effort in data cleansing based on the enterprisewide data standards. The scope of MDM tends to be aligned to the scope of the SAP application deployment so that only those customers and vendors in the scope of the deployment are considered. This can impact the MDM program's ability to scale the solution and slow down the MDM Phase 2 delivery.

After the MDM solution is live and in production, it can be rolled out relatively quickly to the other business units across your organization, whereas a full SAP application deployment takes longer. This may mean that some parts of larger organizations have to wait for new business application to go live before they can realize the MDM benefits.

A Hybrid Approach: Business Solution Illustration

An SAP NetWeaver MDM solution can also be a hybrid of both the consolidation and the central management scenarios. For example, multiple SAP NetWeaver MDM business partner repositories can coexist and be linked to different business applications. This approach is particularly relevant if your organization is taking a phased approach to centralization.

Consider an organization that is implementing an SAP ERP 6.0 deployment and is rolling it out to different locations. As we've discussed, the central MDM approach is a good business fit in this scenario and will go live in parallel with the first SAP application deployment.

This live functionality can then be leveraged to create a data consolidation scenario for the organizational units that are at the end of the queue for the SAP ERP 6.0 application rollout. The data consolidation solution uses the SAP NetWeaver MDM enrichment process to assign the unique identifier (the D&B D-U-N-S Number) for each of its master data records. The unique identifier and the cross references to the business application key fields, such as customer number and vendor number, can be passed on to the BI applications, which leverages this data for both spend and sales analysis.

In this hybrid solution, the central SAP NetWeaver MDM business partner data repository acts as a system of origin for the supplier data for the new SAP ERP 6.0 solution. The business applications consume these MDM services through a combination of request, enrichment, and syndication processes.

A consolidated business partner repository with the same data model as the central repository then leverages the data enrichment architecture to assign unique IDs to the new records that are created in existing legacy transactional systems. The internal matching and external enrichment process ensures that any records created in the transactional systems are assigned the D&B D-U-N-S Number.

While the data cleansing is happening in phases, the cleaned and externally enriched company records can be uploaded into an SAP NetWeaver MDM staging area repository. Data in this area are then imported into the production repositories in subsequent MDM deployments. Figure 6.3 shows the MDM architecture for this solution.

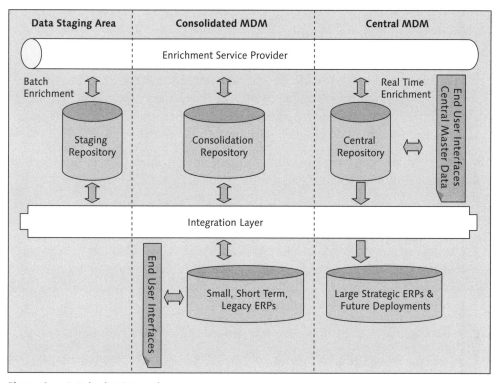

Figure 6.3 A Hybrid MDM Architecture

By using an integration architecture or enabling the SAP NetWeaver Portal to access multiple SAP NetWeaver MDM repositories in sequence, the repositories can make their data available to each other.

Let's assume that there are 500,000 cleansed and enriched business partner records in the staging repository. Each time a new request is raised in the live repositories, the application can match the new supplier request attributes with the cleansed records in the staging repository. If a match is found, an internal enrichment of data can be performed.

This approach has two key advantages. It reduces the steps in data enrichment to get the D&B D-U-N-S Number for the central MDM scenario, and it strengthens both the central and consolidation scenarios by ensuring that there is only one version of truth for the business partner information.

We've now analyzed the various options to address the consolidation, centralization, and hybrid scenarios for MDM. SAP NetWeaver MDM offers you the capability to design open and flexible definitions of repository structures. Your MDM architecture team will define a suitable MDM scenario based on the key business requirements and MDM program positioning in your organization.

Let's now consider the various MDM processes and how they fit into the SAP NetWeaver MDM Technical Framework.

6.1.3 Master Data Management Process Definition

The next step in developing your SAP NetWeaver MDM Technical Framework is to define your MDM processes, which are driven primarily by your organization's data governance strategy and rules. The MDM architecture team carries out the following activities to define the MDM processes:

1. Evaluate the business processes interaction with the master data processes.
2. Identify and design the MDM processes required to maintain a master data object in MDM.
3. Design the business services for distributing the master data to both your transactional and reporting consuming applications.

Master Data and Transactional Business Processes Integration

The assessment of your business process interaction with SAP NetWeaver MDM typically involves understanding the impact of the master data CRUD (create, read, update, and delete [archive]) processes on the transactional business processes. It also helps to determine the requirements for interfaces with the repository and the desired structure and properties of data elements in the MDM data model.

This activity should be executed at a high level. The benefits of a detailed (as-is) impact analysis of the detailed low-level business processes impacted by master data are debatable. If we take the example of vendor master data, it's generally true that your vendor data is referenced throughout the entire purchase-to-pay business scenario. This is supported by the fact that typically the LFA1 table is linked to more than 30 parent tables and more than 700 child tables in the data model. Analyzing and documenting each of these linkages at a low level is a time-consuming activity.

Instead, a practical approach is to identify the unique master data requirements for the business processes and evaluate these. These requirements may include geography-specific legal requirements or requirements that are driven by your organization's manufacturing and shipping scenarios.

> **Business Process and Master Data Process Evaluation**
>
> By involving the appropriate solution architects, business process experts, and the Technical Design Authority in your MDM architecture team, it will be simpler to zoom in on individual business process integration scenarios with master data, rather than revalidating the complete set of process integration touch points.

Design of the Master Data Management Processes

Your MDM processes map the flow, activities, and roles involved in the maintenance of your master data. A good enterprise MDM architecture provides you with the key tools by leveraging the SAP NetWeaver MDM and functionality for each of the tasks in the processes.

Let's now discuss the triggers, actions, and outputs for each of these key master data processes. For details on the roles mentioned in these examples, refer to Chapter 5.

Tables 6.3 through 6.6 illustrate the approach to mapping the MDM processes into your SAP NetWeaver MDM Solution Architecture. By effectively integrating the SAP NetWeaver capabilities, including features from the SAP NetWeaver Portal, SAP NetWeaver MDM, and SAP NetWeaver PI (SAP NetWeaver Exchange Infrastructure [XI]), you can simplify and automate several of these process steps.

Process Rationale	Search provides the enterprise business community with a single view of the data object. Good search capabilities ensure that duplicate requests for master data creation are minimized.
Performed by	Business user teams from your procurement organization.
Triggers	Search the vendor master data in the SAP NetWeaver MDM system to: Validate if the record already exists before requesting a new vendor. Understand the vendor hierarchy and the D&B Corporate Linkages. Understand which business applications are currently consuming the vendor data. View the status of the vendor data; is the record currently active or has it been blocked?
Activities	Provide search parameters. Execute the search. Evaluate the results. Search again if necessary with revised company parameters.
Output	Vendor search executed, and search results displayed.
Possible follow-up actions	Request to create, change, or block a vendor.
SAP NetWeaver enablement	Provide options for search by: Consuming system key. Name and address parameters. D&B D-U-N-S Number. Display search result overview and details for each "hit." Provide links to display the consuming system key information, such as the D&B Worldbase details, and vendor partner function mapping. Seamless transfer of search result information to change vendor and distribute vendor MDM applications.

Table 6.3 Process: Search Vendor Master Data

Process Rationale	Streamlined functions for requesting a new vendor.
	Review, approve, and enrich the master data before it's distributed to the consuming business application.
Performed by	MDM data stewards.
Triggers	Business organization wants to procure services from a new vendor.
	Search for this vendor in MDM was unsuccessful.
Activities	Collect request using electronic form (potentially SAP Interactive Forms).
	Request creation of a new vendor after local organization approvals — requestor.
	Review the request and either approve or reject — MDM data steward.
	Enrich the data with D&B Worldbase — MDM data steward.
	Recheck for duplicate records by comparing the D&B D-U-N-S Number.
	Automatic distribution of the record to the consuming business application.
Output	New vendor creation request processed.
Possible follow-up actions	Local extension of transaction-relevant master data in the consuming system.
SAP NetWeaver enablement	Use MDM matching functionality to compare the new request with existing data.
	Display the matching results in the portal review application.
	Modularize and split the SAP NetWeaver MDM workflow to enable looping in the creation and enrichment process.
	Deploy the enrichment architecture to provide "iterative" look-ups of the D&B company search function.
	Enable automatic syndication of an approved request.
	MDM data model captures requestor and consuming system information.
	Enable offline data capture of the vendor creation requests, for example, SAP Interactive Forms integrated with SAP NetWeaver Portal.
	Email notifications at appropriate stages to the requestor and approver.
	Application to check the status of a request.
	Application to monitor workflow throughput times.

Table 6.4 Process: Vendor Master Data Creation and Enrichment

Process Rationale	Management of change requests for the centrally managed attributes of vendor master data and distribution to all business applications that consume this data.
Performed by	Local and central data stewards.
Triggers	Business wants to change attributes for an existing vendor.
	Lifecycle Management processes through the D&B Worldbase data refresh process have updated an attribute, which is relevant to the consuming systems (e.g., business name or address after a company merger).
Activities	Creation of a change request —requestor.
	Review and approval of the change — MDM data steward.
	Automatic distribution of the change to all business applications that consume this vendor record.
Output	Vendor change request processed.
Possible follow-up actions	Communication to the wider business community about the change.
SAP NetWeaver enablement	Modularize and split the SAP NetWeaver MDM workflow to enable looping in change process.
	Enable automatic syndication of an approved request.
	Email notifications at appropriate stages to the requestor and approver.
	Application to check the status of a request.
	SAP NetWeaver MDM data model captures the requestor and consuming system information.

Table 6.5 Process: Vendor Master Data Change/Block

Process Rationale	Vendor exists in MDM and in one or more consuming business applications. The same vendor now needs to be created in another business application, where it doesn't currently exist.
Performed by	MDM data stewards.
Triggers	MDM data steward has executed a search for a new vendor request. Search shows that the vendor already exists in MDM and is consumed in some business applications.
Activities	Create a distribute request — requestor. Review and process the request — MDM data steward. Automatic distribution to the consuming system.
Output	Vendor distribute request processed.
Possible follow-up actions	Local extension of transaction-relevant master data in the consuming business application.
SAP NetWeaver enablement	Modularize and split the SAP NetWeaver MDM workflow to enable looping in the distribute process. Enable automatic syndication of an approved request. Email notifications at appropriate stages to the requestor and approver. Application to check the status of a request. SAP NetWeaver MDM data model captures the requestor and consuming system information.

Table 6.6 Process: Distribute Vendor Request

Let's now move on to consider data integration and the architecture of the distribution of records to consuming business applications.

6.1.4 Data Integration and Synchronization Architecture

When you define your enterprise integration architecture, this involves connecting SAP NetWeaver MDM with your SAP ERP and your legacy systems through the use of messaging protocols. The following three steps are involved in defining the integration architecture:

1. Evaluate the integration requirements and the design solutions for interfacing SAP NetWeaver MDM with both the system of origin and the consuming business applications.

2. Align the integration requirements with the standard integration content that is provided by SAP NetWeaver PI.

3. Design and prepare the mapping specifications and message routing conditions for the selected master data objects between the source and target systems.

SAP NetWeaver Process Integration (SAP NetWeaver PI) is the new generation SAP NetWeaver Exchange Infrastructure (SAP NetWeaver XI) tool and is the preferred stack solution for building the integration between MDM and your business applications.

SAP NetWeaver PI offers multiple ways of connecting the SAP NetWeaver MDM repositories to your consuming systems. You can integrate using XML files, whereby the MDM syndication process creates an XML file that is then transferred by SAP NetWeaver PI. Text or comma-separated files can also be used instead of XML files if this is your preferred format.

SAP NetWeaver PI can call published MDM Web Services to search and retrieve master data from your repository. It can also be enabled for scenarios where the SAP NetWeaver PI process calls the MDM Java and ABAP APIs to obtain the master data.

SAP NetWeaver PI can use one or a combination of these options to search, update, and distribute data both to and from your SAP NetWeaver MDM repositories. Your chosen implementation method will be driven by your integration architecture principles. Is XML a company standard, and do you strive to avoid file-based interfaces in your organization?

SAP NetWeaver MDM also provides various additional features such as the cloning of attributes (to default an attribute value), transformation rules, and de-duplication during the import process.

Two SAP NetWeaver PI Best Practices

Two simple rules will help you avoid unnecessary effort when architecting your SAP NetWeaver PI solution.

► As a best practice, avoid data transformation or manipulation logic in the integration layer because it becomes opaque to the business users.

► As far as possible, use common master data formats and schemas to transfer data to and from your MDM systems.

6.1.5   Enterprise SOA Principles in Data Architecture

Your enterprise master data architecture will be designed to support the sharing of data across your enterprise applications. Harmonized master data is a foundation for enterprise service-oriented architecture (enterprise SOA), which is intended to be a business-driven software architecture that increases your flexibility and openness. Enterprise SOA introduces the design, composition, and management of Web Services to address enterprise requirements.

In principle, an enterprise SOA can be quickly assembled to develop new applications and to enable business processes. Organizations will improve the reusability of their software components and can respond to business change more quickly.

Enterprise services communicate business logic between software applications running on disparate platforms. By using enterprise services, your IT departments can respond more quickly to changing business requirements and can take advantage of existing functionality in their landscape.

To enable enterprise SOA, several concepts are incorporated in your enterprise master data architecture. Your data layer will be decoupled and kept separate from the applications which use them, and your solution will be modular and based on a services framework.

Your Metadata model adheres to global standards and to global data types and is uniform across the enterprise. The system of origin and the system of reference for each master data object are distinctly defined, and your MDM processes cover the entire lifecycle of the data record.

Finally, your Web Services for accessing the business partner master data are published centrally and are available to be used by different applications across your enterprise landscape.

SAP NetWeaver MDM provides the framework and components for building enterprise SOA-ready solution architectures. When designing the MDM processes, define your data model and workflow design to make it a composite of simple elements.

A good example is the design of the Create Vendor workflow. Chapter 8 covers in detail the SAP NetWeaver MDM workflows, which have the capability to call a workflow B as the last step of workflow A. This can be used to split the Create Vendor process steps into distinct components. The review and approval/rejection steps can therefore be configured as a distinct workflow, which is called by the Create, Change, and Distribute workflows.

Let's now consider the importance of the enterprise data standards to MDM and discuss some examples.

6.2   Enterprise MDM Data Architecture Standards and Requirements

Data standards form the basis for data governance in an MDM solution. Standards are prerequisite for distributing data to multiple consuming systems and for monitoring the quality of data. Your data standards definition captures the business rules to ensure that correct values are entered for each global master data attribute.

6.2.1   Data Inheritance Rules, Quality Standards, and Validations

Defining the appropriate data architecture standards is one of the core activities for the MDM Steering Board and the MDM architecture team. Existing data standards in an organization can help define the standards for the SAP NetWeaver MDM solution.

As discussed in Chapter 2, adopting a new company data standard mandating that "All customers and vendors must be authenticated with a D&B D-U-N-S Number and be maintained with MDM" may initially be resisted. However, when you consider the following questions, this seems a sensible way forward:

▶ How will you create a new company record, in the absence of a D&B D-U-N-S Number?

▶ How do you authenticate that a company is who it says it is?

▶ How can you verify a company's credit status and risk?

▶ How do you search to see if the customer or vendor is already used in your company without it?

The data standard is clear, concise, measurable, and enforceable. You have either tagged a customer or vendor record with a D&B D-U-N-S Number or you haven't. The standards defined should also facilitate easy data maintenance and retrieval. Your standards maintenance starts at the origin of the data creation, so awareness and acceptance of the MDM standards by the wider business community are crucial to a successful SAP NetWeaver MDM deployment.

Table 6.7 shows an illustrative data standard definition for vendor master data.

Field Description	Field Status	Data Standard
Supplier Name-1	M	The legal entity name of a company must be used as required or provided by the D&B legal name.
Supplier Name-2	O	When the D&B legal name exceeds 35 characters, the name is wrapped into the 4 supplier name fields up to 140 characters in length.
Supplier Name-3	O	
Supplier Name-4	O	
Search Term-1 Search Term-2	M	Search Term1: Abbreviation of the legal name to facilitate company searching. Search Term2: Abbreviation of the Global Ultimate company name. No punctuation is allowed.
Street		Should be entered according to the information provided by the vendor. Use mixed case wherever necessary. Enter the name of the street but not the number.
Postal Code	O	The street postal code must be used for this field. It must be entered in the format of the country of the business partner.
City	M	This must be the city name according to the local postal authority.
Country	M	Use SAP default values for each respective country, which is based on the ISO alpha two-digit country codes.
Region	O	In countries where the region (state, province, county) is part of the address, the information must be entered here using the two-digit code from the SAP list of possible entries.

Table 6.7 Example Vendor Data Standard Definition

Field Description	Field Status	Data Standard
Telephone 1 Telephone 2 Fax Number	O O O	The phone or fax number must consist of a dialing code and a number without the country code. Enter the number as it must be dialed within the country (SAP has built-in country codes). Leading spaces are not allowed.
Tax Code 1 and 2	O	There *must* be an entry either in Tax-1 or Tax-2; this will never be blank.
VAT Registration Number	M	Enter the VAT Number specified by the business partner.

Table 6.7 Example Vendor Data Standard Definition (Cont.)

Validations and Inheritance

You will use *validations* to confirm whether a data attribute value meets the standards defined. A good example of this is if the vendor is from one of the European Union countries; if so, then a company's VAT registration number should be a mandatory entry. This can be checked both at the point of requesting the data and also during the review process.

Integration with External Web Services

Another good use of SAP NetWeaver technology can be demonstrated in the VAT number validation process. The European Union offers a public Web Service that accepts a VAT registration number and confirms whether it exists in the EU database. The SAP NetWeaver Portal can make a Java connector call to this Web Service in real time and check that the VAT registration number entered by the business user is valid.

Inheritance is a key property for master data attributes. As an example, your data standards may define that a particular payment method must have a given payment term. In this case, rather than allowing a user input, the payment term can be automatically inherited based on the payment method entered.

The SAP NetWeaver MDM functions, such as validations, assignments, and calculations, can be leveraged to ensure that your chosen data standards are followed. This is discussed in more detail in Chapters 8 and 9.

6.2.2 Global and Local Attributes

A key MDM architecture decision is to classify which attributes are global and which are specific to local transaction applications. The SAP NetWeaver MDM solution, when it's distributing data to multiple business applications, should not aim to master all attributes of the data object in question. Nearly 70% of the master data attributes that are required by an SAP ERP or SCM business application are specific to executing transactions in that particular system. The exercise of porting all of these attributes into MDM is a huge maintenance-intensive activity that delivers few business benefits.

Your MDM solution will be architected to focus on maintaining a single version of truth and uniquely identifying the master data record. Only the attributes that identify the data object as a unique entity should be mastered in MDM. This is all the more relevant if the MDM solution is distributing data to many business applications.

Master data attributes that are relevant only to the execution of business transactions such as vendor bank details will be mastered in the transaction systems directly. Business applications such as SAP ERP 6.0 have comprehensive and robust functionality to cross-validate these transaction-relevant attributes, and it's a redundant exercise to map and maintain these details in an SAP NetWeaver MDM system.

6.2.3 Taxonomy (Hierarchy) and De-Duplication

Taxonomy or hierarchy is used to classify master data and is a powerful tool in SAP NetWeaver MDM. The solution offers the capability to build multiple distinct hierarchies for classifying a master data object.

Taxonomy in SAP NetWeaver MDM is a *classification tree*, the leaf node of which enables you to maintain attributes and values, such as color and power rating. Hierarchies are classification trees for which attribute values cannot be assigned.

Based on this definition, the taxonomy defined in SAP NetWeaver MDM reflects the main characteristics of the master data object. Hierarchies can be used to classify specific structures such as health and safety standards, or geopolitical location. A practical way to architect this is to initially define a central taxonomy and then add the specific hierarchies as required.

For example, in a vendor search, if the drill-down search is performed using a geopolitical location, this increases the probability of identifying and stopping a duplicate request at the source.

In addition, the SAP NetWeaver Portal capabilities can also be used to display the existing records under a taxonomy node, either when a new master data request is created or when assigning the record to that particular node. The business user on viewing this information can clearly decide whether the requested data record is in fact a duplicate.

When you define your taxonomies, consider the industry standard taxonomies such as the UNSPSC hierarchies. You should design the structure of the taxonomy in such a way that there is only one logical place to assign any master data record in the taxonomy.

The taxonomy you design will be a complete classification structure. Be aware that regular updates and changes to the taxonomy can result in it losing its relevance, which means that the taxonomy will not achieve its primary purpose of correctly classifying each master data record.

6.2.4   Optimization — Data Volume and Performance

Your MDM data modeling phase addresses the performance and data volume management. However, before this, your MDM architecture team needs to ensure that the principles for designing a robust and high-performance repository are incorporated in the architecture design phase itself. A good repository design ensures that the master data is in the correct context, that it performs well during the search and maintenance of records, and that there is good performance during the import and syndication processes.

Access to tables and fields in SAP NetWeaver MDM is optimized for the main table in the repository. There are performance implications when other tables such as lookup tables or qualified lookup tables contain large numbers of records. This should be considered during the MDM architecture phase to ensure that the SAP NetWeaver MDM Technical Framework that is defined doesn't require the maintenance of data in a true relational sense.

Your SAP NetWeaver MDM repositories are always designed in a way that the majority of records are kept in the main table with each of the lookup tables containing significantly fewer records. If the repository has a different distribution of records, this indicates that the main table should be a different object from the one chosen or that other errors have been made during the design.

Change tracking is another feature that influences the performance of your SAP NetWeaver MDM repository. The MDM design team validates the audit trails, changes tracking requirements, and ensures that only critical data attributes are enabled for tracking. You'll learn much more about how to improve the performance of your SAP NetWeaver MDM repository in Chapter 8.

6.2.5 Data Security and Data Privacy Requirements

During the MDM architecture phase, the requirements for secure access to the data repositories are evaluated and incorporated in the solution architecture.

SAP NetWeaver MDM offers some robust functionality for meeting your data security and data privacy requirements. This includes role-based authorization to control who can maintain data in your repositories. These roles define the functions, such as data maintenance, workflow execution, and access (read/ writes) permissions.

SAP NetWeaver MDM can be integrated with the Lightweight Directory Access Protocol (LDAP) to provide the capability of logging in with a single Windows NT user account. This is a step towards single sign-on, which is advantageous for business users. By using SAP NetWeaver Portal as the end user data maintenance interface, you can define roles in the portal system that can perform selected functions in the SAP NetWeaver MDM repository. These roles control the level of access to maintenance functions, whereas permissions to read or write data are still controlled by the repository user role.

Typical roles required for business users in an SAP NetWeaver MDM system are listed here:

- ▸ **Search**
  Users can search for records in the MDM repositories to retrieve selected companies and their D&B Corporate Linkage (the "yellow pages" users).

- ▸ **Requestors**
  Business users in the procurement or customer services teams who can request the creation of new customer or vendor data records.

▶ **Request approvers**
Users who have the authority to display/edit a request and make decisions on whether to proceed with or reject the request.

▶ **MDM data stewards**
Users who have the authority to review requests, check for duplicates, enrich the data with D&B Corporate Linkage, and distribute the records to consuming systems.

6.2.6   Key Mapping and Remote Systems

SAP NetWeaver MDM provides remote system and key mapping features that enable it to synchronize data with consuming systems.

Any logical system configured within MDM, which can supply data to or receive data from MDM, is known as a remote system. The logical system can be a consuming business application such as an SAP ERP application or an organizational entity defined within an SAP ERP application.

MDM key mapping maintains the relationship between the remote system's identifier for an object and the corresponding record in MDM. Within a remote system, each type of object can have its own separate collection of keys as well. This enables vendors belonging to different vendor account groups to be mapped to different keys.

6.3   Summary

This chapter discussed designing the SAP NetWeaver MDM Technical Framework, which includes defining MDM scenarios, the data management processes, and the integration scenarios. This phase is driven by the MDM program scope and the identified key business requirements to deliver the business benefits. We described the importance of the people who are designing your MDM architecture, and how the roles for the MDM architecture team should be agreed on upfront.

We described how to evaluate the MDM scenario that is the best fit for your organization, while realizing that the hybrid models can be implemented without waiting for a full centralization exercise to occur.

We then moved on to discuss how to design the SAP NetWeaver MDM Solution Architecture for the master data objects. This involves designing the data model, the context (taxonomy and hierarchy), and the validations and workflows, in compliance with your data standards and security design. The MDM Solution Architecture phase is also driven by your MDM business case and by the SAP NetWeaver MDM Technical Framework definition.

We discussed the importance of accurately defining your MDM processes, and how the MDM team should look to leverage key SAP NetWeaver functionalities to provide a seamless process to the business. The data standards definition and governance holds the key to the long-term success of the MDM program and that the definition should be stated at the master data attribute level. Finally, we described how your MDM architecture team should pay close attention to the optimization, security, and remote systems design.

You'll now understand the differences between a "light" and "heavy" SAP MDM Technical Framework and how key MDM processes can be designed and built using a combination of the SAP NetWeaver components in a Solution Architecture. A sample Data Model was developed and you were given insights into the rules of how to create an effective data model for your organization, recognizing the differences between global and local attributes and the importance of keeping the MDM data layer simple.

Let's now move on to consider the best-in-class approaches to migrating, cleansing, and maintaining data in your SAP NetWeaver MDM repositories in Chapter 7.

This chapter describes the processes and techniques involved in data conversion. We'll evaluate the ways to combine the D&B Entity Matching and enrichment processes together with the SAP NetWeaver MDM repositories and workflow functionality to address the challenges of data cleansing and migration.

7 Converting and Maintaining Master Data

In this chapter, we'll discuss the processes involved in the cleansing and migration of your master data records from your consuming systems into the SAP NetWeaver MDM repositories. The quality of the data in your MDM repositories is the number one critical success factor for your MDM program, so this data conversion is extremely important. Data cleansing and migration is the "engine room" of your MDM program, so you need excellent people, particularly your MDM data stewards, and processes to meet your organization's data standards.

This chapter joins together several of the ideas from the previous chapters. As described in Chapter 2, when an organization starts an enterprise MDM program, the existing master data is often maintained in multiple systems or master data silos and does not follow corporate standards. We'll revisit our case study Company CO1 and describe in detail the data conversion phases that are needed to cleanse and enrich your customer and vendor data records.

In Chapter 3, we introduced the MDM two-phase roadmap. We'll consider how during Phase 2 of the MDM program, you scale your MDM solution to include your entire customer and vendor records and how this impacts your SAP NetWeaver MDM repository design and approaches to data conversion.

In Chapter 4, we discussed the Dun & Bradstreet services. We'll now revisit these to discover how you use a combination of the batch D&B Entity Matching services and D&B MDM Data Enrichment Architecture Web Services to authenticate each of your business partner master data records and to accurately match them to the correct D&B D-U-N-S Number. These D&B services are integrated using your SAP NetWeaver MDM repository design and workflow.

And finally, from Chapter 6, where we initially introduced the SAP NetWeaver MDM repository architecture, we'll now examine in some detail the use of staging, consolidated, and centralized repositories throughout the data conversion and maintenance processes. We'll discuss how the repositories should be maintained in a consistent manner and how the role of the staging repository differs from the other two repositories. We then discuss how the data integrity in the staging repository is managed through the use of workflows and how you manage the Lifecycle Management processes, including updates to the external company details maintained by D&B, and updates in your consuming systems.

7.1 Data Cleansing and Migration

Let's start our discussion by reviewing the MDM Phase 2 roadmap, as shown in Figure 7.1.

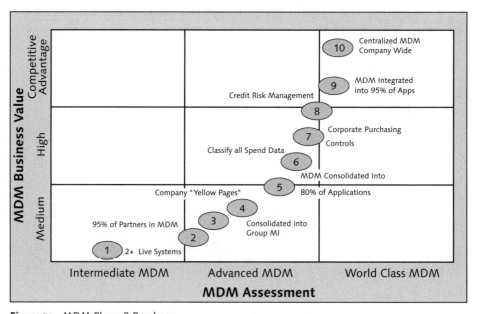

Figure 7.1 MDM Phase 2 Roadmap

Let's now consider how the MDM Phase 2 roadmap impacts our conversion strategies and objectives.

7.1.1 Data Conversion Strategies and Objectives

You can see from Figure 7.1 that one of the major initial objectives of MDM Phase 2 is to store 95% of your business partner records in your SAP NetWeaver MDM repositories. The reasons for this are fairly obvious when you think back to our "yellow pages" analogy. If MDM is the first place that you want your business users to search to find a company record, then you need a full directory in place.

If only a small percentage of your company's records are maintained in SAP NetWeaver MDM, then it serves little practical business purpose. Your business users will continue to only search their local business applications, and the master data silos will continue.

Also, by tagging all of your business partner records with a D&B D-U-N-S Number, you obtain the D&B Corporate Linkages and start to deliver many of the promised business benefits discussed in Chapter 3.

For these reasons, one of your key objectives is to populate and maintain the SAP NetWeaver MDM consolidation repository with the entire set of your customer and vendor records. The consolidation repository will be established with links to the key identifier in each of your consuming systems and will enable you to tag the D&B D-U-N-S Number to your short-term legacy SAP ERPs. In the long term and at the end of your MDM Phase 2, your business applications will also be centralized through SAP NetWeaver MDM, which will then be integral to your customer and vendor maintenance processes throughout your organization. You should design your centralized processes upfront during MDM Phase 1 so that you have the capability and are live with an initial system. You are then ready and able to work with your new business applications deployments and to implement a centralized MDM side by side.

However, changing all of your business applications to integrate with a centralized MDM will take considerable time. With this in mind, we developed the MDM Technical Framework architecture as introduced in Chapter 6.

Figure 7.2 shows the SAP NetWeaver MDM repository architecture. Most of the data migration processes and activity takes place in the staging repository, and you then promote the business-approved records to the consolidation or the centralized repositories.

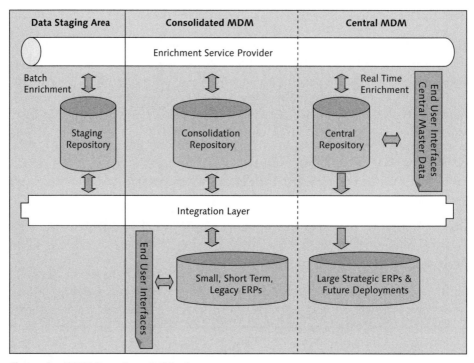

Figure 7.2 MDM Repository Architecture

The MDM staging repository differs from the MDM consolidation repository and the MDM centralized repository in three important respects:

1. The MDM staging repository contains operational data from your live business applications and prospective consuming systems that are not yet integrated into MDM. It's the *"work in progress" repository*, where you prepare your master data records to meet your data standards and can then moved those records to your "live" MDM consolidated and MDM centralized repositories.

2. The MDM staging repository is the only repository that provides you with the *batch D&B Entity Matching* processes.

3. Records in the MDM staging repository aren't retrieved as part of your *MDM company search*. They are not yet ready to take their place in your corporate "yellow pages." The records in the MDM consolidated and central repositories are retrieved as part of your company search.

The MDM centralized and the MDM consolidated repositories continuously get requests for new operational business master data records to be set up, and they also get feeds of data from the consuming systems with which they are already live. The MDM staging repository provides an additional data import into these repositories.

Throughout the chapter, we'll return to Company CO1 as first described in Case Study 1 in Chapter 2 to show how the data matching and conversions principles are practically applied in the MDM staging repository. Let's now consider how to measure your data quality and how it meets your data standards.

7.1.2 Organizational Data Quality Metrics and Standards

Successful interpretation and treatment of master data is derived from both an accurate *Syntax* and *Context*.

Syntax is something that a technology such as SAP NetWeaver MDM is very capable of in that it has good functionality to transform data to a defined syntax with relative ease. An example of this is when telephone numbers should all appear in the same format in a database with international code management.

However, *Context*, or the meaning behind the data, is something that you will need help with from your business users because they are the best sources of information. An example of this is when you discover the repeated occurrence of an undocumented comment or code that is embedded in a search term of a vendor record. Another example is why duplicate master data records are created in a business application to overcome some functional deficiency in the business application, which cannot handle a complex scenario such as a special contract or multiple bank details.

Your data quality metrics will consider the completeness, uniqueness, correctness, and consistency of data of your active records. You'll explore the following types of questions:

▶ What percentage of data meets the data standards?

▶ What are the common definitions of incompleteness or incorrectness of data? Examples include whether a region field is never completed in your address details.

▶ Is the location landmark always put in the Street 2 field?

When defining your data standards and data quality metrics, you'll identify both the immediate and long-term objectives for data cleansing. The immediate objectives are usually to get a set of data clean and ready for the next implementation.

The long-term objectives define the strategy and processes for data cleansing, the provision of tools for data staging, and enrichment for future rollouts of central data management. We consider both the short-term and the long-term objectives throughout this chapter.

You can create metrics to measure your business partner, vendor, or customer system index in a similar way that you can measure your "body mass index "(BMI). In Chapter 1, we introduced the Vendor System Index (VSI) as the following:

Vendor System Index (VSI) = (Number of Available Vendor Records / Number of Unique Active Vendor Records) − 1) × 100%

Number of Available Vendor Records is the number of vendor records currently set up in a system that are not blocked or end dated.

Number of Unique, Active Vendor Record is the number of unique vendor records as matched with the D&B D-U-N-S Number that have been used in a transaction in the system in the past three years. You can count a D&B D-U-N-S Number once only and must exclude duplicates.

The Vendor System Index (VSI), and the similar Customer System Index (CSI), or the Business Partner System Index (BPSI) can be applied to each of the business applications where your customer or vendor records are maintained. They give you a view of the health of your master data records.

A VSI score of 10% or below for a system shows that you have "lean" data under tight control. You have very few duplicates or inactive records left hanging in the system. A VSI score of between 10% and 50% indicates that your data is not being subjected to tight master data management control, and a VSI score in excess of 50% implies that your data lacks internal controls.

Table 7.1 provides some typical results from the first iteration of a D&B Entity Matching process.

CO1 Systems		Vendor Active Records	Used in Past Two Years	Vendor Linked to DUNS	Vendor Unique DUNS Records	Customer Active Records	Used in the Last Two Years	Customer Linked to DUNS	Customer Unique DUNS Records
Customer Relationship Management	CRM1					3,000	1,200	840	790
Supply Chain Management	SCM1	4,500	1,000	740	680				
Sales and Distribution	SD1					2,000	1,100	685	600
Financial Accounting	FI1	6,000	950	845	810	2,500	975	920	900
Business Intelligence	BI1	9,000	1,200	990	940	6,500	1,300	975	905
Totals		19,500	3,150	2,575	975	14,000	4,575	3,420	965

Table 7.1 First Iteration of D&B Entity Matching for Company CO1 (Fictional Example)

239

This initial D&B matching process provides you with a lot of valuable insights and metrics into the state of your existing master data. You now know not only the number of master data records in your legacy systems but also which of these the duplicate records are. This provides an excellent start point for your data assessment phase in which you will conduct a detailed analysis of the state of the current master data. Let's now discuss how you will further investigate your consuming systems data.

7.1.3 Investigating the Source System Data

A data-cleansing project has several distinct phases. In the initial data discovery phase, you address the following questions:

▶ What is the existing set of values in your data in the different systems?

▶ What is the structural integrity of this data, are the primary keys unique, and are there set of records with specific rules?

▶ What percentage of the data values is complete?

▶ Do they follow unique standards in attribute definition?

▶ What does the profile of your data look like?

▶ How many business rule validations does your data adhere to?

During your source system data assessment, you pull together a lot of facts. You collate information on current data quality initiatives in your organization and also collect the data models for the source data from the different business applications. You collect sample data of different business partner types and subsets of data "owned" by different business units and regions.

You also profile sample data and identify quality issues in the sample. Profiling can include null value analysis, maintenance date range checks, and columns analysis to arrive at the likely value sets for text fields. Profiling identifies the relevance and usage of binary value (yes or no) columns. *Is it always a no? If so, is it worth storing this as an attribute?* You also analyze categorization attributes, such as vendor groups, and the business partner hierarchies and the nodes that they fit in.

Based on the data profiling, you gather the known data issues and also define the total volumes and the expected delta volumes to produce an estimate of the baseline data condition.

The source system data investigation must be carried out with the business users. Only they understand the context of the data and the underlying reasons that explain why it's in its current form. The business users are accountable for the cleansing and migration of the data into SAP NetWeaver MDM.

The Importance of Business Ownership in the Data Conversion Process
There is a tendency for the IT communities who can quickly gain an in-depth understanding of the syntax of the data to also try to transform the data without including the business users. This is a big mistake and should be firmly discouraged!
Applying data transformation rules and changing the legacy data without understanding the business context is extremely risky. Customer and vendor records can be lost or duplicated or incorrectly updated if you change the data structure from a current operational system without business validation. Its best practice to work closely with the key business users throughout the process and to ensure that there is a nominated business owner who is accountable for the data migration.
Your MDM program needs to identify the business owner for each application who will be accountable for the migration process and agrees to take ownership of the conversion process. The business owner will sign off that the data has been successfully linked to MDM and that all of the necessary corrective actions have been taken to resolve the issues where the existing data does not meet your data standards.

You can get some good insights by carrying out a full data assessment of some sample records in your existing business applications. You should initially select 10 records of the simple, intermediate, and complex types. We'll focus on the vendor records in this analysis and recognize that the customer records data assessment will be similar.

A *simple vendor* is a vendor whose legal address and all other types of addresses, such as the purchasing address and the payment address, are at the same location. Investigate five of these types of simple records that have successfully matched with a D&B D-U-N-S Number and five records that haven't. For the matched records, review the matched D&B name and address, and confirm that you are happy that the record has been "authenticated" correctly.

Now investigate the five non-matched records. There are many data discovery questions to ask at this point.

▸ When did you last do business with the vendor?

▸ What is the value of the business with the vendor?

▶ When were the vendor record details last updated in the system?

▶ Are the vendor name and address details complete, and do they comply with your data standards?

▶ Is the company linked in some way to another legal entity?

The answers to these questions will provide you with some good insights into the current state of the data in your business application. If you can also assess the total number of "simple" vendors in your application, you'll quickly get a good idea of the total data-cleansing effort that will be required.

An *intermediate vendor* is a vendor with a more complex data structure. Look for multiple payment addresses and ordering addresses and also for situations when the supplier is trading as part of a much larger group. You may choose some vendors who have been know to give your business users payment issue difficulties because of their complex setup. Again assess five records that matched with D&B and five that didn't.

With this data assessment, you'll get a good understanding of the existing legacy system data model and its application. You'll see how the prospective consuming system's relational model will integrate to your SAP NetWeaver MDM repository and its main table, look-up tables, and qualified look-up tables design.

By examining the intermediate records that don't match with D&B, you'll begin to understand how your business application's definitions match with the legal entity definitions. In these cases, look for purchasing addresses and payment addresses that may have been inadvertently set up as legal entities.

Finally, really test your MDM data model with 10 of the most *complex vendors* that you have. In this category, include the vendors with the highest number of duplicate records each matching to the same D&B D-U-N-S Number. You may find that you have 5 or more vendor records linked to the same D&B D-U-N-S Numbers.

Why is this? Is it a limitation of the business application that can't manage the procurement processes with a company with just one vendor record? For example, you may be dealing with multiple payment terms or multiple bank details or multiple departments within the same organization. How will this impact your SAP NetWeaver MDM repository design?

Following are two key points to remember when conducting your sampling exercise:

▶ **Always involve the business users**.

You are looking to understand the context for the data so arrange workshops with the key business users and the business owner. They need to understand what you are trying to achieve and how the current state of the master data records impacts your MDM program.

▶ **Inspect "real" legacy data in the business application**.

There are many good theories about how data may potentially be set up in a business application, but these are often not substantiated by the facts of the real master data records that are actually maintained. During your workshops, ensure that you inspect the data extracts and also the relevant business application screens to obtain a better understanding of why the master data is currently set up in the way that it is.

Let's now move on to consider how to extract and cleanse the data from the prospective consuming systems.

7.1.4   Data-Cleansing Processes: Extract and Cleanse Principles

When you extract the master data from your business applications, the following data extraction principles will help you.

Aim for a repeatable process that can be reused across your various business applications. Define the global attributes that you require, and always try to extract data using common formats across the systems. Also extract only the attributes that are necessary for your MDM design. For example, if the consuming system contains vendor purchasing relevant master data, and this is not mapped in the enterprise data model, then don't extract this data.

Decide on how you want to extract the relational data. You may choose either one full row per relationship, or separate files for the main attributes and the relationships, which are linked by the unique identifier of the record. Ensure that you can identify the extracts from each of your different business applications, and include the application project name and the extract date. Devise a method of uploading the delta records in the extraction load after checking if it's a duplicate.

> **Identify and Match the D&B D-U-N-S Number Only Once**
>
> A key data conversion principle is that after you've authenticated that a business partner record has successfully matched to the appropriate D&B D-U-N-S Number and this has been confirmed by the business owner, then it should be made available to the relevant SAP NetWeaver MDM consolidated or centralized repository.
>
> Extracting data from your consuming systems and loading into your SAP NetWeaver MDM staging repository is an iterative process. However, you shouldn't need to revisit a data record more than once, and there's no need to reprocess the record again in your staging repository after it has been approved.

A SAP NetWeaver MDM repository design option for you to consider in your data extraction and cleansing is the potential use of the SAP NetWeaver MDM master–slave architecture.

Master–Slave Architecture in MDM

Slave repositories are read-only snapshot copies of the master repository, which is the operational repository. All data and schema changes to the master repository are logged by the MDM system. The slave repository initiates synchronization requests, and the synchronization is carried out by the SAP NetWeaver MDM console. Synchronization updates the slave repository with all of the changes done to the data and repository structure in the master repository. The synchronization process cannot be filtered, and the slave immediately after synchronization becomes an exact replica of the master.

Using the Master–Slave Architecture

Staging allows you to create a staging environment on a single machine using a single copy of the software that completely insulates the published slave from changes made to the staging master until you're ready to publish the updates by synchronizing the slave.

Publishing updates allow you to efficiently disseminate updates to multiple slaves across multiple machines that may be geographically dispersed because the synchronization process itself transmits only updates rather than the entire repository.

Let's now move on to consider the various phases of the data conversion process.

7.1.5   Data Cleansing and Enrichment with Dun & Bradstreet

The first objective in the data cleansing and enrichment process is to uniquely identify each of your customer and vendor records. The D&B Entity Matching functionality is initially used to match each of your consuming system's master data records and to find the appropriate D&B D-U-N-S Number. There are four phases of cleansing and enrichment with D&B, and you use a combination of batch and MDM D&B enrichment Web Services. The next subsections cover the four phases in sequence.

MDM Data Conversion Phase 1: Matching the Initial 70% of Records with the D&B D-U-N-S Number

The D&B Entity Matching usually is set up as a batch process, and your MDM data steward arranges for the extracts of the company name and addresses from your consuming systems and sends these to D&B for analysis. The MDM data steward soon builds up specialist knowledge of how your company structures are set up in your business applications and also how D&B Entity Matching processes are best organized.

An initial extract file is therefore produced from your prospective consuming business application and is loaded into the SAP NetWeaver MDM staging repository. The MDM Import Manager maps the relevant attributes to meet the MDM repository design, and the data is imported. The legacy system and legacy identifier are stored in the main table to uniquely identify the record.

Each of the customer and vendor records loaded into the MDM staging repository are set to an initial MDM workflow status of "Send for enrichment" and sent to D&B using the MDM Syndicator process. The records may be sent in various formats, such as an Excel spreadsheet or as a flat file using a secure flat file transfer method.

The functionality of the MDM Import Manager and the MDM Syndicator is described in much more detail later in Chapter 9.

D&B then inspects the records, goes through its batch-matching mechanisms, and returns the matched records. Typically, in the first round of D&B Entity Matching, you can expect somewhere between a 60% and 80% Entity Matching success rate. In these successful matches, a D&B D-U-N-S Number is identified with a confidence code of between 8 and 10 so that you can link it to your customer or vendor record.

In our example of the Supply Chain Management system SCM1 for Company CO1, D&B managed to match 740 out of 1,000 vendor records with a D&B D-U-N-S Number, giving an initial match rate of 74%. You will define some "success" criteria such as only accepting a D&B Entity Match if the confidence code has a score of 8 or higher. You are likely to inspect each of the 120 records where the confidence code is 8 before you send out to the business owner and users to validate the accuracy.

Table 7.2 shows an initial D&B Confidence Code report for the fictional Company CO1's SCM1 application.

	Score	Number	Percentage	Cumulative Percentage
Confidence Code	10	410	41%	41%
Confidence Code	9	210	21%	62%
Confidence Code	8	120	12%	74%
Confidence Code	7	38	3.8%	77.8%
Confidence Code	6	26	2.6%	80.4%
Confidence Code	5	12	1.2%	81.6%
Confidence Code	4	13	1.3%	82.9%
Confidence Code	3	3	0.3%	83.2%
Confidence Code	2	0	0.0%	83.2%
Confidence Code	1	0	0.0%	83.2%
Confidence Code	0	168	16.8%	100.0%
Total Confidence Codes		1000	100	100

Table 7.2 Iteration 1 – D&B Confidence Code Report Produced for SCM1 (Fictional Example)

You create a report of the successful matches and then distribute these records using the MDM Syndicator for the business users and the business owner (the head of procurement) to sign off. These records are given a new workflow status of "Successfully matched with D&B and sent to Business for sign off." The extract may be in the form of an Excel spreadsheet containing the SCM1 vendor name and address details with the D&B Worldbase details alongside for comparison. The extract also contains an Approval column for the business so sign off with a "Y" as well as a Comments field. Signing the approval column signifies that the business owner has formally signed off that these records have successfully matched.

The data is then re-imported into the SAP NetWeaver MDM staging repository through a special port with the import map containing only the MDM ID, the MDM Approval Status field, and Comments field. When the data is imported, its date and time stamped for audit purposes. Any changes made in the other columns on the Excel spreadsheet do not impact the staging repository design. In our process, we're consolidating the SCM1 business application with MDM. We can therefore change the status of the record in the MDM staging repository to "Approved – Sent to Consolidated Repository."

No further action is required for the matching process with D&B. However, depending on the reasons for the duplicates, the business may choose to clean up the duplicate records in SCM1 because there are only 680 unique D&B D-U-N-S Numbers in the 740 records. This activity is required before you can move to a centralized model.

If the duplicate records are end dated or blocked in the SCM1 application, then on the next extract of data from SCM1, these records need to be removed from both the MDM staging repository and the MDM consolidated repository. We'll discuss this process in our Lifecycle Management process later in this chapter.

We've made an impressive start with 74% of our vendor records uniquely identified automatically. Let's now consider how to resolve the data quality issues of the non-matched records.

MDM Data Conversion Phase 2: Resolving the Data Quality Issues

Phase 1 was successful in that we now have reduced our list to investigate to just 260 records instead of the original 1,000 records. The MDM workflow status is now changed to "Send to Business for Investigation – D&B Phase 1 failed to match" for these records. One of the reasons for the failure to match is probably the quality of name and address details, such as incomplete names or missing country, city, or postal code address details.

Establishing and mandating the data entry standards for complete and accurate business name and address data is a key building block for a successful MDM program. However, in the current practices, Company CO1 business users often key the minimal vendor information into a business application as a shortcut to save time, especially if the full details are not readily available. If a country, a postal code, a street, or a city are not mandatory fields and are not provided on a request form, they are omitted from the data entry process.

The business names that are set up may also be partially completed; for example, a system may limit a name field to say 30-50 characters, and a legal name can be over 100 characters in length.

Data may have been automatically added via batch processes to the SCM1 application due to, for example, a previous merger or acquisition or a previous data conversion exercise. Unfortunately, the vendor records were not fully validated due to time constraints before loading, which has caused significant problems for the retrieval and management of the SCM1 vendor data records.

The business data owner may decide to correct the erroneous data in the SCM1 system directly and then to arrange for another extract, which is the cleanest approach. However, if the SCM1 system only has a limited lifespan, and the update processes are cumbersome and expensive, you may decide instead to update the MDM syndicated spreadsheet directly and then to re-upload.

This approach is achievable if managed in a controlled way, and you store the modified data in a separate qualified look-up table (in this scenario, there will be separate qualified look-up tables for the original SCM1 name and address, the D&B legal name and address, and the "cleansed" name and address). Again, you look to the business owner to sign off this iteration of cleansing.

The next iteration of data is imported either from SCM1 or the "intermediate" Excel spreadsheet. The MDM Workflow status for the records is changed to "Data verified by the business – send to D&B for Phase 2 matching."

This MDM Syndication process now re-extracts the 260 records and resends them to D&B. The good news is that when the D&B Entity Matching process is repeated, 80 new records are successfully identified with D&B D-U-N-S Numbers, increasing the total up to 820 successful matches.

Once again, you repeat the approval exercise at the end of Phase 1. The extract may be in the form of an Excel spreadsheet, which contains an "Approval column" for the business so sign off with a "Y" and a comments field. The data is then re-imported in the MDM staging repository through a special port with the import map containing only the MDM ID and the MDM Approval Status and comments fields. The records are date and time stamped in the MDM repository, and you change the status of the MDM workflow to "Approved – Sent to Consolidated Repository."

MDM Data Conversion Phase 3: Batch Use of the D&B Enrichment Architecture

So far we've been using the batch D&B Entity Matching process to identify the appropriate D&B D-U-N-S Numbers, and these numbers have been retrieving records with a confidence code of 8 to 10.

Now let's try a different method, using the D&B MDM Enrichment Architecture but in a "batch-like" way. You can submit the remaining 180 records in smaller batches using the Web Services process and set up the parameter to accept candidate records with the low confidence codes.

Through this process, you can now identify several D&B candidate records, each of which potentially could be the record we're looking for. The MDM data steward now manually processes these records to see if the relevant D&B D-U-N-S Numbers record has been found. This is similar to the usual online look-up processes and follows the same MDM workflow steps.

This method matches 40 more records, taking your total up to 860 records.

Over time, as your MDM repositories become more complete with the entire list of your customers and vendors, you'll rely less on the batch processes and much more on the operational D&B MDM Enrichment Architecture. By sending multiple batched requests, you can speed up the process to ensure a consistent approach between the data conversion approach and the live operational services.

We'll now consider the fourth phase of the data conversion, the manual investigations, in the following section.

7.1.6　Validate Results

As previously stated, the overall aim of the process is to ensure that each third-party vendor and customer record in your business applications is accurately matched to the correct D&B D-U-N-S Number. By using the D&B Entity Matching and the D&B D-U-N-S Number in this way, you're ensuring that each of your vendor's legal entities are uniquely authenticated. The head of procurement signs off on this.

However, it's likely that approximately 10 to 15% of the records in your SCM1 application cannot easily be matched to a D&B D-U-N-S Number. There are several reasons for this, as described next.

MDM Data Conversion Phase 4: Manual Investigations

The only thing to do is inspect each of the 140 records in turn. We'll discuss the reasons for this further in the next section as we validate the results of the MDM matching exercise.

The business partner name and address on your existing record is for a different type of partner account. For a vendor, this may be a purchase ordering address or an address to which payments are sent. In the case of a customer record, it may be a ship-to (or delivery) address, a bill-to (or invoicing) address, or a payer (or payment) address. This often accounts for many of the exceptional cases. You may find one large company with 10 or more ordering addresses or payment addresses set up on the consuming system.

For these records, you have various approached to consider. You may decide to change the records in the SCM1 application to reflect the company's legal structure. Another approach is to manually find out the legal entity that the purchasing address is linked to and then to store the D&B D-U-N-S Number on the purchasing address as well.

Over time, a company may merge, change its name, or move its address. A business partner record in the SCM1 system may have been created several years ago and has not been updated to reflect this. This type of scenario will take some time for the business users to research. In this situation, you should update the records in SCM1 with the latest company details. The updated address will be extracted in the next iteration of the data conversion and imported into the MDM staging repository, and then the record is resent to D&B. For these individual cases, you should individually match them to the D&B D-U-N-S Number using the MDM D&B Enrichment Architecture Web Service.

Relationships with individuals (natural persons) may be set up in the same SCM1 system tables as the company's legal entities. D&B won't recognize these types of records. Natural person's information should be differentiated from third-party companies, and every effort should be made not to send these records to D&B because there are data protection and data privacy rules that must be complied with. In these cases, if possible, you should separate the natural persons into a different vendor type or account group in your SCM1 business application.

Finally, it may be the case that D&B does not have the legal entity set up in the Worldbase database. The reasons already given are more likely to explain why a record cannot be matched to a D&B D-U-N-S Number, but in a small number of developing countries and regions, the D&B match rate may not be as high. Also, in certain circumstances, your business partner may be a brand-new startup company that has yet to be investigated by D&B.

In these exceptional cases, you agree on policies and procedures with D&B, who investigates if the company is a valid one, creates a new D&B D-U-N-S Number in the D&B Worldbase database, and then makes it available to you to import into your MDM repository. This is a different kind of workflow, and it may take two weeks before you can obtain a D&B D-U-N-S Number, so you need to design a separate process for these situations. You may decide to create the record in the consuming system upfront and then update the record with the D&B D-U-N-S Number details when they become available.

Figure 7.3 shows the entire D&B Entity Matching business approval workflow through the four phases. You can see how by combining the end user data cleansing and validation processes with the various D&B look-up techniques, you can progress to an end state of 100% D&B D-U-N-S Numbers authenticated against your business partner records and approved by the business owner.

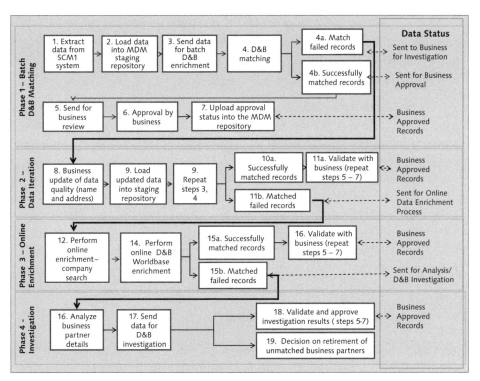

Figure 7.3 D&B Entity Matching Processes by Phase

Let's now consider how you keep your MDM staging repository in line with your consuming systems throughout the conversion phases.

7.1.7 Monitor the Migration Processes

Repeated extracts of data from your consuming systems is part of the data migration process. These iterative extracts are likely to take place monthly or every six weeks during the conversion process. Each time new extracts are produced, during the MDM import process, you manage three different types of maintenance changes.

New records are created in the consuming systems that now need to be stored in the MDM staging repository. These incremental or delta records follow through the same four phases of identification to link to the correct D&B D-U-N-S Number.

There are *updated records* where the name and address has changed in the consuming system since the previous iteration. If the D&B D-U-N-S Number has not yet been found, the existing name and address should be updated in the MDM staging repository and the record reprocessed through the matching phases.

Finally, there will be *deleted records,* which were originally sent through on the extract file but have subsequently been blocked or end dated. If the D&B D-U-N-S Number has not yet been found for these records, then the record can be deleted from the MDM staging repository.

You will need three sets of skilled people to analyze the manual investigations. The business users resolve the data inaccuracies and feed the revised details into the MDM staging repository. The MDM data stewards ensure that the revised data is uploaded and that the outstanding MDM workflow items are progressed. During the MDM Data Conversion Phase 1 and Phase 2, you also need the help of a D&B data analyst to provide you with the batch D&B Entity Matching files and the confidence code reports.

Let's now consider the ongoing data maintenance of the MDM staging, consolidated, and the centralized repositories.

7.2 Ongoing Data Maintenance

In this section, we'll consider the various techniques you use to maintain your three MDM repositories. We'll discuss how the MDM repositories are maintained in a consistent manner and how the role of the MDM staging repository differs from the MDM consolidated and the MDM centralized repositories. We'll discuss how the data integrity in the MDM staging repository is maintained through the use of SAP NetWeaver MDM workflows.

We'll consider how you manage the Lifecycle Management processes, including both updates to the external company details, which are maintained by D&B, and updates in the consuming system, as a result of your company either transacting with new business partners or ending relationships with previous partners. Well also cover how you introduce an initial Phase 0 into the MDM data conversion process so that you can now search your MDM staging repository to find out if the company already exists in MDM before sending the request off to D&B.

Let's get started by discussing the design of the MDM repositories architecture.

7.2.1 MDM Repositories Architecture

In Figure 7.1, you saw both an MDM consolidated repository and an MDM centralized repository. If you are in the process of migrating to a new SAP ERP business application and are close to the final stages of the deployment, you copy the approved data to the MDM centralized repository.

The disadvantage of the MDM centralized repository, however, is that you are dependent on the SAP ERP deployment program. Because these can be large and complex programs, you may have cleansed the data long before the go-live.

In such a scenario, you should continually write the approved records to the MDM consolidated repository during the SAP ERP deployment process. This means that you only have to match the record once; when it has been processed, the record is available to be retrieved using the MDM company search. The record is initially mapped to the "soon to be legacy" system as the consuming system with the key mapping field being the legacy vendor or customer number taken from that system.

If you move your records to the MDM consolidated repository, then when the SAP ERP application cuts over to go-live, the records are imported into the MDM centralized repository. An advantage of the MDM centralized approach is that if you also decide that MDM will externally generate the new vendor and customer numbers for a SAP ERP 6.0 implementation, then these can be loaded as an early cutover activity. You are then in a position to notify your customers and suppliers of their new identifying numbers ahead of the SAP ERP deployment and actual go-live.

You must decide on your strategies for the maintenance of each of the MDM staging, consolidated, and centralized repositories. Key design questions to consider include the following:

► Do you keep all requests in the MDM staging repository and all approved records in the MDM consolidated repository?

► At the time of go-live of the new SAP ERP application, do you keep the key mapping of the legacy system for a period or do you just store this in the SAP ERP record?

A requirement is that whichever MDM Enrichment Architecture design you decide upon, your MDM company search functionality will only retrieve and present the relevant current key mappings that are "live" in your various business applications.

7.2.2 Driving Data Integrity Through SAP NetWeaver MDM Workflows

We've described several workflow statuses throughout the migration process. There are typically fewer statuses for the online process as compared to the batch process, and we'll introduce Phase 0 shortly. Let's now consider the different MDM workflow statuses as shown in Table 7.3.

As you can see, there is an approval process in each of the phases. The date and time and the approver details can be stamped on the record when it's moved to the MDM consolidated repository to provide an audit trail of who agreed, to what, and when. This is particularly helpful for the MDM data steward when there is a subsequent query of a data record in the MDM repository and also enables the "match a record to the correct D&B D-U-N-S Number once" principle, which will save considerable data migration effort.

MDM Data Conversion Phase	Workflow Steps
Phase 0: Batch MDM Repository Company Search	0_Requested 0_Approved 0_No_Match_MDM_Search 0_Under_Business_Review
Phase 1: Match the Initial Extract Records with Batch D&B Entity Matching	1_Sent_to_DnB_Batch 1_Under_Business_Review 1_Approved 1_No_Match_DnB_Batch
Phase 2: Resolve the Data Quality Issues and Second Round of batch D&B Entity Matching	2_Under_Business_Review 2_Sent_to_DnB_Batch 2_Approved 2_No_Match_DnB_Batch
Phase 3: Queue Up Requests in the D&B Enrichment Architecture	3_Sent_to_DnB_web_enrichment 3_Candidates_to_Select_From 3_Under_Business_Review 3_Approved 3_No_Match_DnB_web_enrichment
Phase 4: Manual Investigations	4_Under_Business_Review 4_Approved (** Phase 4 will see an iteration back to Phase 3 on a case-by-case basis)

Table 7.3 MDM Workflow Statuses by Data Conversion Phase

Reports of the workflow status can be regularly produced using the MDM Syndicator. These reports update you as to the latest number of records currently at each MDM workflow status. A detailed report showing all of the "to be approved" records will assist your MDM data stewards.

7.2.3 Lifecycle Management

Throughout this book, we've been repeatedly saying that Lifecycle Management is extremely important for MDM. The data in your MDM repositories must be accurate, comply with your data standards, be complete, and most importantly be kept up to date. Your MDM repositories have to contain simply the best customer and vendor data records in your company!

There are three types of changes you will need to consider in your MDM repository design:

▶ Changes to the external company details, which are maintained by D&B

▶ Changes in the consuming system details as a result of you transacting with new business partners or ending relationships with previous partners

▶ Changes in MDM due to the way you deal with a consuming system's records as they progresses from the MDM staging repository to the MDM consolidated repository and finally to the MDM centralized repository

Let's consider each of these types of changes in turn.

Lifecycle Changes in the External Company Details

Your MDM repositories need to be kept up to date with the latest company details as maintained by D&B. By refreshing the data from D&B, you ensure that the company name and address and Corporate Linkage data is kept up to date throughout a company's lifecycle.

Lifecycle Management changes are made available to you by periodically refreshing your D&B Worldbase data (e.g., on a monthly or quarterly basis) and then importing these details into your MDM staging, MDM consolidated, and MDM centralized repositories. You can review all of the changes that have occurred and decide on the relevant actions.

As an example, if a legal name or address has changed, you can then inform the appropriate consuming systems support team and update your MDM records. Other changes such as bankruptcy or credit rating changes are also significant, and all interested parties should be notified. The D&B Corporate Linkage changes need to be reflected and syndicated to your BI application.

A carefully designed refresh strategy is an important deliverable from an MDM program. You are likely to initially store the latest D&B Worldbase file in another separate "staging" MDM repository and then produce comparison reports to highlight any changes compared to your three "live" MDM repositories. You may consider applying the master–slave architecture discussed earlier in the chapter for this purpose. After careful consideration, the latest D&B Worldbase details are then incorporated into your MDM repositories to keep them up to date. The previous D&B Worldbase details are updated with the latest version, and all changes made in this way to the MDM repositories should be easily auditable.

Lifecycle Changes for Records in Consuming Systems

There will also be changes in your consuming systems as a result of your transactions with new business partners or ending relationships with previous partners. Name and address details can also change either as a result of the MDM conversion initiative or as a normal business process. If you have an MDM consolidated model with the consuming system, you need periodic extracts of all of the active vendor and customer records. You should extract the relevant global attributes and then use the MDM Import Manager to load them into another MDM consuming system staging repository. Again the master–slave architecture may assist you in this process.

You then compare your existing MDM records in the three repositories and identify all of the new, changed, and deleted records. If your MDM design is to adopt a harmonized model where attributes such as the name and address are to be kept in line in both the MDM repositories and the consuming system, then you may also produce some exception reports using the MDM Syndicator processes.

After careful consideration, the consuming system details are incorporated into your MDM repositories to keep them up to date. As with the D&B changes, consuming system updates made in this way to the MDM repositories should be easily auditable.

Lifecycle Changes in MDM and the Consuming System

Another type of lifecycle change in MDM is the way you deal with a consuming system as its records progress from the MDM staging repository to the MDM consolidated repository and finally to the MDM centralized repository.

You may choose to keep all of your D&B records in the MDM staging repository, which means that when you try to search for a company record at the start of the data conversion process, all records are available. You need to carefully maintain your MDM workflow statuses so that you can easily differentiate between the latest records that you're currently in the process of converting, as compared to those records that were previously converted.

Similarly, you may decide to store all of the "approved" records in the MDM consolidated repository, even if they also stored in the MDM centralized repository. This approach simplifies your company search processes but also means that changes made to the MDM centralized repository must be applied to the MDM consolidated repository to ensure consistency.

As you cutover your data as part of a go-live process, you update each of your MDM repositories to reflect the current status of the MDM and the consuming system relationship. An example scenario to consider is when you cutover to a central model as part of a new SAP ERP deployment, when you were previously following a consolidated model with the legacy system.

Let's now move on to consider how the SAP NetWeaver MDM data matching strategies can help you with your data conversion.

7.2.4   SAP NetWeaver MDM Data Matching Strategies

SAP NetWeaver MDM matching strategies become helpful to you when you've already identified a set of D&B D-U-N-S Numbers that your organization uses and now want to match a record from a new consuming system to a record that you've already found.

Consider, for example, that your Company CO1 wants to match all of the vendors in the Financial Accounting (FI1) system with the correct D&B D-U-N-S Numbers. This exercise occurs after the Supply Chain Management (SCM1) records have already been matched.

The process is similar to the one we described earlier in the chapter, with the four phases of MDM data conversion.

- ▶ **Phase 1:** Matching the Initial Records with the D&B D-U-N-S Number
- ▶ **Phase 2:** Resolve the Data Quality Issues
- ▶ **Phase 3:** Batch Use of the D&B Enrichment Architecture
- ▶ **Phase 4:** Manual Investigations

However, there is an initial MDM data conversion Phase 0 to consider, which is described next.

MDM Data Conversion Phase 0: Batch MDM Company Search

When using the online MDM vendor registration workflow processes, an initial step in your process is to search your MDM repository to find out if the business partner already exists. If you can retrieve the record, then the vendor setup process now becomes a distribution request of an existing MDM record to a new consuming system. This is the quickest and best process because it avoids the need for a repeated D&B enrichment process and also prevents the creation of duplicate records at the source.

You now need to adopt a similar kind of process for the management of batch records. The SCM1 and FI1 business applications have many matching vendors as the SCM and FI functions usually combine in an end-to-end process. You would expect at least 80% of the FI1 records are also in the SCM1 business application in an integrated organization.

MDM also provides many helpful normalizing and standardizing functionalities that you can use to match the FI1 records against the MDM staging repository to create candidate records. If an SCM1 key field is also stored on the FI1 business application, this also improves and simplifies the matching process.

Let's now compare how the successful matching record counts compare during the MDM data conversion phases for the SCM1 and FI1 business applications, as seen in Table 7.4.

Data Conversion Phases	SCM1 – Cumulative Total	FI1 – Cumulative Total
Phase 0: Batch MDM Company Search	0	680
Phase 1: Matching the Initial Records with the D&B D-U-N-S Number	740	845
Phase 2: Resolve the Data Quality Issues	820	875
Phase 3: Batch Use of the D&B Enrichment Architecture	860	890
Phase 4: Manual Investigations	880	905

Table 7.4 Example Statistics of Record Matching by Data Conversion Phase (Fictional Example)

When the Business Intelligence (BI1) records are matched, this becomes even more straightforward. Each of the records in BI is tagged with an identifying key such as a SCM1 or FI1 vendor number. This means that you match most of the records to the D&B D-U-N-S Number during your MDM data conversion Phase 0, leaving very few records to be researched through Phases 1 to 4.

7.3   Summary

In this chapter, we discussed the processes involved in the cleansing and migration of your master data records from your consuming systems into an MDM repository. We described these data conversion processes as being the "engine room" of your MDM program requiring excellent people and processes.

We joined together many of our previous ideas. We returned to the master data silos and illustrated in detail how the three MDM repositories can be used to clean up and convert the data for our fictional Company CO1. We considered how MDM Phase 2 of the program, in which you attempt to scale your MDM solution to include all of your customer and vendor records, impacts both your MDM repository design and approach to data conversion.

We discussed how you use the D&B Entity Matching services in partnership with the MDM D&B Enrichment Architecture to authenticate each of your business partner master data records with the relevant D&B D-U-N-S Number.

We considered the importance of your SAP NetWeaver MDM repository architecture, in particular the roles of the MDM staging, consolidated, and centralized repositories throughout the data cleansing and migration processes. We discussed how the repositories are maintained in a consistent manner and how the role of the staging repository differs from the other two repositories. We discussed how the data integrity in the MDM staging repository is managed using SAP NetWeaver MDM workflows and how you will manage the Lifecycle Management processes, including both updates to the external company details and to your consuming systems.

You now have a good understanding of the iterative nature of the D&B Entity Matching process and the techniques you can use to combine business data cleansing and validation with the SAP Netweaver MDM Enrichment architecture. By appropriately maintaining your MDM staging, consolidated and centralized repositories you enable both the consolidated and centralized MDM models, as well as achieving a 100% match of your customer and vendor legal entity records with a D&B D-U-N-S Number.

Let's now move on to consider in more detail the SAP NetWeaver MDM landscape and how to approach your MDM data modeling.

Designing and building an MDM technical landscape involves careful planning and alignment with the objectives of the MDM program. In this chapter, we describe the use of features in the SAP NetWeaver MDM Console and MDM Data Manager, to develop an appropriate data model and business process workflow.

8   The SAP NetWeaver MDM Landscape, Data Modeling, and Data Maintenance

Your SAP NetWeaver MDM system landscape requires a flexible design to enable the continual provision of the MDM project execution, enhancement, and support services. Throughout the lifecycle of the MDM program, different technical environments are needed to enable the various development and support functions. In this chapter we'll describe the options for setting up an appropriate SAP NetWeaver MDM landscape during MDM Phase 1, MDM Phase 2, and beyond.

After the MDM landscape and the environments are established, your next task is to design and build the data model for the individual MDM repository where the business partner data will be stored. Your MDM repository modeling defines the structure and the properties of the data elements and provides a "container" for the complete definition of the master data record. As well as the content, the data model also sets the context of the data by providing a detailed taxonomy and hierarchy classification. We'll consider the best practices for building MDM data models supported by case studies.

The data maintenance functions for the MDM repository are provided in the MDM Data Manager. The MDM Client (or MDM Data Manger) interface provides the functionality to search, create, update, delete, and match data. The MDM Client is also where the data management workflows are modeled using Microsoft Visio as the design interface. We'll consider how to apply the features provided in the MDM Data Manager, including the workflow design functions.

8.1   MDM Technical Landscape and Data Modeling

Your MDM system landscapes are built and adapted based on your IT organization's development and deployment standards. The design is driven by the functions that the MDM solution is expected to perform in the long-term.

8.1.1   Systems Landscape for Production and Continuous Improvement (Projects)

A standard build of a system landscape includes setting up separate development, quality assurance, and production environments for MDM and the associated SAP NetWeaver Portal and SAP NetWeaver Process Integration (SAP NetWeaver PI) servers. These environments can also be augmented by specific data conversion, training, and sandbox environments.

As the first MDM solution goes live, these environments are then converted into a production stack and a separate project stack, with its own development and quality assurance environments. In this design, the project stack is the development environment for the design and build of enhancements and solutions for new master data objects. Figure 8.1 describes this landscape.

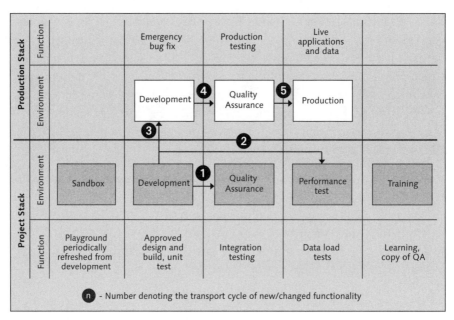

Figure 8.1 Typical MDM System Landscape in a Continuous Improvement Environment

You need a separate development and quality assurance environment in the production stack because over a period of time, major enhancements will be designed and built in the project stack development environment, including enhancements to the SAP NetWeaver MDM repository data model itself. This means that the production and the development environments won't be synchronized, and the changes can't be moved into production unless the required development and testing are completed. The cycle time for executing such MDM enhancements might be a couple of months.

Now, while this development is taking place, there may be a need for a bug fix to the already live objects. The production stack development environment now comes into the picture to enable the bug fix to be done directly into this system, and then tested and transported to the production environment. This fix can then be retrospectively made in the project stack, to synchronize it with the production stack, after the major enhancement is completed.

For enterprisewide MDM initiatives, the two-tier project/production stack MDM landscape provides the necessary flexibility to continue with the development activities while providing the live system support functions in parallel. This two-tier landscape also enables the MDM program team to maintain a holding area for future developments. It provides the flexibility so that the MDM build is synchronized with other transaction/reporting systems rollouts, in cases where the MDM program is also part of an SAP ERP 6.0 deployment initiative.

A typical transport cycle for continuous improvement initiatives in this two – tier landscape is as follows:

- **Step 1:** Approved and unit-tested changes are moved from the development to the quality assurance environment in the project stack.

- **Step 2:** When integration testing is completed, the signed-off changes are then moved to the performance test environment, which in its configuration and setup closely resembles the production server. Performance tests for the applications are then carried out in this environment.

- **Step 3:** After the performance test is completed, the changes are then transported from the project stack development environment to the production stack development environment. Unit testing of the functionality is then completed in the production stack.

▶ **Step 4:** After the unit tests are signed off, the changes are then moved from the development to the quality assurance environments in the production stack, where the business user team carries out testing.

▶ **Step 5:** Finally, when the business team signs off that the functionality meets the requirements, then the changes are moved from the quality assurance to the production environment.

Obviously, the cost of maintaining the two-tier landscape as shown in Figure 8.1 will be higher than a single-tier landscape. Careful planning is needed to evaluate the continuous improvement activities that are required for the MDM functionality to justify the need for the two-tier landscape.

Case Study to Show the Evolution of the MDM Technical Landscape

Let's introduce an implementation program illustration to show how the MDM landscape evolves as the MDM program progresses through its various phases. Company CO1, as referred to in the business case study in Chapters 2 and 4, is now embarking on an MDM journey.

Let's consider the SAP NetWeaver MDM landscape design for Phase 1, Phase 2, and finally beyond Phase 2 of the MDM program.

MDM Landscape for Phase 1

During Phase 1 of the MDM program, you design and build the solution for centralized business partner MDM services. The tasks in this implementation program and the MDM landscape where these are performed follow a defined sequence.

Firstly, you evaluate and build a trial solution in the sandbox environment. You then build a solution based on the approved design in the development environment and perform integration testing for the solution in the quality assurance environment. Performance and load tests are carried out in the mock conversion environment, and you also build a training environment as a copy of the quality assurance environment. Finally, you build the production environment and cutover the data and MDM application to the live environment.

Figure 8.2 shows the MDM landscape for Phase 1 of this MDM program.

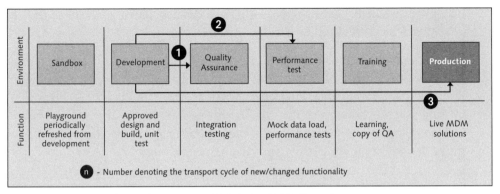

Figure 8.2 MDM Landscape for Company CO1 during MDM Phase 1

Let's now consider how the MDM Landscape changes during MDM Phase 2.

MDM Landscape for Phase 2

After Phase 1 of the project is completed, you need to provide operational support services for the live systems. Meanwhile, Company CO2 has recently been merged with Company CO1, and the mandate of the MDM program is now to integrate the centralized MDM functions into the newly merged company's business processes. This requires some significant MDM enhancements and integration with five more consuming systems. Meanwhile, the MDM program is also starting on an upgrade project to implement the latest SAP NetWeaver MDM service pack. These activities take place during Phase 2 of the MDM program.

The revised MDM technical landscape for Phase 2 needs to provide both the support services for the live processes of Company CO1 and also the enhancements required for the integration of Company CO2 master data processes into the MDM program. The two-tier landscape shown earlier in Figure 8.1 meets these requirements because it enables the streamlined testing of the upgraded functionality without affecting the production environment support operations.

MDM Landscape for "Beyond Phase 2"

When MDM Phase 2 is completed, the master data solution for business partners in the merged Company CO1/CO2 now meets the long-term business requirements for a central MDM solution. The MDM program doesn't now anticipate any major enhancements to the solution, and the focus now moves to the ongoing data governance processes and the data quality metrics.

From this point on, it isn't necessary to maintain the two-tier architecture for the MDM business partner solution. The system landscape can now be revised, and the redundant development and quality assurance environments can be decommissioned. This scales down the maintenance cost of the support services, while still providing ample environments for performing maintenance. Figure 8.3 shows the MDM landscape for this ongoing maintenance phase.

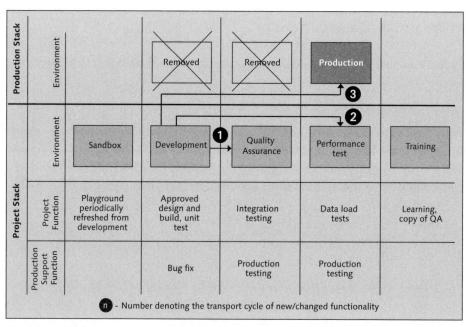

Figure 8.3   MDM System Landscape beyond Phase 2 of the Program

In this case study, we illustrated the evolution of the MDM system landscape through the different phases of the MDM program. The system landscape beyond Phase 2 will depend on the Company CO1/CO2 business strategy, which may continue to evolve with further mergers and acquisitions and the deployment of new business applications and service packs. Let's now move on to the next level of detail to understand how SAP NetWeaver MDM, the SAP NetWeaver Portal, and the SAP NetWeaver PI architectures are integrated.

8.1.2 Technical Configuration of an MDM system

The SAP NetWeaver Landscape in an MDM environment has multiple components that work together to enable the end-to-end master data management processes. Figure 8.4 shows the various SAP NetWeaver components that combine to form an integrated MDM solution landscape.

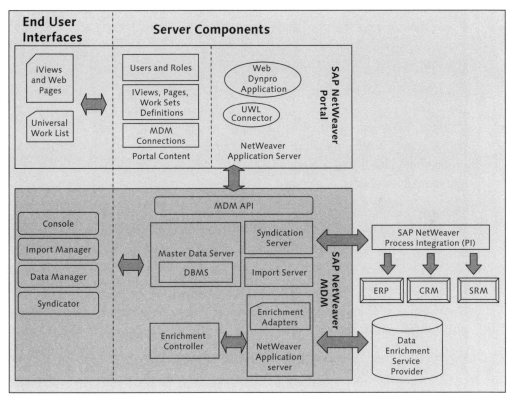

Figure 8.4 Different Components in the SAP NetWeaver Landscape for the MDM Application

We'll discuss the significance of each of these components in an MDM application environment. Our aim is to provide an overview and broad understanding of each of the components that comprise the integrated MDM environment. Let's now look at the components sequentially.

SAP NetWeaver Portal Server Components

Starting from the top of Figure 8.4, we have the end user interfaces that are enabled by SAP NetWeaver Portal. The portal server has two components, the portal content and the SAP NetWeaver Application Server, where the Web Dynpro applications are deployed.

Portal Content

The portal content consists of the definitions of the iViews, portal pages, and work sets; the Universal Work List (UWL) for managing the MDM workflow tasks; the MDM connection settings; and the portal user role definitions.

The *portal iViews* and pages provide the web-based user interface for managing master data processes. These include the search, and the create, read, update, and delete (CRUD) process iViews and pages. SAP NetWeaver MDM delivers standard business content for these processes, and the iViews can also be customized or developed from scratch depending on your business requirements. Figure 8.5 shows a sample iView.

The *Universal Work List (UWL)* is the standard portal user interface for managing the MDM workflow tasks. In the UWL, business users can execute tasks in the workflow, assign the tasks to other users, and display the MDM record details.

The *Connection Parameters* contain the definition of MDM systems and the user mappings in the SAP NetWeaver Portal server, to enable the iViews to connect to the specific MDM repositories. These parameters have to be set up before other portal content is deployed.

Portal pages and iViews are bundled together into different *portal roles,* and the roles are assigned to the business users. The roles assignment manages the access of a given user to a particular portal web page.

Web Dynpros in the SAP NetWeaver Application Server

The Web Dynpro applications contain the programming for the business logic and the user interfaces. These applications are built using the SAP NetWeaver development studio suite and are deployed in the SAP NetWeaver Application Server. When the Web Dynpro applications are executed in the portal, they provide the interfaces for the business users to perform their MDM processes.

The UWL connector for MDM interacts with the MDM server, through the MDM UWL Application Programming Interfaces (API), to enable the workflow tasks and execution methods. The UWL connector is installed in the SAP NetWeaver Application Server, and the UWL configuration file has to be maintained with the MDM parameters so that it can display the MDM tasks.

SAP NetWeaver MDM Portal Business Packages

The SAP NetWeaver MDM software delivers significant functionality in its standard portal business content, enabling you to "plug-and-play" the portal user interfaces to the MDM repositories. An example of this is the powerful search and result set display iViews and pages, which provide the freeform search, the hierarchy search, and the taxonomy attribute search of data in an MDM repository.

In your MDM system landscape, it's a good practice to install SAP NetWeaver MDM, SAP NetWeaver Portal, and SAP NetWeaver PI in separate physical servers to ensure optimal performance. This is a requirement in both the production and project stack environments.

Let's now move on to consider the SAP NetWeaver MDM application components.

SAP NetWeaver MDM Application Components

The SAP NetWeaver MDM application components can be split into the MDM user interfaces and the MDM server components. We'll discuss each of these in turn.

MDM User Interfaces

SAP NetWeaver MDM provides graphical user interfaces in the form of the MDM Console, the MDM Data Manager (MDM Client), the MDM Import Manager, and the MDM Syndicator.

The *MDM Console* enables you to monitor the MDM server through its administration function and provides you with the functionality to create and maintain the MDM repositories. The physical data modeling of the repository is performed using the MDM Console, with your typical users being the MDM solution architects and system administrators. Figure 8.5 shows the MDM Console user interface.

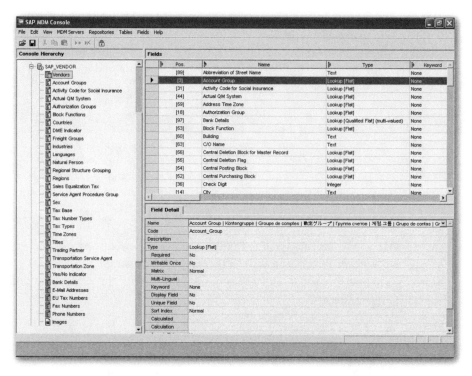

Figure 8.5 MDM Console User Interface

The *MDM Data Manager* allows your users to create and maintain the data records, taxonomies, hierarchies, and other relationships. The MDM workflows and validations are built in the MDM Data Manager, which also provides a powerful search function for accessing the master data records. MDM Data Manager is used by your MDM solution architects and the "power" business users of the system. Figure 8.6 shows the MDM Data Manager User interface, including the search window, the record overview window and the record details window.

The *MDM Import Manager* and the *MDM Syndicator* provide you with the functionality to import and distribute the data to and from the MDM repository. We'll discuss the features of these two clients in detail in Chapter 9. Figure 8.7 shows the MDM Import Manager user interface including the Source and Destination Tables Pane, the Field Mapping Pane and the Value Mapping Pane.

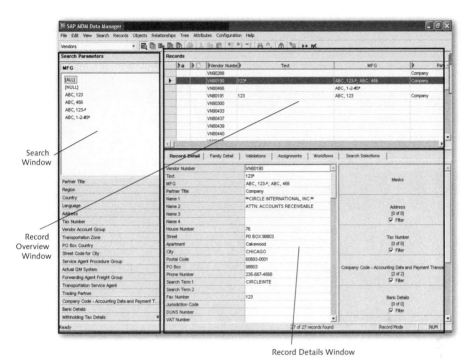

Search Window

Record Overview Window

Record Details Window

Figure 8.6 MDM Data Manager User Interface

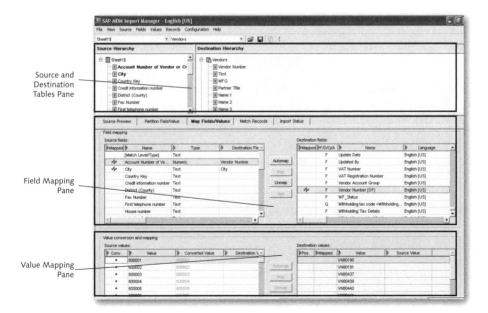

Source and Destination Tables Pane

Field Mapping Pane

Value Mapping Pane

Figure 8.7 MDM Import Manager User Interface

Figure 8.8 shows the MDM Syndicator user interface including the Search Pane, the Record Overview Pane and the Syndication Mapping and Properties Pane.

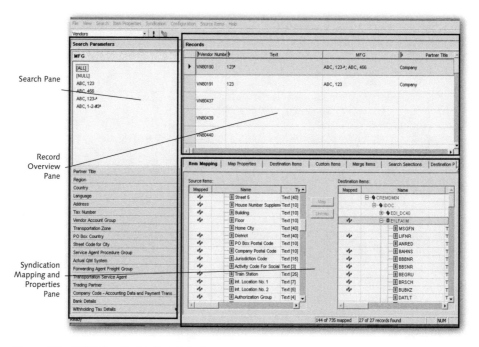

Figure 8.8 MDM Syndicator User Interface

Let's now consider the MDM server components.

MDM Server Components

The *Master Data server* is the central component that manages access to the data based on the structure defined in the MDM repositories. It interacts with the underlying SQL DBMS and has software engines for searching, validating, matching, and running the MDM workflows.

The *MDM Import server* and *MDM Syndication server* automate the task of importing and distributing the master data to and from the MDM repositories. These tasks are driven by the preconfigured import and syndication maps and also include exception handling functionality.

Extended Markup Language (XML) is the standard format by which the import and syndication processes receive and deliver the data record from MDM to the outside world. A Secure File Transfer Protocol (SFTP) server needs to be installed to transfer the XML or text files to and from SAP NetWeaver MDM to your chosen middleware.

In an SAP NetWeaver environment, this middleware is usually SAP NetWeaver Process Integration (SAP NetWeaver PI). SAP NetWeaver PI receives the XML file from the SFTP server, performs any required mapping, and converts the file into a format understandable by the receiving consuming systems. For SAP ERP, CRM, and SRM applications, the XML file is usually converted to an iDoc format by SAP NetWeaver PI.

A key capability of SAP NetWeaver MDM is its ability to interact in real time with third-party data enrichment providers such as D&B. The core module that drives the data enrichment process is the *MDM Enrichment Controller*, which controls and monitors the enrichment process. It has an API that enables you to plug in the external enrichment adapters to the MDM solution. The actions taken by the MDM Enrichment Controller are defined by the enrichment configuration file parameters, which are deployed in the MDM server.

The *enrichment adapters* are the software modules that prepare the master data record in a format that can be understood by the enrichment service provider. These modules call the enrichment Web Service and then feed the enriched data back to the controller. The enrichment adapter's software module is installed in the MDM Web Application Server (J2EE engine).

MDM Server Components Sizing

You need appropriately sized servers for each of your environments to ensure optimal performance and project execution. As a rule, the different SAP NetWeaver components — SAP NetWeaver MDM, SAP NetWeaver PI and SAP NetWeaver Portal —each need to be installed on separate hardware servers.

The SAP installation and help documentation provides you with comprehensive information on the sizing of your development, quality assurance, and production environments. You should closely research the principles and guidelines in these documents and follow the SAP installation recommendations with your company's internal operational infrastructure teams to agree on the optimal sizing.

MDM Server Configuration Parameters

The parameters that control the MDM server are maintained in the MDM server configuration file (.ini file). The three configuration files at the server level are the master data server (MDS) file, the master data import server (MDIS) file, and the master data syndication server (MDSS) file.

You need to accurately set each of the configuration file parameters for the optimal performance of the servers. The SAP NetWeaver MDM documentation provides detailed instructions concerning how to set these parameters. Table 8.1 describes the key parameters in each of the three files.

File	Parameter	Setup
MDS.ini	CPU Count	Define the actual number of CPUs in the server. This improves the data load and repository load times.
MDIS.ini	Interval	The number of seconds the MDM import server waits in between scans for new import files in the MDM server ports. A reduced interval increases the load on performance.
MDSS.ini	Interval	The number of seconds the MDM syndication server waits between scans for new files in the MDM server ports. An optimal interval is 10 seconds.

Table 8.1 Key Configuration Parameters for the .ini Files

Let's now move on to consider the key functionality of the important MDM Console.

8.1.3   MDM Console – Key Functionality

The MDM Console is used to model and administer the MDM repositories. An MDM repository is the container for a specific master data object, which holds the rich, structured information about the data records. For example, an MDM repository for vendors is designed to store the vendor attributes such as the name and address details, and you structure the information into different tables and fields. The repository also enables you to set up the context of this master data through hierarchies and taxonomy attributes. Figure 8.9 shows the structure of SAP NetWeaver MDM Console. You can see the Main Table which is the Vendors table, the Look-Up Tables such as Countries and Industries and the Qualified Look-

Up Tables such as Bank Details and Fax Numbers. You can also see the field in an MDM table and the field properties for a selected field.

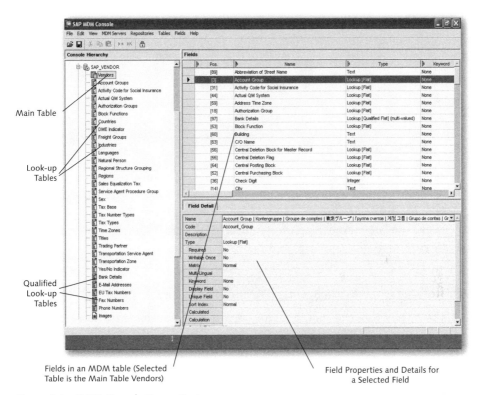

Fields in an MDM table (Selected Table is the Main Table Vendors)

Field Properties and Details for a Selected Field

Figure 8.9 MDM Console Screen Features

As of version MDM 5.5 SP06, the MDM repository can have exactly one main table, which is where the primary master data attributes are stored. For example, in the MDM vendor repository, the main table stores the vendor name and primary address details.

An MDM repository usually has multiple subtables, which are used as look-up tables and store the set of allowed values for an MDM main table look-up field. If a field is defined as a look-up field in an MDM main table, only the values defined in the corresponding subtable can be assigned to the main table record.

A subtable example is the field vendor account group in the MDM main table. The applicable vendor account groups are defined in the subtable called account groups, and this data is available for entry in the main table.

The MDM *system tables* store the administrative information about the MDM repository. Examples of system tables include roles, users, change tracking, remote systems, XML schemas, and logs.

Let's now consider how to design and build an MDM business partner repository.

8.1.4 MDM Repository Design

In Chapter 6, we discussed the data modeling standards and architecture principles to follow when designing an SAP NetWeaver MDM repository. We'll now describe the design of the MDM business partner repository for our Case Study Company CO1, which has now embarked on a central MDM program for its business partners, or customer and vendor records.

Architecture for the MDM Business Partner Repository

First, there are six agreed requirements for the MDM business partner repository design:

1. A central MDM business partner repository will be designed and built to hold the legal entity vendor and customer details, including name, addresses, and other global fields.

2. For each legal entity, the MDM business partner repository will also hold the basic company code-level data, such as the bank details and accounting information. The data will be modeled on the business partner data structure in SAP ERP and will be consumed by Company CO1's five business applications.

3. Requests for new vendors and customers will be processed using this MDM business partner repository.

4. Requests for changes to existing business partner records and for the distribution of existing records to additional consuming systems will also be enabled by this repository.

5. The request details such as the name of the requestor and the request approval details will be stored in the repository.

6. The MDM business partner repository, while processing new requests, will enrich the data with the D&B Worldbase information packet. The enrichment information to be stored will include the D&B Worldbase name and addresses, the Domestic and Global Ultimate details, and the Headquarters and Parent information.

The logical data model is shown in Figure 8.10, and this provides the key inputs for the MDM business partner repository design.

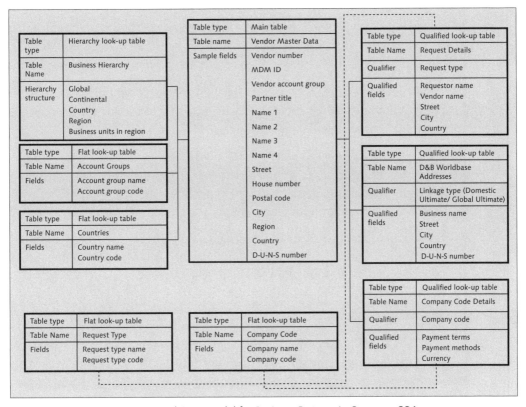

Figure 8.10 Representative Logical Data Model for Business Partners in Company CO1

Now, let's take a step-by-step approach to converting this logical data model into an SAP NetWeaver MDM repository. The first step is to define the main table, the look-ups, and the hierarchies.

8.1.5 Main Tables, Look-up Tables, and Hierarchies

A good feature of the SAP NetWeaver MDM software is that it delivers standard MDM business content in the form of preconfigured repositories. The business partner repository is one of the standard repositories provided by SAP NetWeaver MDM.

The SAP NetWeaver MDM business partner repository is modeled on the SAP ERP business partner structures such as the LFA1 and LFB1 vendor tables and the KNA1 customer table. The standard repository as provided meets most of our requirements for the logical model as shown in Figure 8.5.

Main Table

The main table of your repository is the business partner. Typically, a main table record holds the information about the legal entity of the customer or vendor that Company CO1 transacts with.

The SP06 version of SAP NetWeaver MDM only allows one main table in an MDM repository. In our design, this is the primary reason to move the D&B Worldbase data package, which has more than 100 attributes, to qualified look-up tables, with the D&B D-U-N-S Number of the legal entity as the qualifying criteria.

Workflows and validations are usually executed on the main table records, although it's possible to execute them on the look-up tables as well. Matching and merging processes can also be performed on the main table records.

> **Structure of the Main and Look-up Tables**
>
> By design, the access to tables and fields in MDM is optimized for the main table. This leads to performance implications when other tables such as look-up tables or qualified look-up tables contain a large numbers of records.
>
> Your MDM repository design ensures that the majority of records are kept in the main table with the look-up tables containing only a minor part of the records in the repository. If an MDM repository has a different distribution of records, this indicates that the main table has been designed incorrectly.

The next step in the design is to decide on the required fields in the main table. As a rule-of-thumb, a good MDM repository design ensures that less than 100 fields are in the main table because more than this number may cause performance degradation. If the various attributes of a master data object can't be defined within 100 fields, then the context and relevance of each of the fields should be re-evaluated.

The advantage of using the standard SAP NetWeaver MDM business partner repository is amplified by enhancing it with the provided field definitions. Your MDM solution architect won't have to reinvent the data types that are relevant because for most of the fields, this is already available in the standard MDM repository.

Let's now consider a few rules when you define your MDM field properties to ensure good performance in an MDM repository.

Sort Indices
MDM requires extra memory and processing time to maintain sort indices. Indexing can take a lot of time during the repository load. Having larger repositories with numerous sorted fields can have a dramatic impact on the system performance, especially when it comes to importing and updating records. The fewer sort fields you use, the better your performance.

Display Fields
Display fields are used to create a nontechnical key for the main object and the subobjects and to determine the fields shown to the user for a look-up relations.

Carefully evaluate which fields to use as display fields. The combination of the display fields within a record should be a unique key in the system. The UI clients cache all of the display fields of the non-main table records. The more display fields you create, the more memory is needed.

Keyword Search
Keyword search enables a quick search for a text field in the repository. The system builds the keywords for each unique text element data in the fields to enable a keyword search. Keyword search fields add memory overhead to the system, so try to use them only where absolutely necessary.

When activating a keyword search for a field, you consider whether the set of unique words for all records in the field is fewer, or relatively fewer, than the total number of records. Fields with a unique fields setting should not have keyword search setting enabled because this adds memory load to the MDM server without adding any benefit. The same principle applies for the display fields of a look-up table where once again a keyword search won't add any value.

A business partner number field is an example of a field not to keyword because it's likely to contain a different value for every record. Consider whether to use a free-form search rather than enabling fields for a keyword search.

Calculated Fields

Calculated fields are calculated each time an MDM repository is loaded. The only exception to this is when a field has the setting "Writeable Once," but this is seldom used. The fewer calculated fields a repository has, the lower the CPU consumption during the repository load.

Also, the complexity of a calculation formula makes a difference to the CPU consumption. Although a simple calculation consumes nearly the same CPU time as a normal field, complex formulas for calculated fields can cost a lot of CPU time.

Change Tracking

The change tracking table tells the master data server (MDS) which data modifications to track. Each entry set to "Yes" causes MDS to write one or more rows to the history table in the DBMS depending on the operation. Always set the entries to "No" when tracking isn't needed.

Setting a field such as the Business Partner Name 1 field to "Yes" results in one row being written when a record is added or deleted or when that particular field is modified. Setting x fields in a table to "Yes" causes x rows to be written to the change tracking table when records are added, deleted, or modified. Figure 8.11 shows the Change Tracking Node in the SAP NetWeaver MDM Console Hierarchy and the change tracking properties for individual fields.

Look-up Tables

Reference data in our logical model are created as *look-up tables* in the MDM repository. A look-up table holds the look-up information and is usually used to define the set of legitimate values for which a corresponding look-up field in the main table can be assigned.

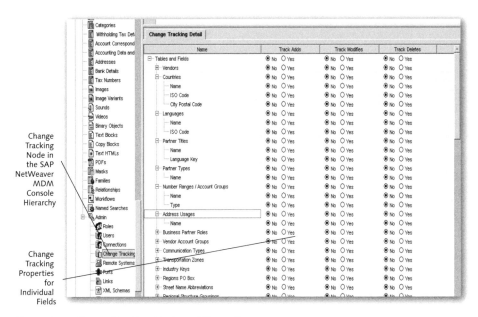

Change Tracking Node in the SAP NetWeaver MDM Console Hierarchy

Change Tracking Properties for Individual Fields

Figure 8.11 Change Tracking Node and Properties

For example, the MDM business partner repository main table includes a field called Account group. The actual list of allowed account groups is stored in a subtable called business partner account groups. Only values that exist in records of the subtable can be assigned to the value of the corresponding look-up field in the main table.

A look-up table should never be used to store thousands of records. If you consider the principle in Chapter 6 that "A well designed MDM repository should be easy to navigate and search," then this goal can't be met when look-up tables have large numbers of records. Selecting a single value from a long list in a dropdown makes navigation clumsy. Storing limited numbers of values in look-ups makes navigation easy and improves performance. The number of fields in a look-up table should be carefully considered because too many fields also make navigation difficult. Therefore, as a best practice, ensure that the number of fields in your look-up tables is limited.

For example, the regions table in SAP ERP has thousands of values in it. Talk to the relevant business process subject matter experts to determine for which countries you want the regions to be imported into the repository.

Each of the discussed conditions will influence your repository design. After evaluation, you'll decide to build the reference data in your logical model, such as countries, languages, currencies, account groups, request types, payment methods, and Incoterms to be physically stored as look-up tables. Let's now consider hierarchy tables.

Hierarchy Tables

A *hierarchy table* organizes information in a hierarchy, where each record is related to a parent record (even if the only parent is the root) and may also be related to sibling records or child records. The main table in an MDM repository typically contains some fields whose data may be hierarchical in nature. Hierarchy tables primarily contain look-up information for fields in the main table.

In our Company CO1 MDM business partner repository design, the business unit and organizational division information is designed as a hierarchy. A key criterion for maintaining data as a hierarchy is the stability of the values. If the values in a hierarchy or the hierarchy structure itself keep changing, then by linking your records to a hierarchy, you'll lose its relevance and gain unnecessary overhead. Only fixed and stable context information should be used as hierarchies in the MDM repository.

8.1.6 Qualified Look-up Tables

A qualified look-up table is a special type of MDM table that is extremely flexible and is defined to map one-to-many relationships of a main record and its subrecords. It's used to store in an efficient way the complex relationships between a business partner record of the main table and one or more look-up table entries that contain additional information regarding this record.

Using qualified look-up tables and qualifiers allow you to store a large amount of potentially sparse data. By using this approach, *n* fields from the main table can be replaced by a single qualified look-up field in the main table. This qualified look-up field takes its values from a qualified look-up table that is linked to it. The qualified look-up table has *n* records corresponding to the *n* replaced fields of the main table. Figure 8.12 illustrates an example of this with the *Bank Key* as a Qualified Record in the Main Table and the Qualified Lookup Table (Bank Key) Details.

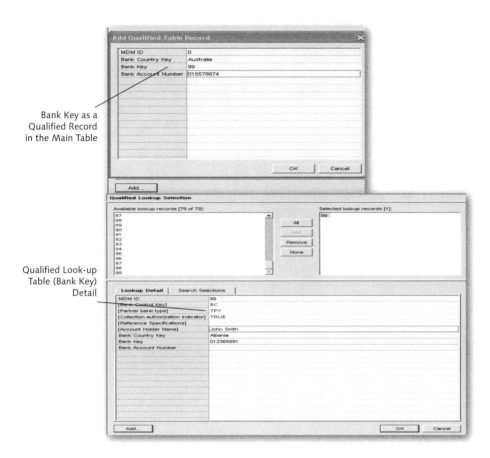

Figure 8.12 Bank Key as a Qualified Look-Up Table

A limitation in the use of qualified look-up tables is the set of look-up records rather than the qualifier fields. Again, the same principle as for the normal look-up tables can be applied, and the overall number of look-up records should be limited.

In our MDM business partner repository, the request details table can be defined as the qualified look-up table. The request type (create, change, distribute) can be taken as a "nonqualifier," and the details of the request, such as the requestor, the approver, the date of request, and so on, can be taken as qualified fields.

The D&B Worldbase package can also be defined as a qualified look-up table, with the D&B D-U-N-S Number of the legal entity and the linkage type (Headquarter,

Parent, Domestic Ultimate, Global Ultimate) as the non-qualifiers, and the name, address, and D&B D-U-N-S Number of each of these sub-records as qualifiers.

Another example is the definition of the qualified look-up table for VAT numbers. The country can be defined as a non-qualifier, and the VAT number that is applicable for that country can be taken as a qualified value.

Overhead Reduction in the MDM Repository

The MDM repositories that are preconfigured and provided by SAP are designed to support numerous languages. These languages add overheads to the system, so you should delete all unnecessary languages. Remember that a language can always be added to a repository later. If you are designing a completely new MDM repository, only activate the languages you require. In our case study, we'll activate only English as the language for the MDM repository.

The same deletion principles apply for all unnecessary preconfigured tables and fields. During the creation of a new repository, tables such as the categories table are also created automatically by the system. Some are linked to the main table and some aren't, such as the PDFs table. Standard repositories provided by SAP may contain fields that aren't required for your business process. You should also remove all unnecessary tables and fields and add them back again later if necessary.

Validate and Review the Data Model

To validate your data model, you should consider the characteristics of a well-designed repository as described earlier in the introductory section.

As well as reviewing the MDM repository structure, which is a service provided by SAP, you should also test your design on your IT/business scenarios by trying to perform business operations on the repository, such as manually creating and updating records, importing records, and syndicating records.

By navigating through the MDM repository, you get a pretty good feel about the quality of your physical design. In some cases, you may consider several design approaches, and the navigation in the MDM Data Manager helps you decide which the best approach is. Usually the easier an MDM repository can be navigated, the better the design.

Perform maintenance and search operations for several records, and see whether the MDM repository does what you originally wanted it to do and whether the business operations on the data can be easily performed. Is the data consistent, and how long does it take to create, update, and search for records?

Trying out the import and syndication operations with sample records provides you with useful insights as to how the repository will perform. Loading your repository with a limited number of records with the update indices option also gives you a good indication as to whether the repository design is sound.

Now, having considered the various design options and principles, the MDM business partner repository is complete. Figure 8.7 shows the data model for this completed design.

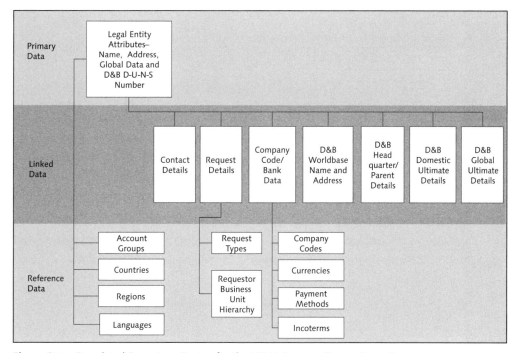

Figure 8.13 Completed Repository Design for the MDM Business Partner Repository

Let's move on to consider the key MDM Data Manager functionality.

8.2   MDM Data Manager Functions

We'll now examine the key functionality of the MDM Data Manager and consider how we design and build workflow. We'll consider other MDM features, including search and report; expressions, validations, and assignments; and data matching and merging.

8.2.1   Key Functionality

The MDM Data Manager operates in multiple modes, and each mode is designed to manipulate specific types of tables and repository information. The key modes that we'll be using to complete the build of the MDM business partner repository are the Record mode, the Hierarchy mode, and the Matching mode.

The *Record mode* allows you to search, view, and edit the records of any table in the MDM repository. This is the mode that you use most often, primarily to view and edit records in the main table, but also to view and edit records in any of the subtables.

The *Hierarchy mode* allows you to view and edit the various hierarchy tables in the MDM repository, including the regular hierarchy tables, the taxonomy tables, and the masks table. Although you can also view and edit the records of a hierarchy table in Record mode, the Hierarchy mode specifically allows you to edit the parent/child relationships and the sibling ordering of the hierarchy.

The *Matching mode* allows you to identify and eliminate duplicate records within an MDM repository. When you view the main table in Matching mode, MDM allows you to perform matching-and-merging processes on and against any or all of its records using various user-defined criteria to decide if a record is a potential duplicate or not.

Now let's consider the features of the MDM workflow design.

8.2.2   MDM Workflow Design

At the outer layer, the MDM workflows consist of a sequence of steps that allow you to orchestrate a series of operations, including user tasks, validations, and approvals, thereby automating business processes at the data management level. A core capability of the MDM workflow integrated with the enrichment model is the ability to push data for the enrichment process.

MDM workflows are a tightly integrated component of the MDM client interface, and the underlying MDM workflow engine includes a number of innovative features that makes designing, modifying, and executing workflows quick and easy for even a nontechnical MDM user. Figure 8.14 shows the Workflow Design View in the SAP NetWeaver MDM Data Manager.

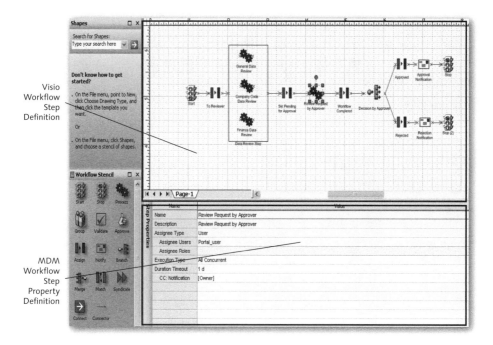

Figure 8.14 Workflow Design View

The useful workflow features are as follows:

▶ **Microsoft Visio design-time environment**
Enables a flow diagram representing a workflow to be designed using a Microsoft Visio plug-in, which makes the workflow definition directly accessible even to end users.

▶ **Task-oriented execution-time environment**
Enables workflows to move from step to step and to be presented as tasks in each user's inbound task queue within the MDM client, ready for processing.

▶ **Multi-record jobs**
Enables each workflow to be invoked as a job that can consist of multiple

records that move through the steps of a workflow as a group while simultaneously maintaining record-level granularity.

▶ **Record filtering**
Selecting each workflow task limits the records in the Records pane to just those records in the relevant job, making it easy to identify and focus in on the particular records that require processing.

▶ **User-based versus role-based execution**
A workflow step can be assigned explicitly to one or more users or can be assigned to one or more roles, which are then expanded to the applicable users during workflow execution.

▶ **Group step**
A series of steps can be organized into a single group, which eliminates much of the complexity of typical flow diagrams, given that a group step has just a single input and a single output.

▶ **Any versus all execution**
Any or all of the steps in a group can be executed, and, similarly, a single step can be performed by any or all of its assigned users.

▶ **Sequential versus concurrent execution**
The steps in a group can be executed sequentially or concurrently, and, similarly, a single step can be performed sequentially or concurrently by its assigned users.

▶ **Push versus pull model**
The receiving users can pull each task as it appears in their task queue, or the sending users can push it to a particular user.

▶ **Validations**
An MDM workflow can run a validation or validation group against the records of a job. If any of the records fails any of the validations, the job is returned to the previous step, with a Validation Result column for each validation indicating the success or failure for each record.

▶ **Approvals**
An MDM workflow can require the approval of one or more users for the records of a job. If any of the records is disapproved by any of the approvers, the job is returned to the previous step, with an Approval Result column for each approver indicating whether each record was approved or disapproved.

▶ **Notifications**

An MDM workflow can send email notifications when a step has exceeded its allotted time or a number of iterations. The notification from the owner of the workflow is sent to all assignees that have received but not yet completed the step, along with a "cc" to the specified users.

▶ **Check out/Check in**

MDM can automatically (1) check out all of the records of a workflow job when the job is launched; and then when the job has completed, either (2) check in the records; or (3) cascade the checkout to the workflow job that is launched by the workflow. Checking out records as part of a workflow allows it to proceed to completion on a private, hidden copy of the records of the job.

Steps in an MDM Workflow

Each workflow consists of a defined sequence of steps. The different types of workflow steps and connectors are summarized in Figure 8.15

Step	Name	Description
	Start	The first step of a workflow.
	Stop	The final step of a workflow.
	Process	A process step that assigns a task to one or more users or roles.
	Group	Groups steps for single, sequential, or concurrent execution.
	Validate	Performs a validation or validation group against the job records.
	Approve	Requires approval by one or more users.
	Assign	Performs an assignment against the job records.
	Notify	Sends an email to one or more users.
	Branch	Breaks a single job into multiple subjobs and threads.
	Merge	Merges multiple threads into a single thread.
	Match	Runs the matching strategy against the job records.
	Syndicate	Syndicates the job records.
	Connect	Connects from one step to another in the workflow.
	Connector	Not a step type, but used to connect two steps.

Figure 8.15 Snapshot of the Different Workflow Steps

The MDM workflow supports two types of steps, either manual or automatic. A *manual step* appears in the cascading next step menus and requires a user action before the task is manually sent to the next user in the step or the next step in the workflow.

An *automatic step* does not appear in the cascading menus and does not require user action. MDM performs the task and then automatically sends the workflow to the next step. Automatic steps include the assign, notify, validate, syndicate, and merge steps.

The MDM workflow emphasizes self-regulating logic rather than command-and-control, and features a relatively small number of step types for conceptual and design simplicity. At the same time, these simple self-contained steps can be combined to build sophisticated workflows that are flexible, configurable, and self-evident.

The validate, notify, merge connect, and merge steps are defined in Microsoft Visio and participate in workflow execution, but they are hidden from the user during runtime. For example, if *Process1* is connected to *Validate1*, and *Validate1* is connected to *Process2*, the user will see *Process2* as the next step when he is finished with *Process1* and is attempting to send the job to the next step.

MDM workflows can be triggered by various events, such as adding, updating, or importing a record. However, such event-driven process execution has its limitations and is effective only in very simple circumstances, when such events all trigger the same simple process.

Unfortunately, in most scenarios, the process flow depends on the type of update or the business intent of the change. For example, changing a vendor description may simply require approval from an MDM data steward, but changing the company code data may require the record to be approved by an accounting user and then to be distributed to a consuming system.

In this example, two very different processes must be chosen as a result of a single type of event. Moreover, as the number of variations increase, building these decisions into a single workflow that is triggered by a change event results in excessively complex and difficult-to-manage process logic.

An alternative to the event-driven approach is based on the SAP transaction model, where a user chooses the process to follow (i.e., the particular transaction) before making any changes to the data. This ensures that the correct downstream steps take place without any ambiguity for the user or the need to build complex decision logic within the process.

Within MDM, the transactional approach can be modeled by displaying a list of available workflows from which the user must choose before any modifications to the records take place. So for the example, the user would choose from the "Update Address Information" workflow or the "Modify Telephone Numbers" workflow before making the change.

This transactional approach isn't only an effective substitute for event-driven execution but is also a superior model, resulting in two very different processes managed by two distinct workflows and making clear to the user what will happen as a result of each of the actions.

Let's now discuss the search functionality provided by SAP NetWeaver MDM.

8.2.3   Search and Report

If you want to locate a particular record or set of related records in a database, then you perform a search. This allows you to view and manipulate a subset of records that matches your search selection criteria. Searches are performed from the Record mode of MDM Data Manager. Let's now describe two extremely flexible and usable types of searches in the MDM client: the drilldown search and the free-form search.

Drilldown Search

With a drilldown search, you can make selections from each search tab that corresponds to a look-up field in the main table (such as Account group or Country). You can also make selections for each of the attributes linked to a selected category and each of the qualifiers of a qualified table record. You can make your selections in any order to constrain the search results and to converge on one or more records. You can also remove search selections in any order to expand the set of search results to find similar records.

Figure 8.16 shows an example of a drill down search for the country "USA."

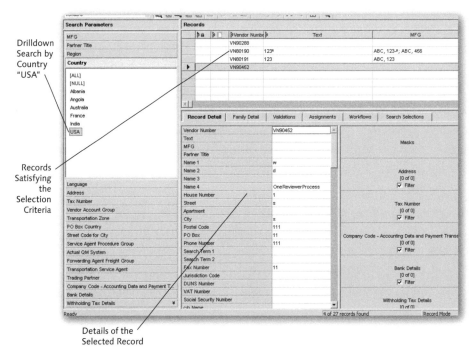

Figure 8.16 Drilldown Search

At each step along the way, the system narrows down the choice of values for each search dimension to show only those that are valid given the current result set based on the previous search selections.

This process is known as *limiting* and guarantees that you can never go down a dead-end search path. For example, if you select "USA" in the Countries tab, and then open the Business Partner Type tab, only partners in country USA will be listed. The result is an extremely flexible and powerful search capability, delivered through a smooth and intuitive process. Limiting also makes it easy to detect errors in your master data, when values that should not be part of the search results are retrieved in the limited list of existing field or attribute values.

Free-Form Search

With a free-form search, you can perform searches on any field that does not look up its values from a subtable. Free-form search also allows you to perform "fuzzy" searches with a variety of search operators. However, the downside of this approach is that you can end up with no matching records, which isn't possible with the drilldown search.

The MDM client includes the ability to save all of the current search selections to a local search in the file system and then restore them later.

Let's now discuss MDM expressions, validations, and assignments.

8.2.4   MDM Expressions, Validations, and Assignments

MDM expressions are Excel-like formulas that are evaluated by MDM and return a distinct value for each record. Using MDM expressions, you can define complex formulas based on the data values of the record and then evaluate those formulas against a group of one or more records, all without using a query language.

You can define category-specific expressions as branches of a single expression, and MDM automatically executes the applicable expression, based on the value of the category for each record. Expressions appear within MDM in a variety of contexts, including validations, assignments, and calculated fields. Unlike an Excel formula, an expression is token-based, so that you don't have to type the field, attribute, qualifier, operator, or function name, and can instead select them from dropdown lists, thus reducing the potential for typing errors.

Figure 8.17 shows an example of an MDM validation expression with the Name of the Bank Country Key being selected from the dropdown list.

Figure 8.17   Validation Expression

MDM validations are MDM expressions that return a Boolean success or failure result. Using MDM validations, you can define complex tests for all types of conditions and then run those tests against a group of one or more records, again without using a query language. You can assign each validation to one or more validation groups so that a set of validations can be conveniently executed as a group with a single selection, rather than forcing you to run each individual validation separately.

Validations offer a powerful and flexible capability to test the main table field and look-up data. Customers can create automated checks for data integrity, which are configured to meet their individual requirements. Because the scripting is easy with no programming required, changes or new validations can be written as circumstances change, without the need to involve significant IT resources. Validations can also be combined with workflows to further automate the quality assurance of the master data.

Similar to validations, *MDM assignments* are also MDM expressions, except that instead of returning a Boolean success or failure result, they can return a data value of any type. Instead of displaying the expression result for each record in a column in the Records pane, the expression result can be assigned as the value to a specified user-editable field.

8.2.5   MDM Data Matching and Merging

MDM matching functionality enables you to consolidate records within an MDM repository. Matching mode is used to identify and eliminate duplicate records within an MDM repository.

When you view the main table in Matching mode, MDM allows you to perform matching-and-merging on and against any or all of its records, using various user-defined criteria to decide whether or not the records are potential duplicates.

Figure 8.18 shows an example of this technique with some transformation rules for the Street field, a matching rule for the Postal Code field and a sample matching strategy.

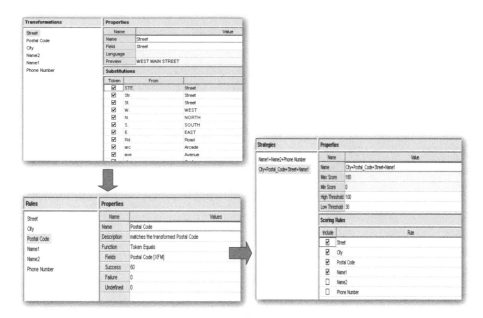

Figure 8.18 Transformations, Matching Rules, and Matching Strategies

The process of matching and merging records typically involves defining the matching strategies, including the various transformations, matching rules, and scoring thresholds that comprise each strategy. You then perform a search to narrow the set of records to just the ones you want to work on and then execute a matching strategy on any or the entire search results against any or all of the records in the repository. Finally, you merge any or all of the potential duplicates into each record.

MDM matching includes the following eight useful features:

▶ Transformations, including substitution lists

▶ Matching functions, including both exact and fuzzy operators

▶ Matching rules, including scores for success, failure, and undefined

▶ Strategies consisting of one or more rules

▶ Thresholds for a record to be considered a low or a high match

▶ Matching groups based on which records meet the thresholds

▶ Manual merge of records in the matching groups

▶ Workflow integration for applying a matching strategy to records in a job

Let's now look at a case study example, where any new business partner requests are compared against the existing D&B Worldbase records to identify potential duplicate requests. This matching process ensures that duplicate requests are captured as the first step in the MDM workflow, thus avoiding unnecessary processing.

8.2.6 Example Case Study – D&B Internal Look-Up Leveraging MDM Matching Strategies

Let's consider our example where your SAP NetWeaver MDM business partner repository stores the D&B Worldbase records in the main table. Your MATCHING strategy compares the new business partner requests with the existing D&B records to arrive at possible match hits. These hits are evaluated by the business users, and a decision is made as to whether to process the new request or to continue with enriching the record.

As described in the previous section, the first step in this matching strategy is to define the transformations, matching rules, and matching strategies.

Step 1: Character Transformation

Many data elements, such as names and search terms, often contain special characters that don't have any semantic meaning, such as dots, hyphens, and commas. Because these will potentially prevent identical real-world entities from being matched in a system, these special characters need to be removed. In this example, you apply the character transformation for the business partner name, which normalizes the Name field.

Step 2: Rules Definition

Each matching rule is identified by its name, and rules can be created from single or multiple fields. You use "equals" or "token equals" for matching and assign different scores, depending on the success or failure of the match. "Equals" matches the content of a complete field whereas "Token equals" splits the text into tokens and then searches for a match on each token in the field.

You can select one or more fields for a matching rule. You select the relevant fields for the current matching rule, with transformed fields also displayed in the list.

You can identify these transformed fields by their name, which is the transformation name with the suffix [XFM].

In our example, the transformed names of the business partner can be compared in the "Token equals" mode, to compare distinct parts of the business name of the partner. You assign scores for the result of the rule execution. A "Success" score defines the score if there is a match, and a "Failure" score defines the score if there is no match. Negative values can also be assigned, as can "Undefined" scores if the content of a field is compared with a NULL value. In our business partner name comparison, the success score is 50, failure is 0, and undefined is also 0.

You also define the rule for comparing the D&B D-U-N-S Number of the new request with the D&B D-U-N-S Number of the existing records. The success score is 50, failure score is –20, and undefined score is 0. This indicates that if the D&B D-U-N-S Number does not match, the probability of the two records being a match is considerably less.

Step 3: Strategy Definition

Your matching strategy combines the defined rules and executes the matching. When a strategy is executed, the minimum score and the maximum score are calculated automatically to get the sum of all individual matching rules in this strategy. You can also define the low threshold and high threshold limits to classify the matching results. Anything that falls below the low threshold won't be displayed as a match.

In this example, you combine the D&B D-U-N-S Number and the business partner name comparison role to execute the strategy. The different types of matching are listed here:

▶ **Selected versus Selected**
  Matches the selected records with each other.

▶ **Selected versus Results**
  Matches the selected records with the record set derived from a search criteria.

▶ **Selected versus All**
  Matches the selected records with all records in the repository.

▶ **Results versus Results**
  Matches all records that result from the search criteria.

▶ **Results versus All**
Matches all records that result from the search criteria with the records in the repository.

In this example, you execute the match type Selected vs. All, which compares the new record with all existing records in the MDM repository. If a match is identified, then the match results are displayed in the matching pane of the MDM Data Manager.

Thus, by executing MDM Matching, potential duplicates can be identified when new business partner requests are created. SAP NetWeaver MDM also provides a matching API, which can execute the matching automatically from the SAP NetWeaver Portal.

8.3 Summary

In this chapter, we discussed the SAP NetWeaver MDM system landscape and how throughout the lifecycle of the MDM program, different technical environments are required to facilitate the various development and support functions. We described the options for setting up an appropriate SAP NetWeaver MDM landscape during MDM Phase 1, MDM Phase 2, and beyond.

We considered how to design and build an appropriate data model for an MDM repository using the MDM Console, with the business partner repository as our example. As well as the content, we described the context of the data, by providing a detailed taxonomy and hierarchy classification. We highlighted the best practices for building MDM data models, supported by case studies.

We discussed how the MDM Data Manager provides the functionality to search, create, update, delete, and match data. MDM workflows were considered using Microsoft Visio as the design interface. We described several other MDM Data Manager features, including search and merge-and-matching.

You now have a detailed understanding of the MDM Console and MDM Data Manager features and how these can be used to create an appropriate repository design for your program. This includes best practices in the use of the main table, look-up tables and qualified look-up tables.

Let's now move on to consider some more technical features, including the MDM Import Manager, the MDM Syndicator, and the SAP NetWeaver MDM D&B Enrichment Architecture.

In this chapter, we describe the MDM data integration and enrichment processes. Using example business scenarios, we explain the key functionality of the SAP NetWeaver MDM Import Manager, MDM Syndicator, and the MDM D&B Enrichment Architecture.

9   SAP NetWeaver MDM Data Integration and Enrichment

MDM data integration drives the information exchange between your central MDM repository and your consuming business applications; it also includes the SAP NetWeaver MDM import and syndication processes. Data enrichment is performed using the SAP NetWeaver MDM Enrichment Architecture.

The *MDM Import Manager* is a powerful graphical user interface tool that allows you to import data from virtually any flat or relational electronic source file and to completely restructure, cleanse, normalize, and rationalize the raw data into rich master data as part of the process.

You'll use the SAP NetWeaver MDM import processes to transform your master data records from a remote system into a suitable format of sufficient quality to load into your MDM repository. SAP ERP 6.0 provides a special MDM transaction with the relevant MDM details, and then SAP NetWeaver Process Integration (SAP NetWeaver PI) transforms the message format to XML and the messages to the MDM file system. There are two different types of import processes with the interactive import allowing you to manually map your field values and records, whereas the automated import uses a previous mapping, which is already proven and tested.

The *MDM Syndicator* is also a powerful graphical user interface tool that allows you to select certain records from an MDM repository and restructure them into a specific format to meet the requirements of a remote consuming system, without modifying the source data itself. You can also use the MDM Syndicator to create reusable syndication maps, so that the actual syndication of data can be performed by users without in-depth knowledge of the data or its structure.

The SAP NetWeaver MDM Syndicator also provides prepackaged business content for data distribution to the major SAP business applications such as ERP 6.0, CRM, and SRM. You use the syndication process to export the master data from MDM to SAP NetWeaver PI using the MDM Syndicator, and then SAP NetWeaver PI distributes the data to the specified SAP ERP 6.0, CRM, SRM, or SAP NetWeaver BI remote consuming system. Again, you can choose between an interactive distribution and an automated distribution, and you can automate the entire syndication process using the SAP NetWeaver MDM syndication server.

A fundamental part of SAP NetWeaver MDM's core capabilities is providing an infrastructure that supports integration with third-party services that support data enrichment services and processes. In this process, MDM sends data elements to an external data enrichment provider and then receives a response containing data to be updated or inserted into a repository.

In this chapter, we'll consider these three integration processes in detail. Let's start by considering the MDM Import Manager.

9.1 MDM Import Manager

Historically, aggregating raw data and improving the data quality into something that deserves to be described as "rich master data" has been an expensive and almost insurmountable challenge. This data-improvement activity often requires a large amount of manual preprocessing that then needs to be repeated for each source data file. In addition, direct user intervention is usually required for exception handling on a record-by-record basis, when the records are actually imported.

Unfortunately, the requirements for a 100% clean import of data that meets all of your data standards are rarely if ever met, and so the master data aggregator must perform a series of labor-intensive preprocessing steps that can take several hours or even days. This activity is required to sufficiently manipulate, massage, and transform the source data into a format that can be properly handled by the import tool. Additionally, during record-at-a-time imports, the import tool needs to flag each discrepancy or unexpected value for exception handling, which means that the import can never proceed smoothly without interruption.

It's these previously difficult challenges that the MDM Import Manager helps you to overcome.

You use the SAP NetWeaver MDM import process for master data objects from an SAP remote system using a special MDM transaction for sending mass IDoc messages (SAP ERP) or client proxy XML messages (CRM and SRM).

SAP NetWeaver PI then transforms the message format to XML and transfers the messages to the MDM file system. You then import the objects to MDM from the XML messages in the MDM file system (ports). The MDM import handles both the loading of the master data records and associated look-up records.

You can choose between the interactive and the automated types of import. For the *interactive import*, you use the MDM Import Manager to map fields, values, and records manually before each file is imported. Figure 9.1 shows the three steps of how to select the mapping tab in the MDM Import Manager screen, map the source field to the target repository field and map the source field values to the repository look-up values.

This method is recommended when you initially load files from new sources, and the MDM Import Manager maps have to be continually adapted. The SAP NetWeaver MDM software provides prepackaged business content to assist with these import processes, which includes the import maps for the major SAP ERP, CRM, and SRM master data objects.

When you use the *automated import*, the MDM import server performs an automated import of the records from the file; this method is recommended for delta loads of data, when the mapping exercise is already completed.

If you choose to use an SAP predefined repository and you don't change the original data model, you can use the automated import from the beginning. However, this is an unlikely scenario given our discussions in Chapter 8 as to how to set up an optimal data model by deleting unused fields from the main table to improve and optimize performance.

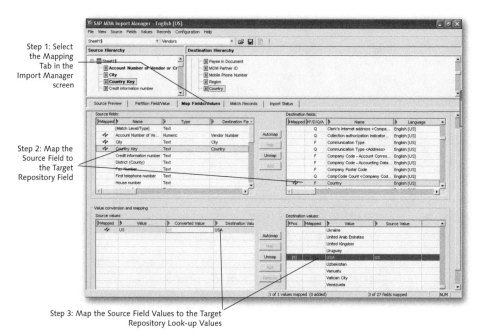

Step 1: Select the Mapping Tab in the Import Manager screen

Step 2: Map the Source Field to the Target Repository Field

Step 3: Map the Source Field Values to the Target Repository Look-up Values

Figure 9.1 MDM Import Manager Mapping Screen

9.1.1 Key Functionality

The MDM Import Manager features an intuitive and highly efficient user interface coupled with innovative functionality that reduces the time and effort required to import raw electronic data by a factor of up to 1,000 times. Instead of performing the import one record at a time, as with other import tools, you can preprocess the source data one field at a time, which can dramatically reduce the amount of time (from several hours to a few minutes) spent processing each source data file.

SAP NetWeaver MDM Import Manager provides several key capabilities that you can consider using. You can combine information from multiple tables, create a pivot table, reverse pivot table, and map fields and values. Additionally, you can convert data types and data values and create measurement values.

Splitting and combining fields provides some useful options. You can split a single field to expand a hierarchy into multiple fields or even into multiple data values. You can combine two fields to build a hierarchy, reconstitute a hierarchy, or create value combinations or a multi-valued field. Additionally, you can combine fields to merge values. Figure 9.2 shows how you can import a source file in the form of a flat table containing a Country/Region/City combination and partitioning the source table to build the data in a hierarchical form.

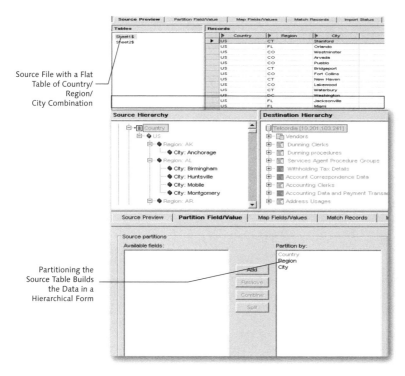

Source File with a Flat Table of Country/Region/City Combination

Partitioning the Source Table Builds the Data in a Hierarchical Form

Figure 9.2 Partitioning a Source Table to Build a Hierarchy

Further functionality for you to consider is the import of attribute data as name/value pairs and match record processing.

Let's now consider two challenges that you'll face when you try to import master data records into MDM and how these innovative functions can help you.

▶ **Challenge 1 – Multiple Source Tables:** All of the source data fields to be imported do not belong to a single source table. In this scenario, the solution may be to initially join the tables together and then to look up fields from each look-up source table into the primary source table, to create virtual extended source records (containing both primary table fields and look-up fields) before importing. Alternatively, the source tables may be "flattened" into a single table as a preprocessing step in your external application.

303

For example, you might consider importing vendor records from an SAP ERP 6.0 environment from the vendor general data and the address data tables. The general vendor data is stored in the LFA1 table, and the address data is stored in ADRC and other multiple address tables. In a typical import scenario, these files have to be extracted separately from the tables and then joined together.

Import Manager Solution: Source data can be imported as multiple tables and combined using the table join and look-up features of the MDM Import Manager. This eliminates the need to "pre-flatten" the source data in an external application.

Figure 9.3 illustrates this by joining the *Company Code* details from three source files to link the *Tax Code, Exemption Rate* and *Vendor Number* details.

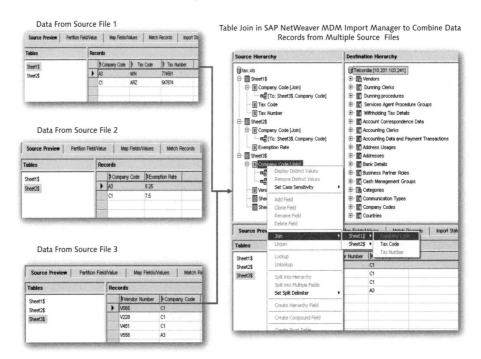

Figure 9.3   Table Join Feature in Import Manager

▶ **Challenge 2 – Look-up Values:** When mapping to destination fields whose values are from a fixed domain of valid values, such as look-up fields and text attributes, the corresponding source and destination values may not precisely match, and some source values may not currently exist as destination values.

For example, the source values USA, UK, and FRA correspond to destination values United States, England, and France, respectively, whereas the source value MEX does not yet have a corresponding destination value.

In this case, a record-at-a-time import tool flags each discrepancy for exception handling during the import process, and the MDM user tediously identifies the corresponding destination value manually or indicates that a new value should be created to correspond to the source value. Alternatively, the data must be meticulously cleansed and scrubbed as a preprocessing step in the external source application.

Import Manager Solution: Source fields that contain text values and are mapped to look-up fields or text attributes can be mapped not only at the field level but also at the value level against the domain of legal destination values, thus eliminating the need to precleanse the source data. For each field, the MDM Import Manager collapses the set of all values across the entire set of source records down to the set of distinct values, whose number is usually dramatically smaller than the total number of records, often by several orders of magnitude.

Let's now consider how to import classifications and attribute data and how to build a hierarchy from a set of fields containing "flattened" hierarchy data.

9.1.2 Import of Hierarchies

Let's consider an example of a non-SAP application, which has information on the core services provided by its vendors in multiple subtables. The information in the source file consists of two fields that classify the vendor type (such as manufacturing, service, agents) and the type of business for each type (such as spare parts supplier, raw materials supplier, health and safety supplier, consulting service provider, or catering service provider).

The SAP NetWeaver MDM design has decided to map this structure into a standard UNSPSC hierarchy structure. The United Nations Standard Products and Services Code (UNSPSC) hierarchy was created for coding and structuring products and services based on industry standards. If vendors are classified based on this structure in MDM, then this information can be distributed to the reporting BI applications. This enables you to segregate and aggregate your procurement expenditure by category of items or services.

An additional benefit is that you can introduce a quick search and discovery of your approved suppliers for a particular category of products or services. The following four-step process explains the procedure for mapping and importing this data as a standard UNSPSC structure.

Step 1: Define Your UNSPSC Hierarchy

You've decided to use UNSPSC hierarchies as the standard way of classifying vendor business operations. The UNSPSC hierarchy has a four level structure with around 28,000 leaf nodes, and not all these classification are applicable for your company's classification of vendors.

So, as a first step, you evaluate the UNSPSC hierarchy with your MDM data analysts and define a reduced structure that is applicable for your company. For vendor classification, it may not be necessary to go to the lowest level of granularity for products and services, and it's sufficient to stop the classification at the family level.

After the correct level and node structure of the UNSPSC hierarchy is finalized, it's imported into SAP NetWeaver MDM using the MDM Import Manager. The hierarchy structure is commonly available as an XML structure, so the import into SAP NetWeaver MDM is a straightforward process.

Step 2: Import Your Classification Data

You'll also import the classification source data into MDM using the SAP NetWeaver MDM Import Manager. The source data in this case is a parent-child relationship table with node names, as shown in Table 9.1.

Parent	Category	Subcategory	Node Name
01			Manufacturing
01	01		Spare Parts
01	01	01	Electrical
01	02		Consumables
01	02	01	Oils and Lubricants
02			Services
02	01		Information Technology
02	01	01	SAP Consulting

Table 9.1 Structure of Classification in the Source File

Step 3: Create MDM Hierarchies

As the third step, you use the *Create Hierarchy* function in the MDM Import Manager to create a hierarchy using this parent-child relationship. The source file data is now modified to represent the linked table structure into a hierarchy. New fields are added to the source file, which represent this hierarchy as shown in Figure 9.4.

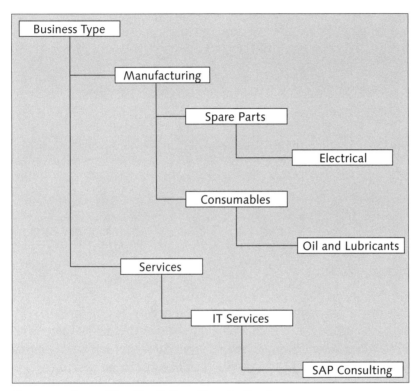

Figure 9.4 Source File with a Built up Hierarchy Structure

Step 4: Perform Value Mapping

The fourth step is to perform a value mapping of this newly created source structure with the imported UNSPSC hierarchy structure using the SAP NetWeaver MDM Import Manager *Value mapping* functionality. Figure 9.5 shows an example Import Manager screen where source and value fields are converted and mapped.

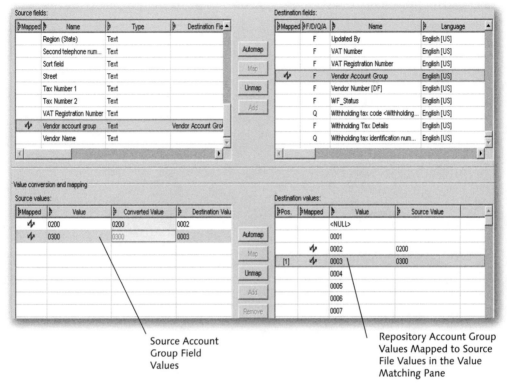

Figure 9.5 MDM Value Mapping Screen

In our case, the source hierarchy names don't correspond to the standard UNSPSC hierarchy names, so this activity is predominantly a manual value-by-value mapping process. However, after the import map is created and saved, it can be reused for all further conversions for the vendor files that have the same structure.

Finally, after performing other import functions for the full vendor record, when the records are imported into the MDM repository, the UNSPSC hierarchy is assigned to each of these vendor records. Thus, you've moved from an unstructured, linked tables-based classification to an industry standard, unambiguous classification structure.

Let's now consider how to handle any duplicate records that are provided in the source file.

9.1.3 De-duplication in the Import Process

The *Record Matching* function in the MDM Import Manager provides you with the de-duplication capability to enable you to identify and to remove duplicate records. After you've completed the field mapping, the value conversion, and the mapping steps, the focus then moves from the field-oriented processing to the more traditional record-oriented processing.

Record matching, which is often called key field matching, is usually the final step in the import process. It shifts the focus from the individual fields (vertical view of the source data) to the individual records (horizontal view of the source data).

Many import tools allow you to identify a single key field to be used to match the source records to your existing destination records so that you can update or replace them rather than create duplicates in the repository. The Record Matching function in the MDM Import Manager takes the basic key field matching and extends it with the functions described next.

You can specify multiple matching fields, for a more precise match if there isn't a single field that is completely reliable as a unique key field. You can also specify matching field combinations if there isn't an individual field that identifies each destination record. For example, you can combine the City and Country fields together to comprise the key field.

Figure 9.6 illustrates this process. In this example, you can see in the *Value matching* pane that the source file vendor number field is matched to an existing repository. The summary results of matching the source file data with the data in the SAP NetWeaver MDM Repository are shown in the *Default import actions* pane. The preview of the source records and the import action that will be performed are shown in the *Record matching* pane.

An additional useful function is the ability to match converted or mapped source values. In this case, rather than using the original source value, matching is based on the normalized, converted, or mapped source value, thereby providing a more accurate match against the destination record values.

You can also break down the matching process into case-by-case operations and record-by-record operations. The case-by-case matching process breaks the source records into different groups based on the type of match such as exact, partial, or conflict, and then allows you to apply a different default import action to each group. These import actions are to skip, create, update, or replace the group of records.

Example
Showing Value
Matching
Executed by the
Vendor Number
Field

Result of
Matching the
Source File Data
with the Data in
the SAP
NetWeaver MDM
Repository

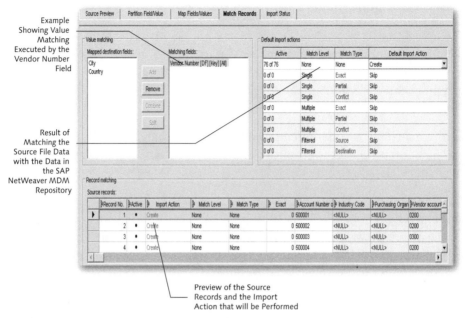

Preview of the Source
Records and the Import
Action that will be Performed

Figure 9.6 MDM Import Manager Record Matching Function

In the record-by-record operations, you can also override the default import action for each individual source record and each matching destination record on a record-by-record basis, for even more precise import control.

Let's now move on to consider how to automate the data import process.

9.1.4 Automating Data Import

The *Master Data Import Server* (MDIS) automates the task of importing source data into your MDM repositories. It's designed to reduce the processing complexity, resource requirements, and opportunities for user error common to data import tasks.

The following MDIS features can be applied:

▶ **Port-driven**
Simply place an import file in a repository's inbound port, and the MDIS processes it automatically.

- **Map-based**
  Each import file is processed according to the predefined import map associated with the inbound port.

- **Streaming-enabled**
  Automatic streaming of text and XML files reduces the resource consumption and results in faster imports.

- **File-aggregating**
  Processing files in batches can improve the efficiency and reduce the total time to import data.

- **Error-handling**
  If MDIS encounters an error in a record or file, it sets it aside, logs the error, and continues to process the remainder of the file.

Both MDIS and the MDM Import Manager can import data from a source file into an MDM repository, and each has unique capabilities that distinguish it from the other. By using each method in an appropriate way, this results in an import strategy that provides the most efficient importing of data possible.

The strength of the MDM Import Manager is its connection to the source data, which enables its interactive map-making capabilities. When the MDM Import Manager connects to a source, it preloads the entire source file, giving it knowledge of every field and every value in the source data. This "total awareness" is crucial for preparing a complete import map.

To help ensure that a map is complete, the MDM Import Manager's *Import Status* tab alerts users to any discrepancies between the source data values and the current map. The user can therefore fix these problems interactively within the MDM Import Manager and then save the corrected map before any data is imported. Preloading an entire source file comes at a price, however. It consumes memory on the computer running the Import Manager, and very large source files may exhaust the computer's available memory.

By contrast, the MDIS strengths are its scalability and automation. For scalability, instead of preloading the entire source file into the host machine's memory as the Import Manager does, MDIS processes the records in a stream by loading the records one at a time into memory. This streaming technique enables MDIS to process much larger source files than the Import Manager because the demand for memory on the host machine isn't affected by the size of the import file.

In addition to file size, file quantity poses a second scalability challenge. For example, a real-time transactional environment may produce a large number of small files, each containing only one or two master data records to process. A good example of this is the import of the D&B Worldbase package, where the mapping has been tested many times. To import each of these files individually through MDM Import Manager would be extremely inefficient. MDIS tackles this problem with a file aggregation feature that processes files systematically in batches rather than as individual files, resulting in a faster, more efficient import of data.

As it relates to automated processes, MDIS requires no user intervention to import files into an MDM repository. Instead, it relies on the maps previously created within the MDM Import Manager. After an import file is placed in the appropriate folder, its data is imported automatically into the MDM repository using the rules of the predefined import map. After a file is processed, MDIS then scans the repository for the next file to import. This process continues 24 hours a day, seven days a week, until either the MDIS or MDM server are stopped.

The trade-off for this scalability and automation is that if discrepancies between the source data and the import map arise, MDIS can't "fix" these problems by itself. Instead, the "problem cases" are fixed manually at a later time using the interactive capabilities of the MDM Import Manager. Unlike the MDM Import Manager, however, MDIS can set aside problem records or files and continue with the file import process.

Let's now move on to consider how to distribute or syndicate the master data to your consuming systems.

9.2   MDM Syndication

When you've completed the creation, enrichment, and validation of your master data records, the final part of the process is to distribute the records to your consuming systems. The *MDM Syndicator* is a powerful graphical user interface tool that allows you to select certain records from an MDM repository and to restructure the record to meet the requirements of a remote consuming system, without modifying the source data itself. As with the SAP Import Manager, the SAP NetWeaver MDM Syndicator comes with prepackaged business content for data distribution to the major SAP business applications such as ERP, CRM, and SRM.

When you run the SAP NetWeaver MDM Syndicator in interactive mode, this data file can be placed in any folder that is accessible to you. When you syndicate a record to a port, the data file is moved to a designated "ready" folder in the MDM server file system. Syndicating a record in SAP NetWeaver MDM creates a data file for the record in XML or text format.

You can also use the MDM Syndicator to create reusable syndication maps, so that the actual syndication of data can be performed by users without an in-depth knowledge of the data or its structure.

9.2.1 Key Functionality

The SAP NetWeaver MDM Syndicator addresses several key business requirements for data distribution that are often covered by your middleware. It's important to understand that the function of the SAP NetWeaver MDM Syndicator stops when you create a file in the file system. The identified middleware such as SAP NetWeaver PI then takes control from this point to move the content in the data file to the system to which the data is to be distributed.

Table 9.2 shows how the SAP NetWeaver MDM Syndicator functionality helps you prepare a suitable data file to distribute from MDM. It provides many additional features when compared to "traditional" distribution applications functionality.

Requirement	Traditional Distribution Applications Functionality	SAP NetWeaver MDM Syndicator Functionality
Source to target data field mapping	Manual maps created by the middleware	GUI-based interface for field mapping that can be saved for future reuse
File formats	Data usually syndicated using text files	Delimited or fixed-width flat files and XML file formats supported
Distribution of changed records only	Explicit identification of change pointers and configuration to process changes	Simple selection of the option to "suppress unchanged records"

Table 9.2 SAP NetWeaver MDM Syndication Functionality

Requirement	Traditional Distribution Applications Functionality	SAP NetWeaver MDM Syndicator Functionality
Include destination-specific keys (country key is US in MDM and USA in a destination system)	Build mapping tables and include program logic in functions to distribute master data	The MDM Remote key feature to map the destination-specific keys
Filtering a subset of records and syndicating them	Requires custom coding to extract a subset of data	Search by a specified selection criteria, which then can be saved for repeated syndication
Combining fields in the source system to make one destination field	Requires custom coding to combine fields	Custom combinations of text fields to arrive at the single value target data
Formatting data values	Requires code and function operations	Data normalization and formatting properties in the syndication map definition

Table 9.2 SAP NetWeaver MDM Syndication Functionality (Cont.)

Three key features of the SAP NetWeaver MDM Syndicator are the syndication maps, ports, and remote systems, and each play an important role in the configuration of the data distribution scenario.

In your *syndication maps*, you define the rules for which records you'll distribute from your MDM repository, which search selections to apply to the current record set, and which data attributes from the matching records to syndicate. You select which remote system is going to receive the syndication file and understand the field structure that this remote system requires. This then defines how your source data maps to this field structure, how the data will be formatted in the syndication file, and how the syndication file itself will be formatted.

Further syndication map design considerations also include whether all records or only changed records are syndicated and whether the remote record keys for the distributed system are generated for the syndicated file. These details enable you to create reusable maps, which contain all of the necessary business logic required for syndication. With this intelligence stored in the map itself, future syndications can be performed automatically or by persons with no knowledge of the data or remote systems.

After the MDM syndication maps are built, they are associated with specific *ports*. The port represents the physical staging location of the data and is a logical way to identify all of the captured information. The port is responsible for selecting the remote system that will receive the data, selecting the applicable MDM syndication map, and identifying the location where the data files should be placed for delivery. From a syndication perspective, any logical system that can receive data from MDM is known as a *remote system*. Each remote system can have one or many ports associated with it.

Let's now consider the four steps involved in setting up a data syndication process.

Step 1: Log in to an MDM Repository

When you start the syndication process, you must connect to an MDM repository. The repository you select serves as the source of all syndications mapped and executed while the MDM Syndicator is open.

Step 2: Load the Syndication Map

By loading a syndication map, you specify what data is going to be syndicated, which remote system is going to receive the syndicated data, and how the data will be formatted when it gets there. By selecting a predefined syndication map, this information is specified automatically.

Step 3: Select the Records to Syndicate

At this point, you're ready to execute the syndication. However, if you execute now, it's possible that all records on the current table will be included in the syndication file. Syndication provides two ways to narrow down the set of records to be included in syndication, either by searching and filtering, or by suppressing unchanged records.

Step 4: Execute the Syndication

After you execute the syndication, the MDM Syndicator prompts you for the file name and location where you want the syndicated records to be saved.

9.2.2 Automated Syndication

The *Master Data Syndication Server* (MDSS) automates the task of syndicating master data from the MDM repositories. This is designed to reduce the processing complexity, the resource requirements, and the opportunity for user errors that are common with data export tasks. At the same time, it ensures that the most up-to-date version of your master data can be made available to your consuming systems throughout your organization.

In addition, significant deployment and scalability benefits can also be gained by offloading the syndications from the server running the MDM Syndicator to the server running MDSS.

MDSS has some important features that you can take advantage of. Syndication will be *port-driven* because you can simply create an outbound repository port, and MDSS keeps populating it with the data that satisfies the syndication map criteria. When MDSS completes the syndication to a port, it places the syndication file in the port's Ready folder.

Figure 9.7 illustrates this process. The Syndication Map Properties drive the creation of an XML document which is written to a Port (Distributions Folder) in the MDM Server file system.

MDSS Syndication is *map-based* and is performed according to the predefined syndication map associated with the outbound port. Syndication from each port can occur at the frequency that is suitable for you and so will be *schedule-enabled*.

MDSS is designed for automation, and under normal circumstances user intervention isn't required to syndicate data from an MDM repository. To reach this state of automation, you complete the following four preliminary set-up steps, as shown in Table 9.3.

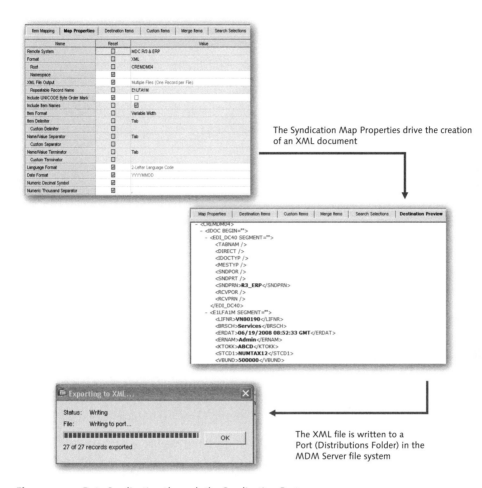

The Syndication Map Properties drive the creation of an XML document

The XML file is written to a Port (Distributions Folder) in the MDM Server file system

Figure 9.7 – Data Syndication through the Syndication Port

Set Up a Syndication Map	Use the MDM Syndicator to create a syndication map.
Set Up an Outbound Port	Use the MDM Console to create an automatic outbound port on the source MDM repository.
Associate a Map to a Port	Associate the syndication map with the port.
Scheduling	Set the port's processing interval and the next syndication date/time, as appropriate.

Table 9.3 MDSS Preliminary Set-up Steps

After these preliminary steps are established, the automated syndication process consists of the following five steps:

1. MDSS finds the automatic outbound port during its scan of the MDM server.

2. MDSS checks the port's processing interval and, if applicable, the next scheduled syndication date/time.

3. If syndication is due, MDSS executes the syndication according to the syndication map associated with the port.

4. MDSS places the completed syndication file into the port's Ready folder, schedules the next syndication date and time (as applicable), and searches for the next automatic outbound port.

5. SAP NetWeaver PI then takes over and imports the syndication file into your target remote system in the usual manner.

9.2.3 Syndication as a Workflow Step

A new feature in the SAP NetWeaver MDM SP05 is the introduction of syndication as a workflow step. This is useful for automating syndication as part of the workflow execution process.

In previous versions of the SAP NetWeaver MDM software, the workflow "stop" step was the last step in the process, and the syndication of a record could happen only after the MDM workflow was completed.

Now with versions SP05 and above, when defining SAP NetWeaver MDM workflows, you can add a step called syndication, which enables you to automate the distribution of records as part of the MDM workflow. The syndication step in the MDM workflow syndicates the records of the job to one or more outbound ports (on an asynchronous basis) and has one input and one output.

The following notification scenario shows how the new feature can be used. The business requirement in this case is to send out dynamic notifications, triggered at preset intervals in the MDM workflow. The triggers can be a request submission into MDM (such as an Adobe form being automatically uploaded into MDM as a request), a request approval, or the distribution of the MDM record to consuming systems. The requirement is also to have a dynamic subject and body content in the email. For example, you can notify the original requestor when the record was distributed to the consuming system, the customer or vendor number in the consuming system and the original request details.

After evaluating these requirements, you decide that this can be achieved by sending the email through SAP NetWeaver PI, which provides the dynamism to build the appropriate mail content. SAP NetWeaver PI will require the email address and the data record details.

In your workflow design, you include the MDM syndication step immediately after the request submission occurs. This MDM syndication step then triggers an XML file, which includes the request and addressee details. This XML file is picked up by SAP NetWeaver PI, formatted, and then using the SAP NetWeaver PI mail adapter, an email is triggered.

By following this approach, whenever a notification is required throughout your process, such as when the workflow status changes to requested or approved or distributed, then the MDM syndication can be included as a workflow step.

9.2.4 Syndication as a Reporting tool

You'll consider how to periodically reconcile the data in your MDM repository and the data in the consuming systems to monitor the ongoing data governance processes. This is especially important when the MDM consolidated and harmonized models are used. For this reconciliation purpose, you can extract the relevant data from your MDM repository using the SAP NetWeaver MDM Syndicator. This extract includes core attributes and the remote key mappings. This data can then be compared with the record details in the consuming systems.

Search and syndication are the two main tools that can be used for MDM reporting. Separate ports and maps can be created using the SAP NetWeaver MDM Syndicator, which can then be used for reporting purposes. Because the mapping of fields to be distributed is flexible, the exported file output can be in XML format or text format.

Taking the reconciliation process a step further, you can also build a duplicate MDM repository that can be used for reconciliation purposes. You can initially populate the repository with a snapshot of the information in the "live" MDM repository. Next, you can import the data from your consuming system, and configure the import matching process to update an indicator if the record already exists in MDM. Any new records imported into this duplicate repository are therefore records that aren't currently maintained in MDM but are available to be used in the consuming systems. These records become the candidate records for investigating non-compliance in accordance with your MDM data governance processes.

SAP NetWeaver MDM Syndicator can also be used to report any records that don't meet a particular validation criterion. For example, you could choose to syndicate all records that satisfy a search criterion of "VAT validation number" is null. This information can then be used to identify records that don't have a VAT number, and the syndication file can be passed on to your procurement team to take the appropriate corrective action.

Another common requirement for reporting in MDM is to provide a list of changes that have been made to critical fields such as Vendor name. This can be achieved by a combination of validations that check for change requests, assigning an indicator if a name change has been identified, and then syndicating those records that have the indicator marked.

Let's now move on to discuss the important functionality of the MDM Enrichment Adapter.

9.3   MDM Enrichment Adapter

In Chapter 4, we discussed the importance of the D&B enrichment process. By integrating the D&B Entity Matching services using the SAP NetWeaver MDM Enrichment Adapter, you enable real-time customer and vendor matching processes to retrieve the best D&B D-U-N-S Number.

In a few seconds, you can search more than 132 million D&B Worldbase records using Web Services to find the best candidate records and then automatically import the appropriate D&B D-U-N-S Number and Worldbase data into your SAP NetWeaver MDM repository.

Let's now consider the technical implementation of this MDM enrichment functionality.

9.3.1   Technical Concept of Data Enrichment

SAP NetWeaver MDM uses the Enrichment Controller and Enrichment Adapters provided by third-party enrichment service providers such as D&B to connect to remote data enrichment services. The process flow for data enrichment is shown in Figure 9.8.

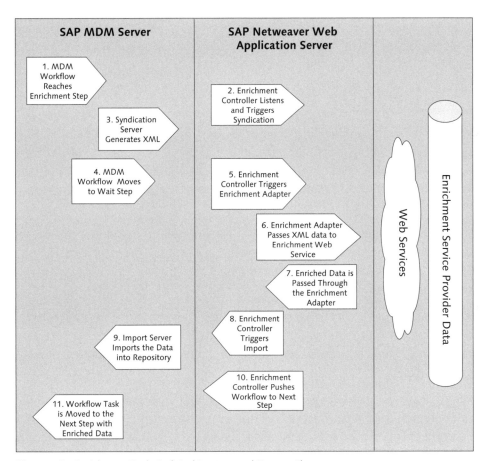

Figure 9.8 Enrichment Technical Architecture and Process Flow

Figure 9.8 shows the different technical components of SAP NetWeaver MDM that combine to make the enrichment process possible. Let's now consider the roles of each of these components.

9.3.2 Key Components and Functionality

We'll consider the roles of the MDM workflow, the Enrichment Controller, and the Enrichment Adapter.

MDM Workflow

The enrichment process is integrated within the SAP NetWeaver MDM workflows. You define a specific workflow "process" step, which triggers the enrichment process. The Enrichment Controller listens to the identified workflow that is being executed by the MDM workflow engine, and when the workflow reaches the specified process step, the controller then starts its actions.

Enrichment Controller

The Enrichment Controller orchestrates the enrichment process from the MDM side. The controller listens to the workflow, triggers the Enrichment Adapter, and activates the MDM syndication server and the MDM import server. During the startup, the Enrichment Controller reads the enrichment configuration file, which is maintained in an XML format.

The enrichment configuration file contains the information about the repositories that the server needs to connect to and the user names and passwords for the MDM repository connection. It defines which workflows to monitor and which steps in the workflow to monitor.

Additionally, the enrichment configuration file also defines the ports and distribution folders that are required for data syndication. It also provides the necessary details for the Enrichment Adapter Java bean to call for the particular enrichment process.

The Enrichment Controller is constantly in a polling loop and is connected to the MDM repositories. After a workflow reaches an identified step, the Enrichment Controller triggers the Enrichment Adapter and the MDM syndication server. An XML file with the specified map is then syndicated to the MDM port by the MDM syndication server, and the file is then passed on to the Enrichment Adapter.

During the enrichment process, the controller also moves the MDM workflow to a wait step, during the period that the external enrichment is happening. When it has been given the information that the adapter has passed on the enriched data to the MDM import server, the controller moves the workflow to the next step. The Enrichment Controller also updates the status of the enrichment in an MDM qualified table called *enrichment statuses*.

Enrichment Adapters

Enrichment Adapters are third-party applications provided by the enrichment service companies. They are Java applications that take the data from the syndication process and use this to call Web Services that connect to the external enrichment tools.

Let's now consider the steps involved in setting up an enrichment process.

Setting Up an Enrichment Process

▶ **Step 1: Adapter and Controller Setup**
Prepare the Enrichment Controller configuration XML file, and place it in the identified location in the MDM server. Deploy the Enrichment Controller application (.ear files provided by SAP NetWeaver MDM) and the adapter application (.ear files provided by the enrichment service provider).

▶ **Step 2: Prepare the MDM Repository**
You'll already have created the MDM repository structure for bringing in the enriched data. Add a qualified look-up table called enrichment statuses, with fields for capturing the error message, the workflow job ID, and the job owner.

  ▶ Create a specific remote system for each enrichment service provider and a port for this remote system. The port should be configured to be in both inbound and outbound mode.

  ▶ Create a user ID with the necessary privileges to access the data. These user ID details are included in the enrichment configuration file.

▶ **Step 3: Include Enrichment Steps in the Workflow**
Your MDM workflows are updated to include two enrichment-specific steps. A trigger step in the workflow starts the enrichment process, and a wait step parks the workflow until the enrichment is complete.

▶ **Step 4: Execute Monitoring**
The enrichment controller operations can be monitored by accessing a URL that is pointing to the controller operations. The web page provided by this URL shows the status of the polling and the repository connections, and any errors in the enrichment processes.

9.3.3 Case study: D&B Data Enrichment, with Iterative Look-Ups, Portal Presentation of Enrichment Information, and Error-Handling Options

Let's now consider a business case study example for the data enrichment process. Company CO1 has decided to use the D&B data enrichment services and to enrich its business partner master data with the D&B Worldbase package plus linkage information. This enrichment happens during the execution of the business partner create process.

The overall objective of the create process is to do the following:

▶ Accept, review, and approve the new business partner request.

▶ Search the D&B Worldbase database for candidate companies.

▶ Enrich the data with the D&B details for the selected company and then distribute the data to the consuming system for which the request was raised in the final format that is required.

Let's now consider in detail the design of these four steps in the workflow, which is componentized to enable looping and iteration of the different process steps. In our review, we'll consider the vendor request process, but the customer request process is almost identical, apart from the approval process and the file format of the distributed data.

Step 1: Review and Approval Workflow

The first step in the appraisal and approval of the new vendor request is to check the completeness and accuracy of the details provided. This task is performed by an MDM data steward, and the workflow is shown in Figure 9.9.

The MDM data steward reviews the request through an SAP NetWeaver Portal application; this review process also includes a search of the existing business partner records to see if the requested vendor has already been created as a record in the MDM repository.

A decision on whether to approve or reject the request is then made. In either case, a notification is sent to the requestor informing him of the decision. If the request is approved, then the current workflow ends, and the stop step of the workflow triggers the next workflow in the process: the D&B candidate search workflow.

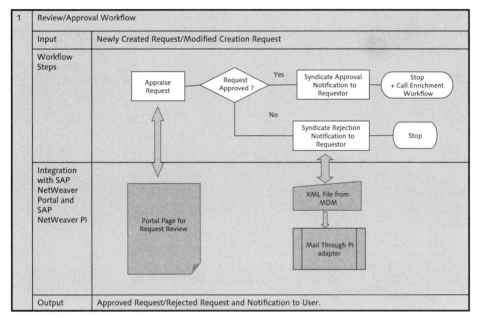

1	Review/Approval Workflow	
Input	Newly Created Request/Modified Creation Request	
Workflow Steps		
Integration with SAP NetWeaver Portal and SAP NetWeaver PI		
Output	Approved Request/Rejected Request and Notification to User.	

Figure 9.9 Review and Approval Workflow

If the request is rejected, the reason for rejection is provided, and a notification goes to the requestor with this reason. The requestor can then decide either to delete the request or to modify the request and resend it for processing again.

Step 2: D&B Candidate Search Workflow

D&B data enrichment is a two-part process. In the first part, the name and address attributes of an approved vendor request are sent to D&B through the "Company search" enrichment process. A key input for this search is the confidence code, which determines the exactness of the matching that will be considered in returning the candidate companies. The Enrichment Adapter then transfers the request attributes out of MDM to the external world of D&B.

The D&B software then normalizes and standardizes the request information and applies matching algorithms to arrive at the candidate companies that match the request information. This information is pulled into MDM by the MDM Import Manager. The candidate companies are then populated into the MDM repository in a qualified look-up table, which holds the name, address, and D&B D-U-N-S Number for each of the candidate companies.

The MDM data stewards execute this operation through an SAP NetWeaver Portal enrichment task list, in which they review and select a candidate company for D&B Worldbase package enrichment.

This process is made iterative by creating two "identical" workflows which each call each other and perform the D&B Candidate search function. Figure 9.10 illustrates this workflow.

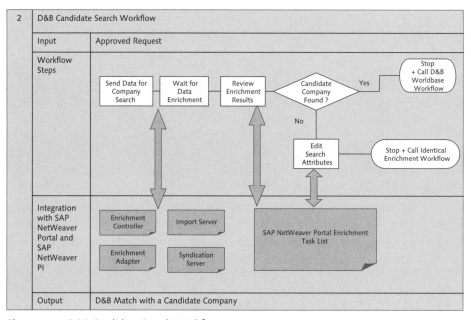

Figure 9.10 D&B Candidate Search Workflow

Step 3: Enrichment and Distribution

After a company is selected from the list of candidates, the second D&B adapter is then invoked, which is the data enrichment with the D&B Worldbase package. The input for the enrichment adapter is the D&B D-U-N-S Number of the selected company, and this information is sent to D&B to retrieve the D&B Worldbase package.

The data from the D&B Worldbase package is then populated into an MDM qualified table for D&B data. The next activity in this step is to finalize the name and address attributes for this vendor. SAP ERP name fields are 35 characters in length, whereas the full legal name as recorded by D&B is 90 characters. Hence, if the

D&B name is to be stored as the SAP ERP 6.0 name, it will be split after every 35 characters and distributed to the Name 1, Name 2, and Name 3 fields of the SAP application.

The vendor record is then distributed to the consuming system through an automatic syndication step. Finally, a notification message is sent to the requestor informing him that the MDM record has been distributed to the SAP ERP system, including the relevant SAP ERP number. Figure 9.11 illustrates this workflow.

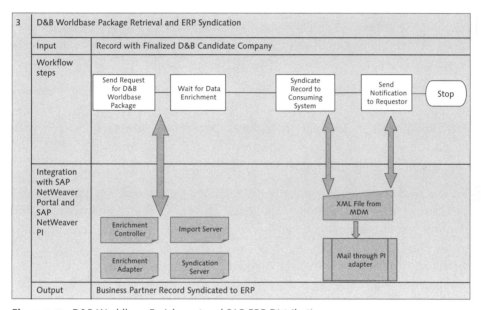

Figure 9.11 D&B Worldbase Enrichment and SAP ERP Distribution

By executing these three steps, an end user request for a new vendor is validated, enriched, and distributed to the consuming system. SAP NetWeaver MDM provides the workflow tool and integration capability to enable this process. Let's now compare the Enrichment Adapter process with SAP NetWeaver Process Integration (PI).

9.3.4 Comparison of the MDM Enrichment Adapter and SAP NetWeaver Process Integration

A key function of the enrichment architecture in SAP NetWeaver MDM is to enable a two way communication between an external Web Service and SAP NetWeaver

MDM. With the advent of the syndication step in the SP05 version of MDM, a question arises as to whether this data enrichment can also be performed using SAP NetWeaver PI.

The answer to this question is yes, SAP NetWeaver PI can also do this job. SAP NetWeaver PI can call external Web Services and can transform the SAP NetWeaver MDM data to the format and map required by the external enrichment Web Service.

However, the SAP Enrichment Architecture adds more functionality to the enrichment service scenario. The Enrichment Controller is more tightly integrated into the MDM workflow, and the enrichment activity is defined as steps in the overall create workflow.

The Enrichment Controller has the intelligence to wait for the enrichment process to complete and then to push the workflow to the subsequent step. The controller also monitors the enrichment process and updates an MDM qualified table with the enrichment status. As seen in the previous section, the controller provides the polling and status monitoring services as well.

Because the enrichment service is provided by a third-party service provider (D&B), it's better to have the mapping and transformation logic for request and response transfer as a bundled application (enrichment adapter) that is provided by the same provider. This will reduce the in-house SAP NetWeaver PI design and build activities each time that the message structure or transformation rules are changed.

9.4 Summary

In this chapter, we discussed three important ways to interface data into and out of an MDM repository. You learned how the MDM Import Manager addresses the key challenges of transforming raw data into rich master data. It's a powerful graphical user interface tool that allows you to import data from almost any flat file or relational electronic source file. You're given the functionality to then restructure, cleanse, normalize, and rationalize the raw data into rich master data as part of the import process.

When you've completed the creation, enrichment, and validation of your master data records, you then use the MDM Syndicator to distribute the records to your consuming systems. We discussed how the MDM Syndicator is a powerful graphical user interface tool that allows you to select certain records from an MDM repository and to restructure the record to meet the requirements of a remote consuming system, without modifying the source data itself.

Finally, you learned how the MDM Enrichment Architecture enables you to search the D&B Worldbase database for candidate companies and to enrich the data with the D&B details for the selected company. You discovered how the data is then distributed to the relevant consuming system in the final format that is required. You also now understand how the use of the SAP NetWeaver MDM Enrichment Adapter compares with SAP NetWeaver Process Integration (PI) to meet these enrichment objectives.

Let's now move on to consider how we integrate MDM with the wider SAP NetWeaver Portal and SAP NetWeaver Process Integration components.

Creating a "best of breed" MDM solution requires other components in the SAP NetWeaver stack. We describe how SAP NetWeaver Portal provides robust end-user interfaces and workflows and how to design an end-to-end messaging architecture using SAP NetWeaver Process Integration (PI).

10 Integrating SAP NetWeaver MDM with the SAP NetWeaver Components

In this chapter, we consider how to integrate MDM with the wider SAP NetWeaver components. We discuss the options available to you to provide end-user interfaces, including the use of MDM Data Manager, SAP Interactive Forms software by Adobe, and the SAP NetWeaver Portal, and describe how you can combine the solutions to enable your end users to execute their MDM tasks. We'll compare the various workflow tools that you can use, including MDM workflows, Guided Procedures, and SAP Business Workflow.

We'll then consider how the SAP NetWeaver PI is used to distribute master data records from MDM to the consuming systems. We'll consider the tools and functions available to you in SAP NetWeaver PI, and explain how the end-to-end data integration scenario is handled using them.

Let's now consider the options available to us for end user interfaces and how the SAP NetWeaver Portal can help.

10.1 SAP NetWeaver Portal Design and Deployment

When designing the end-user interfaces for your MDM data stewards and business users of the SAP NetWeaver MDM application, you need to consider how to use three important tools, namely the MDM Data Manager, SAP Interactive Forms, and the SAP NetWeaver Portal.

Although having such varied choices may initially seem confusing, by using each of these tools in an appropriate manner, you can provide simple but rich interfaces to your end users to enable them to execute their MDM tasks. The three tools complement each other, and each play an important role in your MDM solution landscape.

10.1.1 MDM Data Manager User Interfaces

As discussed in Chapter 8, the MDM Data Manager has a rich graphical user interface client and is an excellent tool for your power users who perform intensive data maintenance operations. These power users typically validate the data after a mass import and also develop and run validation queries on the MDM repository to evaluate the data completeness and accuracy.

MDM Data Manager is also a suitable tool to manage your MDM staging repository as discussed in Chapter 7. The MDM staging repository contains operational data from the prospective consuming systems that aren't yet integrated into MDM. It's the "work in progress" MDM repository, where you'll prepare your master data records to meet your data standards. This is the only repository that provides you with the capability of the batch D&B Entity Matching processes.

MDM Data Manager enables your users to segregate, search, and profile the data. It's a simple way to update the MDM look-up tables and to maintain taxonomies and hierarchies.

However, it isn't the best tool for your operational MDM data stewards, who will primarily progress individual records through a series of workflows, from an initial request to the successful distribution to a consuming system. The SAP NetWeaver Portal is required for this task.

Before we move on to the SAP NetWeaver Portal, let's consider the role of SAP Interactive Forms as a user interface.

10.1.2 SAP Interactive Forms

SAP Interactive Forms are an excellent way to capture requests to set up new customers and vendors. It's important for your MDM program to design suitable maintenance forms that enable you to collect the relevant details for the whole of your organization and not just a subset of data, such as for the Accounts Payable (AP) and Account Receivable (AR) teams. A clear and comprehensive master data entry form helps enforce your MDM data standards and mandate and validate the relevant data attributes.

SAP Interactive Forms Versus HTML Web Pages

Companies may also consider implementing HTML-based web forms as a replacement for paper forms. However, there are several disadvantages with HTML forms in that they can't be made available offline, aren't easy to print, and can't replicate the look and feel of a paper-based form. SAP Interactive Forms offer all of these capabilities.

By implementing an SAP Interactive Forms solution, you improve your master data collection processes. The user interface is slick and flexible; you can enforce mandatory attributes and allow look-ups with dropdown screens. You can also populate application values and provide help values.

The SAP Interactive Forms will be completed by your business end users, such as the customer sales representatives or the vendor procurement teams. SAP Interactive Forms have a natural look and feel and are self-explanatory. They can be printed and saved locally and used in either an online of an offline manner.

An online interactive form has system access and integration into your MDM application, with context-sensitive help and online checks.

An offline form doesn't access your MDM application but does provide static value help, checking, and simple arithmetic calculations in a self-contained PDF that can be printed, emailed, faxed, and archived. Figure 10.1 shows the process for capturing data using an SAP Interactive offline form.

SAP Interactive Forms offers a slick integration into the SAP NetWeaver Portal so that the business partner details can be automatically uploaded without the need for your MDM data stewards to rekey the data. The PDF file can also be stored on the record in the MDM repository to provide a clear audit trail, both to the original request and the requestor.

SAP Interactive Forms are replacements for paper-based forms, not legacy systems. A limitation when compared to direct entry into an SAP NetWeaver Portal iView is that you can't restrict values and carry out validations, depending on the values in other fields at runtime. Also, the SAP Interactive Form should not be designed to have too many pages or fields and be too complex.

It's also possible to dynamically program the SAP Interactive Form using scripting to best capture a particular request. So, in simple cases, the requestor can omit optional sections from a form such as the setup of bidders or customer prospects details for "live" business partners.

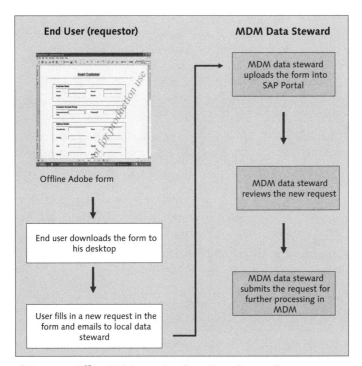

Figure 10.1 Offline SAP Interactive Form Data Capture Process

You can also provide more complex master data collection forms. As an example, if a customer has several ship-to addresses, they can all be captured in a single form, based on an initial parameter provided by the end user.

Let's now consider how the SAP NetWeaver Portal can be used as the primary user interface for your operational MDM data stewards.

10.1.3 SAP NetWeaver Portal and MDM Integration

SAP NetWeaver Portal is tightly integrated with SAP NetWeaver MDM and is the natural choice for implementing web-based applications to maintain the data in MDM for ongoing data governance processes. There are several advantages of using SAP NetWeaver Portal over other third-party portal applications because it provides an integrated authentication mechanism, a roles and authorizations framework, and an integrated change management tool. Only the specific business application needs to be developed and configured into the portal.

If you're considering using any other web-based application or portal, then many additional design and build considerations will come into the picture. You'll need to code the user authentication (with LDAP), develop the roles manually, and develop the user interface applications from scratch.

The SAP NetWeaver MDM solution includes prebuilt portal content business packages that provide end user interfaces for MDM. This business content can be enhanced by further developing more functionality around them. Your MDM deployment team can also develop custom user interfaces using the SAP NetWeaver Portal Java programming tools (Web Dynpro applications).

Let's now consider how the SAP NetWeaver Portal user interface integrates with the MDM repository. Figure 10.2 shows the integration layout.

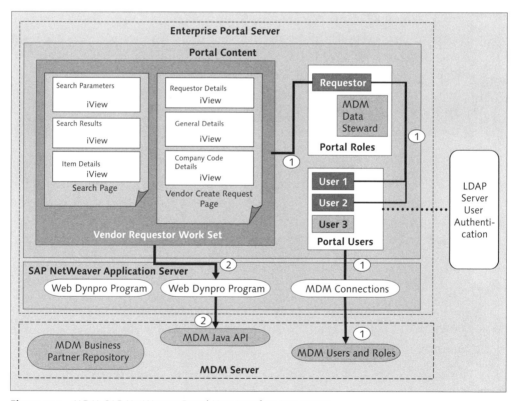

Figure 10.2 MDM-SAP NetWeaver Portal User Interface Integration

We'll now describe the integration of the SAP NetWeaver Portal applications with the SAP NetWeaver MDM server by considering two example processes. The first process is the user sign-on and role validation, and the second is the search and data maintenance functionality.

Process 1 – User Sign-on and Role Validation

The MDM data stewards sign on to the portal server using their user-ID/password credentials. This process is shown in Figure 10.2 with the connectors labeled as "1."

A usual business requirement is to have either a single sign-on or at least reduced sign-on credentials, so that you don't have to remember several user IDs and passwords. The SAP NetWeaver Portal login credentials can be set up to have the same sign-on credentials that are used in your company's Lightweight Directory Access Protocol (LDAP). This means that your users can then use the same login credentials that they already use for logging in to your company's network. The following steps summarize the user connection cycle.

Step 1
The user provides the credentials to the log-on screen to SAP NetWeaver Portal.

Step 2
The SAP NetWeaver Portal connects to the LDAP server and authenticates the user with the information stored in the LDAP server. So, when users key in the credentials (user ID and password) to log in to the portal, the portal server passes the user information to the LDAP server for authentication. If the authentication is successful, then the users are allowed access into the application.

Step 3
Because the role information is stored in the SAP NetWeaver Portal database, after the successful authentication, the SAP NetWeaver Portal retrieves the assigned role information for that user.

Simultaneously, when the user logs in to the portal, the portal user mapping comes into play. The user mapping includes the information on the access the user has to connect to a particular SAP NetWeaver MDM repository (MDM repository, user ID, and password), and the MDM repository connections are also established for the portal user.

The maintenance of the user mapping between the portal user ID and the MDM repository user ID is a one-time activity that is managed by the system administrators when creating a portal user.

Step 4

The user then navigates through the application depending on the role that he has been assigned. Each user is assigned to a portal role that map to his business function. In the example given in Figure 10.2, User 1, when logging in, will have access to perform the role of a requestor.

So, by using simple credentials and a single login, the users log in to the portal and are then connected to the MDM repository at the backend. Let's now move on to consider how the end user searches and maintains master data using the Vendor Requestor work set as shown earlier in Figure 10.2.

Process 2 – Data Search and Maintenance

Let's start by defining a work set and an iView. A *work set* is typically a combination of SAP NetWeaver Portal web pages that provides the user interface to the MDM data maintenance functions. An *iView* is a portlet, an application window that has elements of information and data fields structured within it.

On logging into the system, the portal user is provided access to the menu and pages that are configured in the Vendor Requestor work set. In our example shown in Figure 10.2, the portal content, the role "requestor" is assigned to the work set Vendor Requestor.

In a typical vendor-creation process, the user first uses the Search Page to check if the vendor record already exists in the MDM repository. The connector 2 in Figure 10.3 illustrates how the data maintenance function is performed.

The Search Page in our example has three iViews: Search Parameters, Search Results, and Item Details. We'll now describe how these iViews are linked together.

The first iView contains the search parameters, where the MDM data stewards enter the search criteria. Figure 10.3 shows an example of this Search Parameters iView screen.

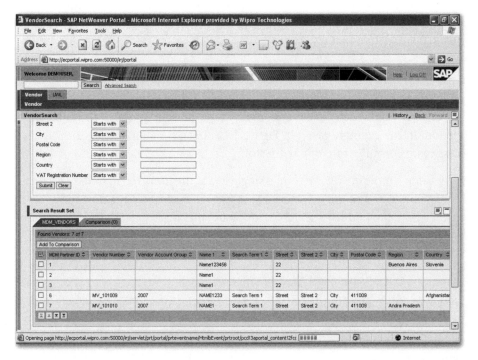

Figure 10.3   Search Parameters iView

When the user submits the search criteria, the search application uses the connection with the MDM repository to retrieve the relevant data in the form of a result set.

The data from the Search Parameters iView is passed to the SAP NetWeaver Application Server. The application programs for the search process then connect to the MDM server APIs to access the MDM repository and to retrieve the vendor records that satisfy the search criteria.

This result set lists all of the vendor records in the MDM business partner repository that satisfy the search criteria. Figure 10.4 shows an example of the Search Results iView.

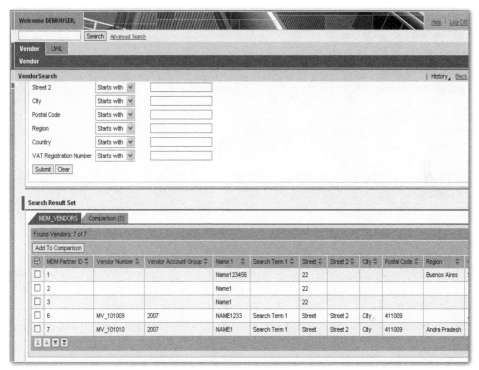

Figure 10.4 Search Results iView

Now, the MDM data steward reviews the search results in this iView and may choose to display the details of one or many of the retrieved records. The user can select multiple records and compare them in the same page in the portal. The portal content usually has the details of the records stored in memory, so the user is able to view the details instantly when a record is selected. Figure 10.5 shows an example of the Item Details iView for a business partner record.

This example illustrates how the integration between the MDM server and the SAP NetWeaver Portal server is established and how a user-friendly interface is provided for the MDM data stewards to manage their master data processes.

Let's now consider the standard business content that is provided with the SAP NetWeaver Portal to enable you to perform your MDM activities.

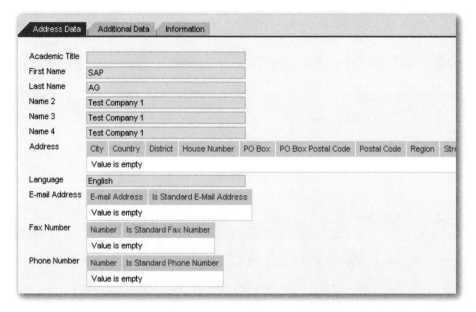

Figure 10.5 Item Details iView

10.1.4 SAP NetWeaver Portal Standard Business Content

The SAP NetWeaver Portal standard business package is delivered along with the MDM software. The business package components enable the deployment of web-based interfaces to maintain, search, and compare master data in an MDM repository.

If your organization's MDM architecture and design is similar to the standard SAP NetWeaver MDM data model and business scenarios, you can use the portal standard business package to provide the user interfaces for master data maintenance. You only need to deploy and configure the standard portal user interface web content, the Universal Work List (UWL) application, and the portal security and roles. In this case, with very little effort, using the SAP-provided business content, the MDM solution will have portal-based user interfaces to maintain your master data.

For the standard business partner MDM repository, the portal content has predefined work sets, roles, and pages to manage the data. The business package also provides iView templates as a starting point to enable you to create custom iViews and pages.

The search content in the business package provides iViews and pages that enable you to search the MDM business partner repository using either a drilldown search based on look-up fields or a free-form search based on any field in the repository. Searches based on hierarchy drilldowns or taxonomy attribute values are also provided.

The business package provides result set iViews that display the search results in the form of an overview of matching records. Further iViews providing the details of a single record are also available.

The record details iView is the starting point for the master data maintenance transaction. The functionality to change a record, to create a new record, and to add a record to a workflow is provided.

The *Universal Work List (UWL)* is the portal task list container that provides a user interface for managing the MDM workflow jobs. The MDM business content for UWL provides an inbox that displays all of the workflow tasks available in one or more MDM repositories. Using UWL, you can assign tasks to specific MDM data stewards, process the workflow steps, move them to the next step, and navigate to review the record details. Figure 10.6 shows a snapshot of the UWL application in the SAP NetWeaver Portal.

Figure 10.6 shows the task list pane in the UWL, which lists out the new and pending tasks for the user profile. The user can select the task in the task list pane and use one of the radio buttons at the bottom to process the workflow task. When the user processes the task in UWL, the MDM workflow step at the backend is processed. The functions in the UWL are standard business content delivered by SAP.

If you deploy the SAP NetWeaver Portal business package, then the connections to the MDM server are maintained internally by the business packages, managed by the system object definition.

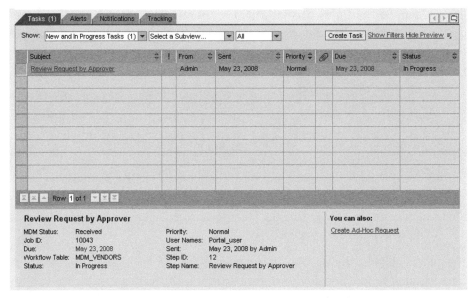

Figure 10.6 Universal Work List in SAP NetWeaver Portal

10.1.5 Custom Portal User Interfaces – Java Web Dynpro Development

As well as the functionality provided by the MDM business package, Web Dynpro Java development then allows you to create highly customized applications. The individual process requirements that can't be met by the MDM business package content can be implemented by developing Web Dynpro Java coding. This enables you to process the specific event triggering, to access and update multiple repositories simultaneously, to send custom email notifications, and to perform data validations. We discussed an example of this in the previous chapter.

Requirements for Customized Portal Applications

The SAP NetWeaver Portal standard business content is useful for providing simple portal pages for searching and maintaining master data in the MDM repository. However, your MDM deployment team is also likely to find some business requirements for the data capture and validation of specific data-management scenarios. These requirements, which incorporate business rules and validations, primarily drive the development of custom portal applications.

Compliance to organizational standards for SAP NetWeaver Portal architecture, usability guidelines, designs, and build specifications may also necessitate the build of custom applications.

Business Rules and Validations

The validations provided by standard portal business content are limited to the provision of dropdown lists for look-up values. However, ensuring that the right data is captured during the initial point of entry itself could require custom rules such as mandating data entry for certain fields depending on the business partner type, and checking for data integrity based on a combination of data values.

Selective inheritance of data values in different fields based on the data input in key fields at runtime is another likely requirement. Building additional data capture iViews for your organization-specific data elements in the repository is also a common requirement. Finally, providing direct connections to external systems through remote function calls and Web Services may be needed to validate the accuracy of the data that is entered.

Your MDM data model might also store and update data from a single process into different repositories. An example of this is a type of business partner address being stored in a different repository.

Another requirement may be to access look-up values from a different repository. For optimal performance, SAP recommends that if the look-up table values for a particular data element are high, then this information should be stored in a different repository (e.g., a list of around 10,000 original equipment manufacturers that are associated with vendor records might be stored in a different repository).

The design of your MDM processes may mean that data from different repositories are made available in the portal during the search, create, and change request process.

Your company might also have specific standards for end user portal applications in the form of usability guidelines, allowed page structure and measurements, icons and visual elements design, data entry form design, and display of error messages. You can adhere to these requirements by either enhancing the standard portal content or by building custom Web Dynpro applications.

Let's now consider the components of the SAP NetWeaver Java Web Dynpro development environments.

SAP NetWeaver Java Web Dynpro Development Environment

The development infrastructure in the SAP NetWeaver environment is a robust platform for application developers that consists of the following:

► **SAP NetWeaver Developer Studio**
This is the tool used for developing the Web Dynpro applications and deploying them as a part of the development configurations.

► **Java Development Infrastructure (JDI)**
This provides the development team with a consistent development environment and also the required software to support developers through the whole development lifecycle. It consists of the following three components:

  ► **Design Time Repository (DTR)**
  Provides central storage of the source code and maintains versions of the source code. It allows for concurrent access of the source code to the development team and manages the conflicts that arise when more than one developer works on the same source code at the same time.

  ► **Component Build Service (CBS)**
  Provides the environment for the storage and generation of the built application objects and for the maintenance of the source code and archives.

  ► **Change Management Service (CMS)**
  Used to configure the transport route from the development to the quality assurance (test) and production systems, and to transport software changes from the development system to the other environments.

Use of Java APIs and MDM Connectors

SAP software provides you with MDM Java APIs to enable you to access the data in an MDM repository through a Java-based application framework. You can create Web Dynpro applications as a complementary set of business package contents. This hybrid approach for development can reduce your development efforts.

An important component in the development infrastructure is establishing and maintaining connections at runtime between MDM and the SAP NetWeaver Portal. Both the SAP NetWeaver MDM business package and Web Dynpro Java use the MDM Java connector to obtain a connection to the MDM server. The MDM connector in turn uses the connector framework of the underlying J2EE Engine, where the connection container uses a connection pooling technique to efficiently use the MDM connections.

You need to implement a reliable connection handling strategy to meet the best practices and security requirements. There are two approaches for addressing this requirement: you can either implement a dedicated connection handling application or implement the connection handling in a J2EE library.

The first approach refers to a dedicated application that maintains the connection data in a secured way: the MDM hostname, the port number, the user, and the password. The application also handles the connection look-up and connection close. Ensure that all of the applications that use the MDM backend have access to use the connection handling application.

The second approach is a J2EE library implementation. The J2EE library is a component that is visible for use from all of the J2EE applications. However, the J2EE library is a static component and does not support data maintenance, like the J2EE applications and the J2EE services. If some configuration data need to be changed in the library, you need to redeploy it and then restart the cluster to effect the changes. You can find out how to implement a J2EE library in the SAP online documentation at *http://help.sap.com/saphelp_nw70/helpdata/EN/ee/6ede3f7bc1eb06 e10000000a1550b0/content.htm.*

ABAP Web Dynpro Development

If your organization isn't using the NetWeaver Portal, you can use the Web Dynpro for ABAP technology to develop applications in the SAP ABAP environment. The concepts in the Web Dynpro for ABAP development are similar to the Web Dynpro Java development. The MDM software includes the MDM ABAP API, and these enable ABAP programs to perform most of the functions of the MDM Data Manager and MDM Console. The user interface for Web Dynpro for ABAP can be either HTML web pages or the SAP core GUI. You can find information on implementing user interfaces using Web Dynpro for ABAP in the SAP online documentation at *http://help.sap.com/saphelp_nw04s/helpdata/en/77/3545415ea6f523e10000 000a155106/frameset.htm.*

10.1.6 Case Study: Portal User Interfaces Build for Vendor Maintenance Processes

Let's now consider a business case example for building portal user interfaces for the vendor master data maintenance process. Company CO1 has decided to use SAP NetWeaver Portal to enable user interfaces for the vendor master data maintenance processes. The objective of this portal build is to provide interfaces for MDM data stewards to perform the following functions:

1. Create and upload new vendor requests.

2. Manage the vendor creation workflow tasks.

3. Drill down from task lists to request review applications.

In the background, this process is driven by the MDM workflow tasks, which typically include request review, enrichment, and final data preparation tasks. During the project design phase, you gather the business requirements so that you can build the user interfaces to execute these tasks.

In this scenario, the portal application development team develops the solution using custom Web Dynpro applications. Distinct portal applications are built for each of the process steps, which are integrated into the MDM workflow to provide a seamless user interface for the MDM data stewards.

Let's now analyze how the business requirements are gathered and then met by the portal applications development team. We'll illustrate this by considering two example processes: "Capturing the Vendor details in a Request form" and "Submission of a Vendor request."

Example Process 1: Capture the Vendor Details in a Request Form

The process is performed by the business end users, such as the procurement team.

Business Requirements
Vendor request data are captured in an SAP Interactive Form. The form captures all relevant data about the vendor, including the address details, purchasing details, and accounting information. Certain fields such as the Vendor Account Group, Name1, City, Country, and Search Term are mandatory. Many data elements in the form are dropdown lists, and the dropdown values are populated from the MDM repository.

SAP NetWeaver Solution

AN SAP Interactive Form is used to capture the vendor details. The form is used in the offline mode, and users enter the vendor details into the form and then email it to the MDM data stewards. Look-up values are periodically updated by generating new versions of the form online from the SAP NetWeaver Portal.

End users are instructed by the MDM data stewards via email or intranet communication to download and use the new version of the form, whenever it's released.

The mandatory fields as specified in the requirements are checked when the form is saved, and the appropriate error messages are issued if these fields aren't populated.

Example Process 2: Submission of a Vendor request

The uploading of the SAP Interactive Form to create an MDM record process is performed by the MDM data stewards.

Business Requirements

The request data entered into the SAP Interactive Form is uploaded into the SAP NetWeaver Portal without the need for any manual rekeying of data.

For U.S. vendor addresses, the tax jurisdiction code should be populated automatically. If multiple tax jurisdictions are determined, then a window pops up with the matching jurisdiction codes from which the MDM data steward can choose. The matched code is updated as the tax jurisdiction code.

For E.U. vendor addresses, the VAT number if entered in the form should be validated using the VAT validation services provided by the European Union.

Based on the chosen vendor account group selected during the request creation, certain fields are mandatory at runtime. Once submitted, the request triggers different workflows based on the vendor account group selected.

SAP NetWeaver Solution

An option for uploading the SAP Interactive Form into the SAP NetWeaver Portal is provided. When a form is uploaded into the portal, the data is automatically populated, and the SAP Interactive Form is rendered in the portal. The local data stewards can then review and edit the data online.

Before submitting the request, the MDM data steward can search for matching records in the MDM repository to retrieve vendor records with information similar to the newly requested vendor. If any match results are found, they are displayed in a pop-up window. This check ensures that duplicate vendor records aren't created in the system.

The integration of SAP ERP with Taxware is already established. The SAP NetWeaver Portal makes a Remote Function Call (RFC) call to the SAP ERP system, which triggers the SAP ERP ABAP function module for calling Taxware, passes the address parameters, and retrieves the tax jurisdiction code. This information is provided in the portal as a portlet window.

The different workflow names that correspond to different vendor account groups are maintained in the MDM repository in a look-up table. SAP NetWeaver Portal obtains the workflow name from this look-up table based on the vendor account group in the record and then triggers the corresponding workflow. The portal application is built with multiple segments, with each segment fitting the normal monitor size. This avoids scrolling up and down in the screen.

A further example of a customized portal application is the D&B enrichment process, discussed next.

Example of a Customized Portal Application Using Web Dynpros

In Chapter 9, we described how the D&B enrichment process is integrated within the SAP NetWeaver MDM workflows. You can define a specific workflow "process" step, which triggers the two-part enrichment process. In the first part, the name and address attributes of an approved vendor request are sent to D&B through the "Candidate Search" enrichment process. The candidate companies are then populated into the MDM repository in a qualified look-up table, which holds the name, address, and D&B D-U-N-S Number for each of the candidate companies.

The MDM data stewards execute this operation through a customized portal enrichment task list, in which they review and select a candidate company for the D&B Worldbase package enrichment. This process is made iterative by creating two "identical" workflows, which each call each other and perform the D&B Candidate Search function.

10.1.7 Portal Guided Procedures, SAP Business Workflow, and SAP NetWeaver MDM – Managing Complex Iterative Workflows

Guided Procedures (GP) is the process orchestration layer in the SAP Composite Application Framework (SAP CAF). GP can orchestrate a master data maintenance workflow by calling various MDM functions to update data in an MDM repository and to route steps in the MDM workflow to various functions.

Using the native SAP NetWeaver MDM workflow capabilities, you can only define and execute predefined process steps available in the MDM workflow engine (approve, match, syndicate, process, branch, group, and merge).

Using GP's open modeling and object calling functionality, custom steps and step routing can be configured for data maintenance workflow. Routing of MDM tasks to different departments or groups of users based on business rules and the status of data can also be configured.

The process steps in MDM workflow tasks are defined as callable objects in GP, and the sequencing and routing of tasks is managed through GP's orchestration functionality. The callable objects of GP's can access the MDM repository information through Web Services or connect to MDM APIs through custom Java program calls.

For example, an MDM data maintenance workflow with data updates from different departments, who review, approve or reject, and then reroute to the department concerned, can be configured by building the GP's callable objects and making them access MDM Web Services to search, create, or update the business partner data.

Before moving on to compare the functionality of SAP NetWeaver MDM workflow and GP workflow, SAP Business Workflow integration with MDM also requires a mention. SAP Business Workflow is a versatile tool for managing workflows in an SAP ERP environment and can be integrated with the SAP NetWeaver MDM data maintenance processes through ABAP APIs or by even calling MDM Java APIs. For integrating the SAP Business Workflow in the Java platform, a Java bean object is constructed to establish the connection and communication between the MDM Java APIs and the SAP Business Workflow object.

Let's now evaluate the technical functionality available in these three workflow management tools.

Function 1: Building Custom Process Steps

For example, you can assign a next step to a particular user at runtime, while processing a step in the workflow.

The SAP NetWeaver MDM workflow engine provides the 10 most commonly used workflow process steps but you can't add a custom step. It's possible to build a custom step with both GP and SAP Business Workflow.

Function 2: Dynamic Notifications

Based on the process step, define the user or group to which the notification (email) should be triggered.

This isn't possible with the standard MDM workflow but can be done by integrating with SAP NetWeaver PI and SAP NetWeaver Portal technology. Dynamic notifications can be constructed with both GP and SAP Business Workflow.

Function 3: Routing of Workflow Process Steps

For example, if the Vendor Account Group is changed during review, a different set of steps needs to be executed based on who the reviewer is.

The SAP NetWeaver MDM workflow engine provides routing functionality in the form of predefined branch, merge, and grouping steps. Basic dynamism in routing can be achieved through the validations attached to the branching step.

GP provide complex routing conditions, and dynamic determination of the next step is possible based on the rules defined in the orchestration process, data status, and data attribute values.

Complex routing logic can be built with SAP Business Workflow.

Function 4: Integration with Portal Universal Work List

All three workflow tools can display and execute workflow tasks.

Function 5: Integration with Other External Systems

With MDM workflows, this is achieved either through the MDM Enrichment Architecture or by integrating the syndicate workflow step with SAP NetWeaver PI.

GP, with its callable objects, is better suited for integration with other applications. Business workflows can be integrate through Web Services

Function 6: Graphical User Interface for Designing and Building Workflows

The SAP NetWeaver MDM workflow engine is integrated with VISIO, which provides an easy interface to the user.

There is no graphical user interface for design in GP. The workflow process is built by custom coding.

SAP Business Workflow has a graphical user interface, available in the ABAP stack.

Function 7: Monitoring and Logs

With MDM workflow, history is standard, and other logs are available at the MDM console level. Monitoring is possible with GP and SAP Business Workflow has good monitoring capabilities

Summary of Workflow Tools

The business requirements for workflow determine the selection of the tool used to build and manage your workflows. SAP NetWeaver MDM workflow provides good capabilities to manage most of the design requirements.

If you do decide to use GP, you should also keep in mind that GP will be replaced by a new tool in SAP NetWeaver called Galaxy, which is the SAP long-term approach to provide a business process modeling notation. Support for GP will be available in the medium term, but in the long term, you'll consider the Galaxy tool for complex workflow management.

Having understood the different SAP NetWeaver Portal components, let's now consider the interfacing technology that's available in the SAP NetWeaver platform.

10.2   Process Integration Using SAP NetWeaver PI

Our objective now is to distribute the vendor and customer master data from the MDM repositories to the consuming systems, both SAP and non-SAP. To achieve this, you need SAP NetWeaver Process Integration (PI) software.

SAP NetWeaver PI provides standard and easily customizable functionality for the master data integration between SAP NetWeaver MDM and other business applications. Standard business content delivered with the SAP NetWeaver MDM software provides the data structure mappings for SAP ERP, CRM, and SRM, and the business content for SAP NetWeaver PI to deploy and run these scenarios.

The interface architecture in your organization provides an information exchange layer between the central MDM system and the consuming system that it interacts with. This information exchange can import the data by pulling records from the source systems into SAP NetWeaver MDM or distribute the data from a centrally mastered MDM system to a consuming application.

The information exchange can also occur without an interface layer, if you decide to build point-to-point file transfers. However, this adds to complexity when there are several consuming systems, resulting in the duplication of efforts in interfacing data, and doesn't provide any message monitoring functionality.

The SAP best practice is to implement the message interfacing using the SAP NetWeaver PI technology. An alternate option for integration is to use the MDM APIs to retrieve data directly from the MDM system. The business application concerned, through its technical layer, can call the MDM system, access the APIs, and extract the data required. However, this process isn't driven by SAP NetWeaver MDM, so it isn't easy to implement in a master data creation process flow, which is completed in MDM and where the distribution needs to be triggered by the SAP NetWeaver MDM system.

Therefore, the use of an integration layer, using SAP NetWeaver PI as the middleware, is the preferred solution to integrate MDM with the consuming business applications.

In many ways, this is one the most straightforward technical pieces of the MDM solution architecture. If SAP is the consuming system, there is no need to build any additional interfaces, and you can use the standard SAP NetWeaver PI interfaces to populate the customer (KNA1) and vendor (LFA1) SAP tables. In this section, we'll focus on the vendor interfaces, but the same principles equally apply for the distribution of customer data.

However, it can be time consuming to set up and test the entire end-to-end process. You need to work closely with both the SAP ERP team and the SAP NetWeaver PI team who support the local consuming systems environments. You need to coordinate activities in both of these areas before the MDM data can be successfully distributed.

The MDM program should own the overall end-to-end setup process. The team drives through the changes required in the SAP ERP and SAP NetWeaver PI systems to ensure that the records can be distributed. You'll find that as more consuming systems are integrated, it's possible to follow similar implementation procedures and to achieve this quickly.

Let's now consider the steps involved in integrating SAP NetWeaver MDM data with business applications using the SAP NetWeaver PI middleware.

10.2.1 SAP NetWeaver PI Interface Architecture and Design Considerations

The SAP NetWeaver PI team is likely to have established the architectural rules, which need to be understood and followed by your MDM development team.

The first best practice at this stage concerns the use of secure file transfer between the MDM server and the SAP NetWeaver PI server. SAP NetWeaver PI can directly poll the MDM syndication port distribution folder, where the XML or text file of an MDM record is placed on syndication from MDM. In a scenario with multiple interfaces, this polling by the SAP NetWeaver PI system increases the performance load on the SAP NetWeaver PI server and does not provide a monitoring or fully secure standard for the transfer of files from MDM to SAP NetWeaver PI. A secure file transfer protocol (SFTP) deployment, whose function is to monitor the MDM distributions folders and to transfer the file from MDM to the SAP NetWeaver PI folder, is considered as a best practice.

The second best practice is to use XML as the file format for the data transfer between MDM and SAP NetWeaver PI. XML is increasingly becoming the global standard format, and SAP NetWeaver PI considers XML as the standard format. If possible, the use of text file formats should be avoided.

A typical integration design for Company CO1, which we have followed through in this book, is shown in Figure 10.7.

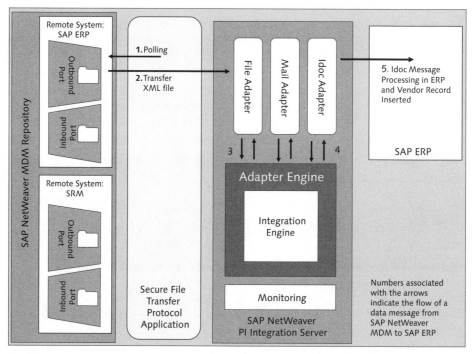

Figure 10.7 Integration Using SAP NetWeaver PI Between MDM and SAP ERP

Let's now consider how we implement an SAP NetWeaver PI interface to the SAP ERP 6.0 system.

10.2.2 Implementing an SAP NetWeaver PI Interface to an SAP ERP System

The SAP NetWeaver PI interface consists of the following five steps as shown in Figure 10.7.

Steps 1 and 2

MDM distributes the request using the MDM Syndicator. An XML file is placed in a specified directory in the MDM server folder structure.

Creating the CREMAS/ADRMAS XML file

As a first step, using the MDM Syndicator, you create the XML file and place it in a specified directory.

A sample CREMAS XML code, which is used to create a vendor record in an SAP ERP 6.0 system, is as follows:

```
<?xml version="1.0" encoding="UTF-8" ?>
- <CREMAS04>
- <IDOC BEGIN="">
- <EDI_DC40 SEGMENT="">
<TABNAM />
<DIRECT />
</EDI_DC40>
- <E1LFA1M SEGMENT="">
<LIFNR>9000999</LIFNR>
<KTOKK>XX01</KTOKK>
<LAND1>GB</LAND1>
<NAME1>Company Name </NAME1>
<ORT01>Town</ORT01>
<PSTLZ>ZZ9 9ZZ</PSTLZ>
<REGIO>ZZ</REGIO>
<SPRAS>EN</SPRAS>
<TELF1>0999 999 9999</TELF1>
<TELFX>0999 999 9999</TELFX>
<MCOD1>1727</MCOD1>
- <E1LFA1A SEGMENT="">
<LFURL>www.vendorurl.com</LFURL>
</E1LFA1A>
- <ADDRESS Address="">
<House_Number>1</House_Number>
<Street2>Street</Street2>
</ADDRESS>
</E1LFA1M>
</IDOC>
</CREMAS04>
```

The vendor number is populated in the SAP LIFNR field on the LFA1 table:

```
<LIFNR>9000999</LIFNR>
```

The XML file is picked up from the MDM distributions folder using the SFTP application and passes this on to the SAP NetWeaver PI file adapter.

Step 3

The SAP NetWeaver PI adapter passes the XML content to the runtime integration engine. The SAP NetWeaver PI engine then uses the interface mapping and communication settings to transform the XML data message from MDM into CREMAS and ADRMAS IDoc messages.

Step 4

The generated messages are passed by the SAP NetWeaver PI integration engine to the IDoc adapter, which transfers the IDoc messages to the SAP ERP application.

Step 5

The SAP ERP application then processes the IDoc messages based on the configuration settings in the partner profile for the interface, and the ABAP BAPIs or function modules update a vendor record into the SAP ERP master data tables such as LFA1 and ADRC.

10.2.3 Required Setup Activities in MDM, SAP ERP, and SAP NetWeaver PI

We've already mentioned that various setup activities are needed in the MDM, SAP ERP 6.0, and SAP NetWeaver PI environments before a record can be successfully distributed. These activities are repeated in each of the development, the quality assurance (test), and the production environments. The activities are as follows.

MDM Setup

Following are five key setup activities:

1. Create the remote system.
2. Create a port for the object map and the remote system.
3. Copy the vendor syndication map into the remote system.
4. Provide preload configuration data for look-up tables such as Countries, Regions, Vendor Account Groups, Languages, and Number Ranges for different vendor account groups.
5. Load the configuration data.

SAP ERP Setup

Create the partner profile with custom inbound process codes and create authorizations for master data objects. These are the technical settings in SAP ERP 6.0 that correctly identify the programs to process the MDM interface.

SAP NetWeaver PI Setup

There are seven setup activities in SAP NetWeaver PI:

1. Export the MDM software components to the SAP NetWeaver PI directory.
2. Establish the HTTP connection.
3. Provide system details for SAP NetWeaver PI (IP address, system name, port information) and SAP NetWeaver PI RFC user information.
4. Load the Metadata for the respective message types.
5. Check for business systems in the System Landscape Directory (SLD), and if not available, create a new one for the interface.
6. Configure SAP NetWeaver PI for routing to the target SAP ERP application.
7. Create a user ID in the SAP NetWeaver PI environment for the MDM SAP NetWeaver PI person for monitoring purposes to ensure that the interface is working successfully.

External and Internal Numbering

For external numbering, MDM maintains the number range, generates the numbers, and sends the range along with the IDoc (CREMAS/ADRMAS). Turning external numbering on for a Vendor Account Group is a good process because it ties the consuming system to the MDM application. It's a true centralized model with all new vendor records being created first in MDM and then distributed to the consuming SAP ERP system, which means you don't have to reconcile MDM and the consuming system to see if new records have been created.

Internal numbering implies that MDM isn't as tightly coupled to the consuming SAP ERP application. It's still possible to create records directly in SAP ERP. Also, MDM needs to find the vendor number generated by SAP to store as the key mapping. The vendor number is also needed to inform the local business users who will then extend the vendor for a company code and purchasing organization in the SAP ERP 6.0 application.

Technically, however, internal numbering is still straightforward to achieve. In this case, prior to the distribution process, you make a Remote Function Call (RFC) to the SAP ERP 6.0 (BAPI_VENDOR_GETINTNUMBER) application from the portal/ MDM application. This enables you to obtain the next available vendor number in the range and then to syndicate the vendor record with the vendor number populated.

Advantages

By following this technical approach, it enables you to use the same CREMAS/ ADRMAS interface for both internal and external numbering. For message type ADRMAS, a custom process code needs to be created. This process code must launch the function module IDOC_INPUT_ADRMAS. You can reuse the same interface from MDM to SAP ERP 6.0, and no local development is required on the SAP ERP 6.0 application. There are no changes in the current support mechanisms. The same interface can be used for change/created vendor, instead of building multiple interfaces.

SAP NetWeaver PI and Large Data Loads

For large business partner loads, SAP NetWeaver PI isn't the preferred option for flat file transfer. A likely scenario for a large number of MDM records is a new SAP ERP deployment or a merger or acquisition. In these situations, you should use the usual data conversion processes to initially populate the customer and vendor records in the SAP ERP 6.0 application. The MDM program must work closely with the SAP ERP deployment team to ensure that all data standards are followed. MDM then manages the operational processes immediately after go-live if the preferred MDM centralized model is followed.

10.3   Summary

In this chapter, you learned how to integrate MDM with the wider SAP NetWeaver components. We discussed the options available to you for the provision of end user interfaces, including MDM Data Manager, SAP Interactive Forms, and the SAP NetWeaver Portal, along with how you'll implement the solutions to enable your end users to execute their MDM tasks. You understand how the various workflow tools that you can use compare, including MDM workflow, Guided Procedures (GP), and SAP Business Workflow.

You discovered how the middleware, SAP NetWeaver Process Integration (PI), is used to distribute the master data records. We considered the functions available to you in SAP NetWeaver PI, and explained how you handle the data integration scenario using them.

Let's now move on to our final chapter where we'll consider the deployment of some of MDM's advanced technical features, including the use of the MDM Java API and Web Services.

In this chapter, we consider the application layer and the use of the MDM Java API and Web Services. We describe how to plan for MDM service pack upgrades and the key features of recent releases.

11   Advanced Features

In this chapter, we'll discuss how an MDM application is developed using the MDM Java API and Web Services. The MDM Java API allows you to write customized applications for interacting with the MDM server. We'll discuss the significant recent improvements and changes to the MDM Java API. We then describe how search Web Services can be used to enable your business users to retrieve customer and vendor data from the MDM repositories.

You'll learn how to plan for upgrades to your SAP NetWeaver MDM landscape, and finally, we'll the latest technical features provided in the service packs SAP NetWeaver MDM 5.5 SP05 and SP06.

11.1   Introducing Application Programming Interfaces and Web Services

The SAP NetWeaver MDM architecture follows a classical "three tier" model with the presentation layer, the application layer, and the data layer separated on different servers. Figure 11.1 shows how the three tiers are linked. The application layer consists of the MDM Java API and Web Services and both reside on the SAP NetWeaver Application Server.

We discussed the *presentation layer* in Chapter 10 when we described how to design the portal content in the form of iViews and roles to present the screens to your business users. In Chapter 8, we described the *data layer* and how you design your MDM repositories in the form of main tables and look-up tables. We'll now consider the *application layer,* which is hosted on the SAP NetWeaver Application Server.

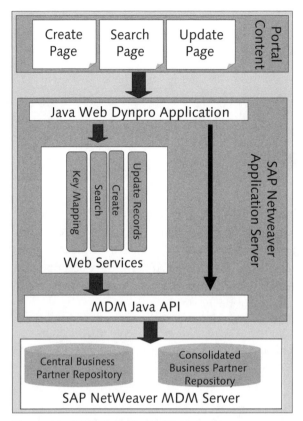

Figure 11.1 MDM Three Tier Architecture

There are several choices of programming tools to use in your SAP NetWeaver application layer. Following are the three primary MDM application programming languages:

▶ MDM Java API for access from Java programs

▶ MDM COM API for access from Windows programs

▶ MDM ABAP API for access from SAP applications

This chapter focuses on the MDM Java API, but even then, there are choices because there are two different types of API. The "new" MDM Java API replaces the recently deprecated MDM4J API, and we'll consider the implications of this.

Additionally, you have the option to use the MDM Web Services. Web Services represent a self-contained subset of application functionality allowing different applications from different sources to communicate with each other without time-consuming custom coding. Because all communication is in XML, Web Services are not tied to any one operating system or programming language.

Service-oriented architecture (SOA) is an architectural style aimed at achieving loose coupling and thereby permitting the reuse of interacting software agents/components. Although these concepts have existed for decades, the adoption of SOA is accelerating due to the emergence of standards-based integration technologies, mainly Web Services.

In Figure 11.1, you can see how the Web Services call the MDM Java API to interact with the MDM data server. SAP provides you with eight individual Web Services:

```
MDMGetKeyMapping
MDMAddRemoteKey
MDMSearchRecords
MDMCreateRecords
MDMUpdateRecords
MDMCreateBP
MDMUpdateBP
MDMSearchBP
```

So a fundamental question for you to consider is, "When do I use an MDM Java API and when do I use an MDM Web Service?"

The answer to this question depends on your enterprise architecture standards. If your company is a passionate adopter of SOA you may choose to implement Web Services for all of the MDM server interactions.

However, a more pragmatic solution is to provide a Web Service only when you want to make your MDM data available to the rest of your company. In large organizations, you may have several business users (maybe even hundreds of business users) who want to search the business partner records stored in MDM to decide whether to set up a new customer or vendor, or maybe to see where else a particular customer or vendor is used in the organization.

Earlier in this book, we described MDM as the "yellow pages" of an organization. By providing the MDM company search as a Web Service, you make the MDM data more accessible to your organization so that it can be presented not just through the SAP NetWeaver Portal but also through any other portal you may have in your company.

However, the end-to-end process of creating a new vendor or customer record in MDM — from handling a request using workflow, enriching the data with D&B Corporate Linkage details, and then distributing out to a consuming system — is a complex one.

This CRUD (create, read, update, delete) application is used by a relatively small number of MDM data stewards. Each of these users has access to the SAP NetWeaver Portal, and there is no requirement to publish this "work in progress" information to a wider user community across your organization.

For these CRUD processes, it seems sensible just to use the MDM Java APIs and don't take on the extra work of creating, publishing, and maintaining the Web Services, which your wider business users will never use. Back to our "yellow pages" analogy, as a consumer, you would only expect to read the finished book listing of all of the validated companies, rather than see those new companies that are currently in the process of being set up.

If you adopt this approach, you use both the MDM Java API and the Web Services in the application layer, but you'll only use the search Web Services. The `MDMSearchRecords` and `MDMSearchBP` Web Services are described later in Section 11.3.

Let's now consider the "new" improved MDM Java API and how you can establish connections and create sessions to maintain the data in your MDM repositories.

11.2 The MDM Java API

The source of the information in this section is the MDM 5.5 SP06 SAP Java API Migration Guide and the MDM 5.5 SP06 SAP Java API Guide.

The MDM Java API allows your developers to write customized applications for interacting with the MDM server.

MDM4J is the part of the API that was released with the initial shipment of SAP NetWeaver MDM 5.5. The functions offered are limited to those dealing with the repository content, such as searching for records or creating records. No functions are available to modify the repository structure or to administrate the MDM server.

In contrast, the "new" MDM Java API, which was introduced with SAP NetWeaver MDM 5.5 SP03, follows a completely different architecture. It separates connections on the network layer from logical sessions that are used to execute commands. This command-oriented approach offers a broad set of functions covering data and repository management as well as MDM server administration.

11.2.1 Background to the MDM JAVA API

As shown in Figure 11.1, the "new" MDM Java API is designed to provide a flexible and robust interface to the MDM server. The API command classes expose a granular and comprehensive set of functions for basic operations such as editing data and searching, as well as advanced functionality such as repository administration.

The core API is built on top of basic Java to make deployment as simple as possible. The development of the new Java API has undergone several stages. The original MDM Java API, as introduced with MDM 5.5 SP03, only included four JAR files supplying functionality for server and repository administration.

An additional JAR file was added to the API for SP04 and SP05, enabling management of the repository content as well. We'll refer to this set of five JAR files as the Basic MDM Java API:

```
mdm-admin.jar
mdm-common.jar
mdm-core.jar
mdm-data.jar
mdm-protocol.jar
```

In SP06, the API was extended with an extension layer that includes more functionality to enable more convenient and user-friendly use of the API. The new mdm-extension.jar extends the commands from the mdm-data.jar. Using the features in the extension layer isn't mandatory and only supplies an alternative to similar features provided in the Basic API set. However, these features can simplify application development significantly and are recommended by SAP as best practices for using the MDM Java API.

11.2.2 Comparing MDM4J API and the New MDM Java API

The legacy MDM4J API has now been deprecated in favor of the MDM Java API and will no longer be supported starting with version SAP NetWeaver MDM 7.1.

In this section, we'll compare important aspects of both APIs to help you if you need to rewrite your application to use the new MDM Java API instead of MDM4J.

MDM4J implements a monolithic approach where sessions (login), connections, connection pool, and cache are coupled. Using the `CatalogData.Login()` method, you create all of these at once.

The new MDM Java API takes a different approach where physical connections can be used by several sessions. Physical connections are established using the MDM network protocol on top of TCP/IP. The MDM server binds to port 20005, and any client application using the Java API creates a TCP connection to this port.

Searching

Search operations with the new MDM Java API work in a similar way to those based on MDM4J. The concept is based on a search object that specifies the search criteria (such as which keyword to search for). In addition, there is the `Result-Definition` class for specifying which data should be retrieved from the repository for the records that are found.

In MDM4J, the corresponding class name is `ResultSetDefinition`. Using this class, the fields, as well as the taxonomy attributes, can be selected, and the API returns their values.

The basic usage pattern for searching with the new MDM Java API differs in two major aspects, namely the command pattern and how to retrieve additional values for referenced look-up tables.

Working with Identifiers

MDM4J uses integers as identifiers for records and strings for tables. For example, if you want to add a field to a `ResultSetDefinition`, you need to pass the field code in method `AddField()`.

In contrast, the new API follows a typed approach. It uses subclasses of `com.sap.mdm.ids.AbstractID` to reference objects such as records, tables, and fields. There are dedicated classes for record, field, and table identifiers, which avoids mixing them up by accident. You can find these in the package `com.sap.mdm.ids`.

11.2.3 API Structure and Basic Concepts

From a functionality point of view, all Java classes representing the MDM Java API can be divided into the following groups.

Commands

A set of command classes is the core of the MDM Java API. The design follows the command pattern, which requires that each API feature is represented by one dedicated command. Each command contains all of the information necessary to make requests to and receive results from the server.

Each API command, in order to be created and executed, requires a socket connection to the MDM server and a `Session ID`, which is a unique string specifying a user session for the MDM server or for a specific repository in the MDM server.

Connectivity Classes

These classes supply connections and sessions needed for command execution. The extension layer includes an additional concept called the MDM Session Context, and the MDM Session Context class helps to simplify the creation of API commands and the management of connections, sessions, and Metadata.

Repository Metadata Structure Classes

These classes represent properties of Metadata elements (components that can be viewed and explored through the MDM Console). Examples are table, field, relationship, and user classes. Usually these classes are named according to the name template `XXXProperties`, for example, `TableProperties`, `FieldProperties`, `RelationshipProperties`, and `UserProperties`.

Repository Data Structure Classes

These classes represent the content of the repository (all components that can be viewed and explored through the MDM Data Manager). Examples include records, attributes, field/attribute values, and workflow tasks.

Utilities

These classes supply services that can simplify the application development process:

▶ `ConnectionManager` creates any type of `ConnectionAccessor` instances.

▶ `SessionManager` creates and caches any type of session.

▶ `MetadataManager` caches the repository Metadata.

▶ `MeasurementUtilities` supplies useful methods for operations with measurement values.

▶ `MdmValueFormatter` enables the formatting of any type of MDM values.

Let's now consider how connections and sessions are established in SP06 using the new MDM Java APIs.

11.2.4 Connections and Sessions

As we've described, the new MDM Java API takes the approach where physical connections can be used by several sessions. Physical connections are established using the MDM network protocol on top of TCP/IP. The MDM server binds to port 20005, and any client application using the Java API creates a TCP connection to this port.

The MDM Java API provides pooled access as well as simple (meaning single or dedicated) access to connections through the two factory classes `ConnectionPool-Factory` and `SimpleConnectionFactory`. After a connection is established, a session can be created on top of it.

Session Types

There are three types of sessions, and, depending on which action is to be performed, the corresponding session type must be created.

A *server session* is used for the general management of running an MDM server, such as mounting a repository, stopping the MDM server, and unarchiving a repository.

A *repository session* is used for managing an MDM repository. A repository session is created for a specific MDM repository, and after it has been created, it can only be used in conjunction with this repository. Repository sessions are used to create, delete, or modify administrative parts (such as users or roles) and data model-related parts (such as fields and tables) on a repository. If for any reason a repository isn't mounted, the repository session becomes invalid.

All activities that are interactively performed using the MDM Console require either a server session or a repository session.

A *user session* is used for repository content management. User sessions allow you to search for records but also any other content-related activity such as updates of records or creating attributes. Again, if a repository is unloaded, the user session becomes invalid.

In general, all activities related to repository content and for which you would use MDM Data Manager require a user session. Sessions are created by issuing one of three commands:

- `CreateServerSessionCommand`
- `CreateRepositorySessionCommand`
- `CreateUserSessionCommand`

Commands

Any action to be performed from the MDM Java API requires the use of a dedicated command. Commands are grouped in Java packages according to their function; for example, you find all of the commands for working with validations in the package `com.sap.mdm.validation.commands`.

Each command requires a set of arguments that are specified using several setter methods. For some arguments, built-in default values exist (optional arguments); other arguments must be set before the command can finally be executed. One of the mandatory arguments is the session to be used for the command.

Depending on the command, a specific session type must be used which is given in the `Javadoc` of the corresponding command class. Some commands don't have a session argument. They don't require a session and are session-less. Typically, these are all of the commands that are used to create a session.

Authentication

The MDM server executes a command only if the corresponding session has been authenticated beforehand. Exceptions are the session-less commands that don't use a session at all. For each session type, there is an authentication command that takes the session to be authenticated, a user name, and a user password as arguments:

▶ Server session: `AuthenticateServerSessionCommand`

▶ Repository session: `AuthenticateRepositorySessionCommand`

▶ User session: `AuthenticateUserSessionCommand`

In use cases where the user has already been authenticated by some other means, for example, by a web application, an authenticated session can be created using these commands:

▶ Server session: `TrustedServerSessionCommand`

▶ Repository session: `TrustedRepositorySessionCommand`

▶ User session: `TrustedUserSessionCommand`

These commands require only a session and a user name as arguments and create an authenticated session. In order not to compromise security, a trusted connection needs to be established between the MDM server and the client using the MDM Java API. This needs to be configured on the MDM server side.

11.2.5 Summary – The Basic Building Blocks

Using the MDM Java API for accessing data that resides in an MDM repository requires the implementation of the following basic building blocks:

1. Create a Connection

The first step is to obtain a `ConnectionAccessor` via the `getInstance()` method of either `SimpleConnectionFactory` or `ConnectionPoolFactory`. This method requires the mandatory parameter `connectionTag` to have the destination server name as the value.

2. Create a User Session

Using the ConnectionAccessor, create an instance of the command class CreateUserSessionCommand, and execute it. Mandatory parameters for this command are the repository to which the sessions should be established and the data region to be used. These parameters are set via the methods setRepositoryIdentifier() and setDataRegion().

3. Authenticate the Session

Before any command can be executed via the user session, successful authentication needs to take place. Typically, this is done with the command AuthenticateUserSessionCommand, which requires the session to authenticate the user name and the password as parameters.

4. Work with the Session

The authenticated session is then used to execute one or several further commands. This comprises creating an instance of a particular command class using ConnectionAccessor and passing the session as well as any other mandatory parameter via the respective setter methods. For commands that return data, the result can be retrieved using the respective getter method(s) after the execute() method has returned.

5. Destroy the Session

After all work has been completed, the session needs to be destroyed by executing the DestroySessionCommand. This frees the reserved resources on the MDM server.

6. Close the Connection

In the case of simple connections, if the connection is no longer needed, SimpleConnection.close() should be called. If pooled connections are used, connections are created and closed by the pool handler according to the settings of minConnections and maxConnections. Unused connections can be closed on request with method ConnectionPool.freeUnused().

11.2.6   Searching

Search operations with the new MDM Java API work very similarly to those based on MDM4J. The concept is based on a Search object that specifies the search criteria, such as which keyword to search for. In addition, there is the `ResultDefinition` class for specifying which data should be retrieved from the repository for the records that are found.

In MDM4J, the corresponding class name is `ResultSetDefinition`. Using this class, the fields as well as the taxonomy attributes can be selected, and the API returns their values.

The basic usage pattern for MDM4J looks like this:

▶ Create an instance of Search, and add the search criteria to the class.

▶ Create an instance of `ResultSetDefinition`, add the fields for which the values should be retrieved, and optionally set a flag indicating whether attribute values should also be retrieved.

▶ Call `CatalogData.GetResultSet()` to execute the search and to retrieve the record details in an instance of `ResultSet`. To get values of referenced look-up tables, create additional instances of `ResultSetDefinition`, and perform additional calls of `CatalogData.GetRecordsById()`, which potentially result in several additional `ResultSet` instances.

▶ For accessing the search result, use the multiple instances of `ResultSet`.

The basic usage pattern for searching with the new MDM Java API differs in two major aspects: first the command pattern, and secondly, how to retrieve additional values for referenced look-up tables.

Create an instance of Search, and add the search criteria to the class. Then create an instance of `ResultDefinition`, and add the fields whose values should be retrieved. There is also a flag to request the retrieval of attribute values.

To get the values from fields of referenced look-up tables, create additional instances of `ResultDefinition`. Then, instantiate a search command, such as `RetrieveLimitedRecordsCommand`, and set the command's arguments for the search and the result definitions. With the new API, it's possible to do this for the search table and the look-up tables in parallel. Finally, execute the command, and retrieve the search result in one single result instance of `RecordResultSet`.

11.2.7 Working with Identifiers

MDM4J uses integers as identifiers for records and strings for tables. For example, if you want to add a field to a `ResultSetDefinition`, you need to pass the field code in method `AddField()`. In contrast, the new API follows a typed approach. It uses subclasses of `com.sap.mdm.ids.AbstractID` for referencing objects such as records, tables, and fields.

There are dedicated classes for record, field, and table identifiers, which avoids mixing them up by accident. You find these in the package `com.sap.mdm.ids`. We'll now introduce the most important identifier classes.

TableID

The first identifier class to use when working with the MDM Java API is the `TableID`. The `TableID` is required to instantiate a search, for example:

```
TableID myTableID;
(...)
Search mySearch = New Search(myTableID);
```

One way to create the `TableID` is to use the constructor `TableID(int ID)`. This is only possible if the integer identifier is known, although typically this isn't the case because this number isn't displayed in the MDM Console. The information you have in the MDM Console is the field code, a language-independent identification string of the table, but there is no constructor of `TableID` into which you can feed this code.

You need to use the method `RepositorySchema.getTable(String code)` to retrieve the `TableProperties` first. After that, the ID can be obtained using the method `TableProperties.getID()`.

A typical process you'll follow during the initialization of any program is that you'll retrieve the complete schema of the repository you are working with, using the command `GetRepositorySchemaCommand`. Then using the returned instance of `RepositorySchema`, you can easily convert from table code to `TableID`.

> **Note**
>
> There is a constructor `TableID(String IDString)`, but this argument is a special string notation of the identifier, and this constructor isn't meant to be used directly.

FieldID

Following the same approach as for table identifiers, you need to add fields to a result definition for field identifiers, for example.

`ResultDefinition.addSelectField(FieldID myFieldID);`

Again, you can instantiate the `FieldID` directly if the integer identifier is known. The field code used in the MDM Console can be converted to `FieldID` using this method:

`RepositorySchema.getField(String code)`

This method returns an instance of `FieldProperties`, which makes it possible to get the `FieldID` by method `getID()`.

> **Note**
>
> As for the constructor `TableID(String IDString)`, you can only use the constructor `FieldID(String IDString)` using the special string representation of a field identifier.

AttributeID

Knowing the identifier of an attribute is especially important if you want to set the value of a particular attribute via method.

`Record.setAttributeValue(FieldID taxonomyFieldID, AttributeID attributeID, MdmValue value)`

Because attributes and their assignments to taxonomy nodes are not part of the repository schema (they are not maintained using MDM Data Manager), attribute identifiers can't be obtained using the class `RepositorySchema`. Attributes are created and modified when a repository is loaded, and, therefore, attributes can possibly change during run time.

For this reason, any information about attributes must be retrieved using specialized commands. The first command `RetrieveAttributesCommand` is useful if you need a complete list of all attributes defined for a given taxonomy table.

The second command `RetrieveAttributeLinksCommand` is preferable if you want to get a list of all of the attributes of a specific record that are available for setting their value. This command evaluates the existing linkages to attributes of a given taxonomy node and therefore returns only the valid attributes for a record that is already assigned to a taxonomy node.

This command returns an array of `AttributeLink`. From each of the array elements you can retrieve the respective `AttributeID` and, for example, use this identifier for composing the call of `setAttributeValue()`.

Let's now move on to consider MDM Web Services and specifically how you create a Web Service to enable your business users to search MDM records to find a customer or vendor record.

11.3   MDM Web Services

Web Services for MDM are open interfaces to the MDM server. They are based on the Simple Object Access Protocol (SOAP) and Web Services Description Language (WSDL) standards.

They provide data management capabilities (create, read, update) and access to central key mapping (create, read). MDM Web Services provide synchronous access to MDM for the consumer of the Web Services.

The source for the information in this section is the SAP NetWeaver MDM 5.5 SP06 Web Services document.

11.3.1   General Concept of Web Services

Web Services are web-based interfaces that can be integrated into business scenarios of a company based on open and commonly accepted standards. They describe a standardized way of integrating Web-based applications using the XML, SOAP, WSDL, and UDDI open standards.

Web Services represent a self-contained subset of application functionality allowing different applications from different sources to communicate with each other without time-consuming custom coding. Because all communication is in XML, Web Services are not tied to any one operating system or programming language.

SOA is an architectural style aimed at achieving loose coupling and thereby permitting the reuse of interacting software agents/components. Although these concepts have existed for decades, the adoption of SOA is accelerating due to the emergence of standards-based integration technologies, mainly Web Services.

You can best benefit from SOA by assembling/combining existing services and reusable components into new applications called composite applications. A *composite application* describes the combination of services into new functionality.

SAP has coined the term enterprise SOA (previously Enterprise Service Architecture). Technically speaking, an enterprise service is a Web Service with business functionality and enterprise quality (with regard to scalability, robustness, and security). Looking at the bigger picture, enterprise SOA is more than a collection of Web Services; it's a comprehensive solution for the new emerging requirements for enterprise applications. The ability to search for customer and vendor master data stored in an MDM repository is a classical enterprise SOA service.

11.3.2 Introduction to MDM Web Services

The MDM Web Services can be used to manage master data objects and to check for the existence of a central master object before local creation. You can retrieve details and create or update master data objects on MDM. SAP provides eight individual Web Services:

```
MDMGetKeyMapping
MDMAddRemoteKey
MDMSearchRecords
MDMCreateRecords
MDMUpdateRecords
MDMCreateBP
MDMUpdateBP
MDMSearchBP
```

MDM Web Services operations use the following eight XML data types: Repository Information, Execution Status, Configuration Data, Data Element, Record Identifier, Record, Query Interface, and Key Mapping Query.

Let's now focus on the two search Web Services: `MDMSearchRecords` and `MDMSearchBP`. We earlier described MDM as the "yellow pages" of your organization so by providing the MDM Company search in the form of a Web Service, you make the MDM data more accessible across your organization. We'll also consider the XML data types used in the `MDMSearchRecords` Web Service.

11.3.3 MDM Search Records

The Web Service `MDMSearchRecords` has the following Web Service operations:

```
MDMSearchResponse searchRecords(Query query, RepositoryInformation
repositoryInformation, ConfigurationData configurationData)
```

MDM SearchRecords Functionality

This Web Service searches for records in one MDM repository. One search request can return multiple records in an array of MDMRecord. Depending on the query instance used for the request, the resulting records may consist only of RecordIdentifiers or a DataElement data type. The resulting record can be based on all fields, only display fields, or a specific custom-defined field list.

Depending on the constraints defined within the query instance, the returning MDMSearchResponse instance contains the resulting data in record array MDMData and/or array ExcecutionStatus. These results provide feedback about errors that occurred during the request. If an error occurred, the ExcecutionStatus data type contains at least one fatal or error instance. If no errors occurred, it returns the searched data.

Each request is based on a specific main table. The main table is currently used for the request as well as for the result. At the moment, it isn't possible to have the request and result in different tables, but this will be possible in future releases.

Each record returned within MDMData consists of a RecordIdentifier and several DataElement data types (if defined in this way within the query constraints). If DataElements are also returned, each instance of them contains either the value(s) of a specific field of the requested table or an attribute related to a specific field of the requested table. Look-up values are attached recursively as records to the corresponding DataElement, if the field is of type look-up. Qualified links contain a specific link ID to identify them as unique.

The input consists of the following data types: Query to describe the requested data constraints, RepositoryInformation to describe where the request should be performed, and ConfigurationData.

MDMSearchBP Functionality

MDMSearchBP is a Web Service for searching a business partner repository. This Web Service finds business partner records in an MDM repository based on the parameters passed to it. The format of the result may also be defined. This Web Service is based on the generic MDM search Web Service (although it isn't a composite Web Service).

The Web Service name is MDMSearchBP and the Web Service operations are the following:

```
MDMBusinessPartnerSearchResponse searchBusinessPartners(Query
query,RepositoryInformation repositoryInformation, ConfigurationData
configurationData)
```

Return Messages

In MDMSearchBP, the return type is MDMBusinessPartnerSearchResponse. This type contains both ExecutionStatus and BusinessPartner.

ExecutionStatus data types may indicate that the status of execution was OK, PARTIAL, or FAIL. If it was PARTIAL or FAIL, details of the exceptions caught are represented in an array of Fail objects.

BusinessPartner holds the results of a PARTIAL or OK search result.

Error Handling

Errors are caught and returned as ExecutionStatus data types. The exception MDM-WebServiceException is declared in the method searchBusinessPartners, but this should never be thrown.

Let's now consider the data types contained in the search Web Services.

Repository Information

Each Web Service contains the RepositoryInformation data type that defines which MDM repository is to be addressed by the service.

Table 11.1 shows the data elements that are required.

XML Element	Description
serverName	Name of the MDM server
repositoryName	Name of the repository
repositoryPort	Port of the repository (optional)
schemaLang	Language of the schema, for example, table or field names
dataLang	Language of the data in particular values of multilingual fields

Table 11.1 Repository Information Web Service XML Elements

Execution Status

All Web Services contain an `ExecutionStatus` data type in the return parameter. All errors, warnings, and information are appended to this data type together with information that identifies the corresponding record.

Table 11.2 provides a description of each element that make up the `Execution-Status` data type.

XML Element	Description
Description	General description of the operation useful especially in case of failure
Status	Information indicating whether the operation was executed successfully (SUCCESS) or not (ERROR)
DataObject	Information about the object as a string
DataObjectID	Set of variables that identifies the object
Fault	Set of error messages
Severity	Type of message (INFORMATION, WARNING, or ERROR)
ID	Internal technical identifier of the error
Text	Message text detailed description of the error or warning

Table 11.2 Exception Status Web Service XML Elements

Configuration Data

The `ConfigurationData` data type is used to configure the behavior of an MDM Web Service. It contains an array of `ConfigurationDataElements`, each one wrapping a key/value pair. The key defines the name of the element, and the value specifies its value.

Table 11.3 shows the `ConfigurationData` data type supported for `searchRecords`.

Key	Description	Value
PopulateRecord Identifier	Specifies whether the returned record identifier within the returned record is populated (value = true) with `AutoId` and/ or unique fields data, (if the record contains these fields).	If the value specified isn't null and equals true, (not case sensitive), `PopulateRecord Identifier` has a true value. The default value is set to false.

Table 11.3 `ConfigurationData` Data Type Supported for `SearchRecords`

Data Element

MDM Web Services use the `DataElement` data type to represent the fields and attributes of an MDM repository. The following fields and attributes can be represented: simple fields, date time fields, measurement fields, name, look-up fields, qualified look-up fields, and MDM attributes.

Table 11.4 provides a description of each element that makes up the `DataElement` data type.

XML Element	Description
DataElement	List of field values as name/value pairs
displayValue	Contains the display value of a field (e.g., for look-ups).
field	Field/attribute in which the data is stored.
DataType	Data type of the field (is returned by retrieve not needed for add and update).. Data types: Integer (Maximum Value 231-1), Boolean, Create Stamp, Currency, GM Time, Literal Date, Literal Time, Log, Measurement, Name, Text, Text Large, Text Normalized, Real, Time Stamp, User Stamp.
unifiedField	Metadata of field or attribute.
Code	Language-independent code of the field.
objectName	Language-dependent names of the field/attribute.
Name	Name of the field/attribute.
Language	If the value is initialized, the logon language is used.
taxonomyField	Used for attributes, contains the data of the field to which the attribute refers. In this case, `unifiedField` contains the attribute Metadata.
simpleValue	Contains the values for a field/attribute of simple data type (no look-up).
Position	Represents the order of values for multivalue fields.
unifiedValue	Represents the value of a field or an attribute.
value (1..n)	Values of a field (multiple in case of multilingual field).
Value	Single of multivalue.
Language	If the value is initialized, the logon language is used.

Table 11.4 DateElement Web Service XML Elements

XML Element	Description
Unit	Unit of measurements and currency
remoteKey	Contains the remote keys only of the attribute values if key mapping exists.
look-upValue	Refers to the record of the look-up.
linkID	Link of a qualified look-up needed to identify the qualified link in case of update.

Table 11.4   DateElement Web Service XML Elements (Cont.)

MDM Attributes

If an attribute is set for a taxonomy field, the attribute has its own data element object. The field object specifies the attribute name and the taxonomy field to which the attribute belongs.

▶ A taxonomyField object is nested in the field object to specify the taxonomy field to which the attribute belongs. The taxonomy field is identified by the code.

▶ A unifiedField object is nested in the field object to specify the attribute. This attribute is identified by a combination of name and language.

The attribute value is specified by the unifiedValue nested in a simpleValue object.

Record Identifier

The RecordIdentifier data type contains the information that identifies the record and is used for records of all table types. It is used in certain Web Services for identifying records and represents the MDM internal identifier (integer) and the MDM external identifier (the first display field of a record). Table 11.5 shows the RecordIdentifier XML elements.

XML Element	Description
RecordIdentifier	Contains the information for identifying the record.
RecordID	Internal record ID (integer).

Table 11.5   Record Identifier Web XML Elements

XML Element	Description
ExternalID	Value of first display field normally used by the user to identify the record (e.g., in the Data Manager).
RemoteKey	(0..n) Remote key in remote system (one tag per remote system).
ClientSystem	Code of the remote system as maintained in the MDM Console and in the key mapping of the Data Manager.
Key (1..n)	Key (identifier) of the record in the remote system.
Value	Value of the key.
IsDefault	Indicates if key is the default key for this remote system.
Table	Identifies the table in which the record is stored.
Code	Language-independent code of the table.
TableName (0..n)	Language-dependent names of the table.
Name	Name of the table or field.
Language	If value is initial, the logon language is used.
AutoId	Record's auto Id(Integer). This element isn't part of the interface of the MDMAddRemoteKey Web Service.
uniqueFields	A unique constraint that consists of one or more fields that are represented by DataElements. This element isn't part of the interface of the MDMAddRemoteKey Web Service.

Table 11.5 Record Identifier Web XML Elements (Cont.)

Now that we've covered the MDM Web Services, let's move on to how to plan for upgrades to your SAP NetWeaver MDM landscape and then consider the functionality provided in the service packs MDM 5.5 SP05 and SP06.

11.4   Planning for Service Pack Upgrades and Recent Service Pack Functionality

MDM is a recent SAP product and has been subject to considerable changes and improvements over the past three years. There have typically been one or two service packs introduced in a given year.

Primarily, MDM releases provide you with enhanced functionality and additional tools and capabilities. You'll see from the long list of new features in this section that this was the case for both SP05 and SP06. An MDM release will also fix defects in a proactive way before you encounter them. Systems constantly change, and technical structures need to adapt accordingly. You also need to apply the service pack to keep you within the SAP support window guidelines; it's also beneficial to be on the latest available version whenever you need to raise an SAP OSS note.

We'll first consider how you plan for MDM and SAP NetWeaver upgrades.

11.4.1 Planning for MDM Service Pack Upgrades

Take the service pack changes as positive improvements. SAP is continuously improving the NetWeaver components, and this is a good thing for your organization because you get better value from your investment. In most cases, you see only benefits and very few negative impacts.

An exception to this is the change to deprecate the MDM4J API in favor of the MDM Java API and no longer support if from version MDM 7.1. Both APIs have been available during SP03 and SP04, and for those organizations that chose the original MDM4J, there will be rework and testing to migrate the code. If your organization faces this issue, plan the exercise sensibly, and try to change the code at the same time as other functional changes to minimize your regression testing effort.

In most cases, applying a new service pack is a straightforward exercise. The MDM repository that you have developed based on an existing template to meet your business requirements can be simple upgraded by a "repair" of the repository. Don't think of it as a big deal; it's a simple process when compared with an SAP ERP 6.0 type upgrade. You can usually fully test and upgrade your SAP NetWeaver MDM landscape within a two-month period.

You need to establish the appropriate governance processes for each of the shared SAP NetWeaver components, including the NetWeaver Portal and XI. The service pack patching schedule should be agreed on both with your MDM Steering Board and the wider SAP NetWeaver Steering Board.

You should include in your MDM roadmap the application of new service packs. This plan will include the following steps.

Step 1: Produce an MDM Service Pack Assessment Report

Assess the impact of the service pack within four weeks of release. Your skilled SAP NetWeaver resources will review the SAP NetWeaver MDM service pack release notes to assess the following:

▶ What's new?

▶ Will it provide a quick win to help out with a current existing issue?

▶ How will it benefit the MDM program?

▶ What is no longer supported? Recent examples include starting with MDM 5.5 SP05, the MDM Import Manager Batch and MDM Syndicator Batch will no longer be delivered, and the legacy MDM4J API has now been deprecated in favor of the MDM Java API and will no longer be supported starting with MDM 7.1.

Also consider what else is happening in your MDM program:

▶ What is your MDM roadmap for the next three to six months?

▶ Are you about to go-live with integration into some major new consuming systems?

▶ What MDM enhancement work is about to move to production?

▶ What is the wider SAP NetWeaver roadmap (including SAP NetWeaver Portal and SAP NetWeaver PI)?

▶ What are the dependencies of group policies such as accounting procedures and financial period end closes?

The output from this exercise is an *MDM Service Pack Assessment Report*, which answers these questions and includes a plan as to when to implement the new service pack in your sandbox, project, and production MDM environments. When planning the implementation of a service pack, also consider your entire SAP NetWeaver landscape.

Step 2: Install Service Pack on a Sandbox Environment

This is an excellent way to start your service pack testing. The sandbox is usually a "play area" where you can test without any impacts for your end business users. In the same way that we encouraged you to be bold with your MDM proof of concept and to try out as many things as possible, the same principle applies with your sandbox testing. Be innovative and test the new software from all angles. The more issues you can find during this period, the better.

If any rework is required to your MDM applications, prioritize these activities so that they can be retested before you decide to apply the service pack to your development environment.

Step 3: Test in Your Development Environments

You need to plan both Step 3 and Step 4 in a clearly defined and short time frame so that changes can be controlled. Ensure that you have the skilled business users and SAP NetWeaver technical experts available to test and fix any issues that you find.

Aim to promote from your development environment to your production environment within one month. It's not a good practice to have the two environments at different service pack levels for longer than this because it impacts both your development program and also the testing of any defects found in your live system.

Step 4: Move the Service Pack into the Production Environment

And finally, hopefully you can make a smooth transition to the production landscape. Ensure that you document all changes in a formal MDM release note so that your business users and MDM data stewards are prepared for any changes that arise in the MDM applications.

A final piece of advice for a "startup" MDM implementation is to use the latest available version of the SAP NetWeaver MDM software at the start of your implementation, and also upgrade to the latest versions before you go-live. It's much easier to test when there are no live consuming systems and business users to impact!

Let's now move on to consider the latest functionality, which was provided in the service packs SAP NetWeaver MDM 5.5 SP05 and SP06.

11.4.2 Service Pack Enhancements Up to MDM 5.5. SP06

Most of the information in this section has been taken directly from the SAP NetWeaver MDM 5.5 SP05 and SP06 Release Notes.

The most recent SAP NetWeaver MDM 5.5 service packs at the time of writing are SP05 and SP06. SP05 was made available for general release in April 2007 and SP06 in February 2008.

Whereas SP05 delivered several functional enhancements, SP06 focused more on the performance, quality, and supportability of MDM.

As a high-level summary, SP05 and SP06 improved the MDM Console security and the repository reconciliation (schema migration). There were improvements in the functionality of the import server and the syndication server, as well as MDM Data Manager enhancements. Solution Manager Diagnostics is now supported, and there is a new user interface for the Enrichment Architecture. There is enhanced MDM portal content with Enterprise Portal Connectivity Framework (EPCF) events from standard iViews and also improvements in the UWL.

We'll now consider the new functionality provided in SP05 and SP06, starting with the enhanced administration and repository reconciliation functionality.

11.4.3   Enhanced Administration and Repository Reconciliation (Schema Migration) in SP05 and SP06

In SP05, there is improved MDM Console security with a login per repository now required. This allows you to restrict the authorization in the MDM Console to change the administrative settings, to perform data modeling maintenance, and to execute schema migration tasks. The login to the repository is integrated into the repository's user and role management. An audit trail is now kept of schema modifications and security-related activities.

In SP05, a role can now be maintained even when users with that role are currently logged in. You can define how the MDM Console handles this by a setting in the `mds.ini` file (`Logged-In Role Maintenance=True or False`). In SP06, roles may now include constraints based on Named Searches.

In SP06, the `Relationships` table in the MDM Console now contains the Code field and the default remote system is created as type `Inbound/Outbound` (previously `Inbound`).

In SP05, the repository reconciliation (transport of repository changes from one repository to another) has been extended so that now changes to role definitions, expressions of calculated fields, and relationship definitions can be transported. A higher granularity on change handling (field/table detail level) is provided. Automated mapping has been enhanced for the mapping of source to destination field/table, and the manual assignment of source to destination is available.

In SP06, in the repository reconciliation, the Ports able is now supported (schema migration), as are validations and assignments. There are also new command-line interface (CLIX) commands available.

11.4.4 MDM Data Manager in SP05 and SP06

In SP05, with the improved stemming engine, a multilingual sounds-like search and a search for word roots (such as conjugated verbs) is possible. You can now search for measurements in the keyword search field and save search criteria in Named Searches, which can be reused by any user who logs in to the MDM repository.

In SP06, Adobe Illustrator images (AI) are now supported. The editing of multiselect qualified look-up fields is improved, and individual values for the same look-up records are now possible. Role constraints for Named Searches defined in the MDM Console are applied in the MDM Data Manager. Not initialized Named Searches behave like empty searches; that is, all records are presented in the MDM Data Manager.

11.4.5 MDM Import Manager and MDM Syndicator Enhancements in SP05 and SP06

In SP05, the import performance was improved. The virtual match class field was extended (e.g., to detect if a record was created or changed during an import). During an import, filtering can be used to filter records in the source and destination tables, and you can now delete records in the source and destination tables. You can import attribute values for records as name/value pairs.

In SP05, the MDM import server (MDIS) automation was enhanced. There is now support for hierarchy and relationships, the definition of inbound port sequence for MDIS, and inbound port status in the MDM Console. File aggregation via MDIS to optimize data transfer is now available as well.

In SP05, the syndication performance was improved. Automated syndication can be configured per port to be either no automatic syndication, continuously/direct (on change), or scheduled (automatic). The new workflow step syndicate is also provided.

From SP05, the MDM Import Manager Batch and MDM Syndicator Batch will no longer be delivered. For automated import and syndication, you can use the MDM import server and MDM syndication server.

11.4.6 MDM Portal Content in SP05 and SP06

In SP05, several additional MDM data maintenance functions are available. You can now create, read, update, and delete relationships, image fields and blobs, and hierarchy multivalue look-ups. There are enhanced qualified fields editing options and a change tracking application to check the changes made to the data in the MDM Console.

The MDM iViews user interface integration options were improved. Enterprise Portal Connectivity Framework (EPCF) event auto-firing and URL/EPCF table event are enabled, and dynamic URL and EPCF events for Result Set iViews and Item Details iViews are also available.

The Universal Work List (UWL) and the MDM workflow functions were enhanced. The Next Step function of the MDM workflow is supported, and the priority of the workflow task is displayed in the UWL. You can create and launch a job when master data is changed in iViews. The workflow is available in UWL.

In SP06, the MDM portal content provides several more new functions. If the checkbox column in a Result Set iView isn't used, it is disabled. The Save action triggers an event (EPCF) in an Item Details iView that can be used by other applications. A full view of the entries of a qualified table is supported in an Item Details iViews (pop-up).

A new unlaunched MDM workflow job without records can be created in the SAP NetWeaver UWL, allowing the addition of optional records. Depending on what role has been assigned to a user, the page on which the result set is placed can be more controlled (read-only or editing permissions). The workflow validation step is supported in Result Set iViews.

A new locking mechanism on record level is supported, and only unlaunched Workflows can be deleted.

The Java code of MDM UWL and of all launched MDM iViews (History, Next Step, Create Job) now only use the new Java APIs of MDM.

Field display can now be changed from vertical to horizontal to align fields that shift when editing an Item Details iView.

11.4.7 System Monitoring and Support Enablement in SP06

In SP06, there has been an improvement in the log files and trace files, and the content has been enhanced significantly (e.g., thread numbers, user names, and error descriptions). The new formatter allows easier reading and analyzability of the log files (e.g., sorting by thread, or filtering by error/all).

In SP06 the *Solution Manager Diagnostics 4.0 (SMD)* is now supported. All MDM log and trace files are visible in SMD via a file system browser using the MDM browser format. The OS command console allows you to call operation-specific commands out of the SMD user interface. For MDM, you can call the CLIX to perform activities on the MDM host such as monitory activity (e.g., `clix mdsMon host`) or setting log levels.

SMD provides a configuration browser to display the MDM configuration files. A comparison between different states is also possible. SMD provides remote monitoring of all databases underlying MDM. The workload analysis is based on the E2E Workload Analysis provided by SMD and the integration of Wily Introscope, which is now supported. Wily Introscope is a standard third-party tool that is integrated into the SMD workload analysis. It can be used for performance measurement and specific root cause analysis.

11.4.8 MDM Java API in SP05 and SP06

In SP05, the MDM Java API offers a broad functional coverage. You can now execute matching strategies, execute matching searches (existence check), access and modify master data and model repositories, and administrate MDM servers. The Java API can be consumed by J2SE applications (including the JARs in the JVM `classpath`), J2EE applications (using J2EE library and/or JCA connector), and portal applications (via the SAP Connector Architecture).

The *MDM Connector* is based on the SAP Connector Framework and provides connectivity between the MDM server and J2EE applications. In particular, the connector can be used within the SAP NetWeaver Portal and allows the configuration of connections to MDM repositories in the portal system landscape.

Besides the SAP NetWeaver Portal, any J2EE application can use the MDM Connector to establish physical connection to an MDM server, while allowing J2EE server-wide connection pooling, configuration, and monitoring.

(Old) MDM Java API – MDM4J

With SP05, the Java library MDM4J is considered deprecated. The next major release of SAP NetWeaver MDM won't support MDM4J anymore. MDM 5.5 SP05 is the last version to introduce new features in MDM4J with only the new Java API now being continuously extended. MDM4J is deprecated with SP05 because MDM4J will be completely replaced by the new MDM Java API in the next release of SAP NetWeaver MDM.

(New) MDM Java API

In SP06, the MDM Java API is further enhanced. New commands support masks, locking and unlocking records, and protecting sets of records. New methods support units and new attributes support sorting. A new command cancels syndication, and a new event indicates a failed syndication. A new command also specifies an admin role user instead of the default "Admin."

A new constructor has been added for all API commands obtaining MdmSession-Context as the input parameter, and a new class MetadataManager retrieves the Metadata information by demand and caches it. A new mdm-extension.jar extends the commands from mdm-data.jar. Extended commands enable you to manipulate the record data through the element codes (table code, field code) instead of element IDs.

11.4.9 Miscellaneous SP05 and AP06 Functionality

Several other additional pieces of functionality are provided in SP05 and SP06, which we'll now consider.

MDM Workflow in SP05

The Next Step function of the MDM workflow is supported in the SAP NetWeaver Portal. You can assign LDAP users to workflow steps. Two automatic steps can now be executed one after the other (back-to-back), and you can define dynamic texts in workflow notifications (such as the repository name). The new workflow step `Syndicate` is now provided.

MDM Business Content/SAP NetWeaver Exchange Infrastructure (SAP NetWeaver XI) Content in SP05

There is now an optimized business partner data model (for Customer Data Integration (CDI) and master data consolidation). The SAP NetWeaver XI content was extended to support business scenarios based on SAP NetWeaver 7.0.

Matrix Application in SP05

Taxonomy data is now loaded by the MDM Import Manager only. The pre-load and post-load applications are no longer used. The inbound process is more automated because the generic extraction framework is used for the extraction of the customizing data, the hierarchy data, and the characteristics. Ports are used for the import. The SAP NetWeaver XI content was modified to include new XSLT transformations.

The matrix user interface supports the deletion of matrix type records and also supports empty (NULL) values in variant fields and attributes. The Select All function is available in the matrix user interface.

MDM Enrichment Architecture (Data Quality Services Framework) in SP05

For monitoring purposes, the adapter interface was changed to include two new methods. Therefore, adapters that have been developed for SP04 have to be adapted to work with SP05.

A new administrator web tool for managing the Enrichment Controller process is available. The Adapter Tester enables you to test your adapter without a configured MDM installation. With the simulators, you learn how to develop an MDM Enrichment Adapter by deploying the simulator package.

MDM-BI Integration in SP05

The MDM-BI integration provides a direct integration of SAP NetWeaver BI and MDM. This integration is used to consolidate SAP NetWeaver BI master data in MDM. The MDM-BI integration will be available with SAP NetWeaver 7.0 (2004s) BI SP12 as a pilot shipment.

11.5 Future Roadmaps

The next major release will be SAP NetWeaver MDM 7.1 scheduled in 2009. Until the release notes are produced, we won't know for sure, but we anticipate the following changes:

A significant extension of the MDM data modeling capabilities will be accomplished through the introduction of multiple main tables per repository. This will allow different master data objects, such as vendor and material, to reside in the same repository. In addition, this will also provide mechanisms to relate records of different main tables. As an example, vendors could be linked to the particular materials they supply. These meta-model extensions will provide an additional modeling alternative for complex structures that today are handled via qualified look-up tables.

Further core enhancements will include performance and scalability improvements. To ease the transport of MDM repository schemas and contained instruments such as workflows and validations across the development, test, and production environments, the change and transport management will be improved and integrated to the SAP transport mechanisms for non-ABAP.

A deeper integration to infrastructure components of SAP is targeted. An example is the native adapter for SAP NetWeaver PI, which will ensure reliable message transport and monitoring.

There will be process-centric application enablement characterized by tightly integrating MDM services with enterprise SOA (Enterprise Services Repository (ESR) connectivity). MDM operations will be integrated with SAP NetWeaver administration and Lifecycle Management standards, and MDM scenarios will be integrated with the SAP application infrastructure.

SAP NetWeaver MDM will be able to consume content from BusinessObjects™ Data Quality Management software for SAP ERP in 2008 through data cleansing and de-duplication before load into the master data repository. By 2010, SAP will deliver tight integration of the software with an enhanced version of MDM. Data Quality Management for SAP ERP and MDM will also continue to be available as a standalone offering.

11.6 Summary

You learned how an MDM application is developed using the MDM Java API and Web Services. We described in detail the significant improvements and changes in the recent MDM Java API. You now understand how Web Services can be created to enable your business users to search for business partner records in an MDM repository.

You discovered how to plan for service pack upgrades to your MDM NetWeaver landscape and the latest technical features, including the functionality provided in the most recent service packs MDM 5.5 SP05 and SP06.

This now completes both this chapter and the book. In Part 1, you gained an understanding of the issues faced by companies if they don't manage their master data and allow it to reside unconnected in multiple silos. You discovered how to develop an MDM business case and how the D&B services can help you. You also learned how to establish an MDM program through its various phases, and the business and technical skills that are required.

In Part 2, you learned about the SAP NetWeaver MDM technical framework and solution architecture and how to cater for both the consolidated and centralized scenarios. You understand the iterative nature of MDM data conversion and the need for business ownership of the master data processes. You gained an insight into how the SAP NetWeaver components can be combined to provide a "best-of-breed" MDM solution.

We hope that you have enjoyed reading and have gained some useful insights into why MDM is so important to you and your organization and how to implement a practical SAP NetWeaver MDM solution.

Thank you,

Andy Walker and Jagadeesh Ganapathy,

June 2008

A   The Authors

 **Andy Walker** works for a large global energy company and lives in Ascot, London. He has spoken on the subject of MDM at the SAP Sapphire Orlando conference in May 2008, the Vienna user conference in May 2007, the MDM Gartner conference (Florida) in September 2007 and the CDI MDM Summit (New York) in November 2007. In addition to MDM, Andy's areas of expertise include ERP deployment, with both SAP and non-SAP systems. Andy graduated from Loughborough University with a First Class Batchelor of Science Honours degree in Computer Studies in 1985.

 **Jagadeeshwaran Ganapathy** leads the SAP MDM Competency at Wipro, and has served as a lead Architect in multiple MDM projects across the US and UK. He has spoken on the topic of SAP MDM Best Practices at SAP Sapphire 2008 Conference in Orlando, US. He has 14 years of work experience with a rich background in SAP ERP and Functional consulting. Jagadeesh holds a Bachelors Degree in engineering, and CPIM (Certified in Production and Inventory management) certification from APICS (American Production and Inventory Control society).

Index

T

MDM technology, architecture, and solution landscape

Detailed technical description of all three usage scenarios

Includes highly-detailed, proven guidance from real-life customer examples

331 pp., 2007, 69,95 Euro / US$ 69,95
ISBN 978-1-59229-131-1

SAP NetWeaver Master Data Management

www.sap-press.com

Loren Heilig, Steffen Karch, Oliver Böttcher, Christiane Hofmann, Roland Pfennig

SAP NetWeaver Master Data Management

This book provides system architects, administrators, and IT managers with a description of the structure and usage scenarios of SAP NetWeaver MDM. It uses three comprehensive real-life examples to give you practical insights into the consolidation, harmonization, and central management of master data. Plus, more than 120 pages are dedicated to an MDM compendium, complete with detailed information on individual components, data extraction, options for integration with SAP NetWeaver XI, SAP NetWeaver BI, and the SAP Portal (including user management), as well as on workflows and the Java API.

Learn how to import, maintain, and export your data

Uncover the extensive data maintenance capabilities of the Data Manager tool

Get in-depth details on the consolidation and harmonization usage scenarios

76 pp., 2008, 68,– Euro / US$ 85
ISBN 978-1-59229-176-2

Mastering SAP NetWeaver Master Data Management

www.sap-press.com

Bernd Schloemer

Mastering SAP NetWeaver Master Data Management

SAP PRESS Essentials 36

This highly-detailed guide uses a real-life scenario to take you step-by-step through a complete master data management project with SAP NetWeaver MDM. You'll tackle all of the essentials, from importing your data into the MDM sys- tem, to maintaining it with Data Manager, and exporting it into your local systems.

More specifically, you'll quickly master all repository tasks, and learn how best to import data using the Import Manager, or the batch import functionality. This book also shows you how to export the data back to local systems using the MDM Syndicator tool, or the batch export functionality. Plus, you'll also learn how to create a typical workflow, and much more.

Learn how to use SAP NetWeaver MDM to design, implement and maintain your Enterprise Data Management system

Discover master data basics and explore SAP's powerful MDM tools

584 pp., 2008, 69,95 Euro / US$ 69.95
ISBN 978-1-59229-115-1

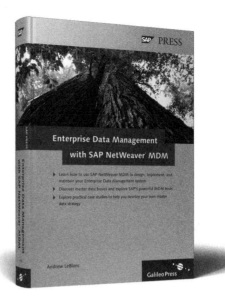

Enterprise Data Management with SAP NetWeaver MDM

www.sap-press.com

Andrew LeBlanc

Enterprise Data Management with SAP NetWeaver MDM

Build Foundations for Continual Improvements with SAP MDM

Master data is your company's DNA, and effective master data management demands extensive preparation. This book is the key to developing and implementing your own comprehensive SAP MDM strategy. Readers get all the essential prerequisites for building a successful and sustainable MDM strategy. Fully up-to-date for SAP MDM 5.5 SP04, this comprehensive book contains all the resources needed to set your own MDM strategy.

Learn the most efficient ways to implement SAP-related change in your organization

Understand the unique challenges of change in an SAP environment and avoid problems before they occur

Learn strategies for successfully conquering each phase of your implementation

364 pp., 2007, 69,95 Euro / US$ 69,95
ISBN 978-1-59229-104-5

Managing Organizational Change During SAP Implementations

www.sap-press.com

Luc Galoppin, Siegfried Caems

Managing Organizational Change During SAP Implementations

Many SAP implementations are not successful because proper change management procedures are ignored. This book helps you prepare for change in an organized manner. This practical guide takes a holistic look at an organization, the impact of an SAP implementation on it and how negative impacts can be lessened or, in most cases, negated early on. Taking a real-world, practical approach this book focuses on actual challenges and details how they can be overcome with relative ease.

Interested in reading more?

Please visit our Web site for all
new book releases from SAP PRESS.

www.sap-press.com